ALWAYS AT WAR

Titles in the Series

Transforming War

Paul J. Springer, editor

To ensure success, the conduct of war requires rapid and effective adaptation to changing circumstances. While every conflict involves a degree of flexibility and innovation, there are certain changes that have occurred throughout history that stand out because they fundamentally altered the conduct of warfare. The most prominent of these changes have been labeled "Revolutions in Military Affairs" (RMAs). These so-called revolutions include technological innovations as well as entirely new approaches to strategy. Revolutionary ideas in military theory, doctrine, and operations have also permanently changed the methods, means, and objectives of warfare.

This series examines fundamental transformations that have occurred in warfare. It places particular emphasis upon RMAs to examine how the development of a new idea or device can alter not only the conduct of wars but their effect upon participants, supporters, and uninvolved parties. The unifying concept of the series is not geographical or temporal; rather, it is the notion of change in conflict and its subsequent impact. This has allowed the incorporation of a wide variety of scholars, approaches, disciplines, and conclusions to be brought under the umbrella of the series. The works include biographies, examinations of transformative events, and analyses of key technological innovations that provide a greater understanding of how and why modern conflict is carried out, and how it may change the battlefields of the future.

ALWAYS AT WAR

Organizational Culture in Strategic
Air Command, 1946–62

MELVIN G. DEAILE

Naval Institute Press
Annapolis, Maryland

Library of Congress Cataloging-in-Publication Data

Names: Deaile, Melvin G., author.

Title: Always at war : organizational culture in strategic air command, 1946-62 / Melvin G. Deaile.

Other titles: Origins of organizational culture in Strategic Air Command, 1946-62

Description: Annapolis, Maryland : Naval Institute Press, [2018] | Series: Transforming war | Includes bibliographical references and index.

Identifiers: LCCN 2018004419 (print) | LCCN 2018009700 (ebook) | ISBN 9781682472491 (epub) | ISBN 9781682472484 (alk. paper)

Subjects: LCSH: United States. Air Force. Strategic Air Command--History. | United States. Air Force. Strategic Air Command--Organization. | Strategic culture--United States.

Classification: LCC UG633 (ebook) | LCC UG633 .D467 2018 (print) | DDC 358.4/23097309045--dc23

LC record available at https://lccn.loc.gov/2018004419

26 25 24 23 22 21 20 19   9 8 7 6 5 4 3

*This book is dedicated to all SAC warriors who
demonstrated throughout the Cold War that
"maintaining peace was their profession."*

Contents

Acknowledgments

No work of this magnitude could have been accomplished alone. There is not enough space to thank everyone who encouraged, supported, or aided me in the completion of this book. The following only serves as a beginning and recognizes those who made completing this project in three years possible.

Special thanks and appreciation go to the Air Force's School of Advanced Air and Space Studies (SAASS), particularly Col. Thomas Griffith and Col. Stephen Chiabotti (Ret.), for securing the funding and providing me the opportunity to attend the University of North Carolina (UNC)–Chapel Hill. Throughout these three years, SAASS provided financial and administrative support, which allowed me to travel to various locations throughout the United States to find the material necessary to finish this project.

I would not have completed this academic journey had it not been for the guidance and direction of my adviser and mentor, Dr. Richard Kohn. He opened my eyes to the greater purpose of history and skilled me in the proper investigation of the past. He is owed a great debt of gratitude for having to read and edit multiple versions of this work to the point that he suffered from "MEGO" (My Eyes Glaze Over). Dr. Alex Roland, likewise, provided incredible critical analysis of this project and challenged me throughout the entire history program to become "a thinker." The other members of the committee—Dr. Gerhard Weinberg, Dr. Joseph Glatthaar, and Dr. Karen Hagemann—kept this work true to its purpose and offered sound and crucial criticism.

As I gathered evidence for this work, my travels took me to many archival locations, individuals' homes, and the sites of several *Strategic Air Command* (SAC) reunions. The people at the Library of Congress, the National Archives, and the Air Force Historical Research Agency

(AFHRA) were always professional and helpful. One person at AFHRA, Toni Petito, deserves special mention. Not only did she provide guidance and support, but she also must have gone through a box of black markers making sure that my documents were in compliance with "Safe Paper." I truly appreciate former Air Force generals David Jones, Russell Dougherty, and John Shaud, who shared their insights and recollections of SAC and its organizational culture. Those associations responsible for preserving the memory and experiences of former SAC members played a significant role in providing the anecdotal and historical evidence needed to uncover the culture of SAC. Specifically, the SAC Airborne Command and Control Association, the SAC Association, the B-47 Association, the B-52 Association, and the Air Force Missileers Association provided terrific support throughout this process.

I also had the support of friends and colleagues in the Duke and UNC–Chapel Hill history programs. Tim Schultz, Robin Payne, and Kelly Morrow helped guide me through the highs and lows of this entire process. Finally, I must offer my sincerest appreciation and thanks to Paul "P. J." Springer for his insight, edits, and guidance as he helped me to make this first book a reality.

One person made this all possible. My grandfather, Melvin A. Deaile Sr., passed away before he could see this project completed. The need to work during the Great Depression prevented him from finishing his education, but that did not stop him from creating and building a profitable family business and corporation. He always valued education, and this work is a testament to the ideals of hard work and determination he instilled in me at an early age in the grape fields of Fresno, California.

First, I want to thank God for His Spirit, strength, and guidance, not only these past ten years but throughout my entire life. My three children, Faith, Melvin, and Joy, were great supporters and showed understanding when research and writing kept Dad confined to his office for days on end. Their love, devotion, and understanding were always appreciated and needed to help me see this book to the end. I also appreciate the support of their mother, Rachel, who stood by me through this endeavor as she has throughout my military and academic career.

Acronyms and Initialisms

7 AD	Seventh Air Division
2 AF	Second Air Force
8 AF	Eighth Air Force
15 AF	Fifteenth Air Force
20 AF	Twentieth Air Force
AAA	anti-aircraft artillery
AAF	Army Air Forces
ACTS	Air Corps Tactical School
AEC	Atomic Energy Commission
AEF	American Expeditionary Force
AF	Air Force
AWPD-1	Air War Planning Document 1
CBI	China-Burma-India
CIA	Central Intelligence Agency
CSAF	Chief of Staff of the Air Force
DEFCON	Defense Condition
EP	Emergency Procedures
EWP	Emergency War Plan
FEAF	Far East Air Forces
FM	Field Manual
GHQ	General Headquarters
ICBM	intercontinental ballistic missile
IFI	in-flight insertion
JCS	Joint Chiefs of Staff
MITO	minimum interval takeoff
NATO	North Atlantic Treaty Organization
ORI	operational readiness inspection
SAC	Strategic Air Command
SIOP	Single Integrated Operations Plan
SOP	standard operating procedure

TAC	Tactical Air Command
TDY	temporary duty
UMT	universal military training
USAFE	United States Air Forces in Europe
USSBS	United States Strategic Bombing Survey
VD	venereal disease

Introduction

"KLAXON! KLAXON! KLAXON!" When public address systems sounded this alarm at Strategic Air Command (SAC) bases across the United States, red lights flashed, and SAC's warriors rushed to their waiting bombers and tankers. As pilots brought their nuclear-armed planes to life, navigators decoded emergency action messages to determine if the alert response was an actual launch against the Soviet Union or just another exercise.

Deep below the earth, missile launch officers inserted coded keys into their guarded slots and stood ready to launch nuclear intercontinental ballistic missiles (ICBMs) at predetermined targets throughout the Soviet Union. SAC's crewmembers never executed their preplanned missions against America's enemies, but for thirteen days during October 1962, the nation came as close to nuclear war as it would during any other time during the Cold War.

President John F. Kennedy learned on October 16, 1962, that the Soviet Union had placed missiles on Cuba. Repeated calls by the president for the Soviet Union to remove the missiles went unheeded. Therefore, Kennedy announced on October 22 that he would impose a blockade (labeled a "quarantine" so as to avoid an act of war) around the island.[1] The following day, SAC raised the number of its bombers on airborne alert from twelve to sixty-six. One hundred and eighty-three of SAC's bombers flew to civilian airfields to sit nuclear alert to make sure the Soviet missiles could not wipe out the nation's nuclear force in a massive attack.[2] When the quarantine went into effect on

1

October 24, 1962, the president raised the readiness of the nation's military forces to Defense Condition (DEFCON) 2, one step away from imminent war (DEFCON 1).[3] Elevating the nation's readiness level meant that the tempo of SAC's bomber, tanker, and missile operations would increase even further. SAC raised the number of its bombers on alert from 652 to 912. Missile readiness grew by over 50 percent as SAC put an additional 60 nuclear missiles on alert, increasing the total to 182. This meant that SAC had close to 2,950 nuclear warheads armed and ready to go.[4] Operating under these emergency conditions placed a high burden on the organization and increased the possibility of a serious nuclear accident or even a flight accident, but neither happened. On October 28, 1962, the Cuban Missile Crisis ended without a serious incident, and SAC returned to normal operations within a month. The Cold War and SAC's alert operations, however, would continue.

Reflecting on the Air Force's performance during the crisis, Gen. Curtis LeMay, chief of staff of the Air Force, said, "At Cuba, we saw deterrence in action. Our superior strategic delivery capability was not challenged."[5] In fact, the Air Force and the nation had begun to rely on SAC as the pillar of Cold War deterrence as early as 1948. From SAC's inception in 1946, the organization had grown in size, strength, and power, reaching its peak in 1962. By the mid-1960s, SAC bomber generals held over 50 percent of the senior command positions within the Air Force.[6] These leaders, largely veterans of World War II strategic bombing campaigns, believed that the threat of nuclear bombs, and later the additional risk of a nuclear missile attack, was *the* way to deter potential adversaries. In the 1960s, the U.S. entry into the war in Vietnam shifted the focus of the Cold War. The threat of head-to-head confrontation between the superpowers became less pronounced, and the two nations demonstrated their resolve through war in peripheral Third World countries.[7] The concentration on smaller countries focused airpower on tactical aviation in support of ground troops. SAC's primacy in the Air Force began to wane.[8] Despite a decreased emphasis on nuclear bombing, SAC's nuclear forces continued to sit alert, ready to launch on a moment's notice.

When the Cold War ended, the Air Force reorganized for a new international environment and disbanded Strategic Air Command.

Although SAC no longer exists today, it left an indelible imprint on the Air Force because the organization developed a strong, distinctive culture that for a time dominated the Air Force and that continues influencing it today.

Discovering SAC Culture

This is the story of Strategic Air Command during the early decades of the Cold War. More than a simple history, it describes how an organization dominated by airmen developed its own unique culture. The Air Force formed SAC because of a belief in the military potential of centralizing strategic bombing under one commander. Strategic Air Command's formulation put it within the generally recognized definition of an organization: it was goal directed, maintained within boundaries (socially constructed ways to identify the organization and its members), and comprised active systems accomplishing particular work.[9] Military organizations exhibit certain characteristics that distinguish them from civilian organizations. Their goals relate to victory in armed combat and include accomplishing defined objectives and missions, managing the battle space, organizing and employing people and weapons, and supplying those forces in battle. Boundaries—both operational and geographic—are controlled by civilians overseeing the military and often defined by legislation. Finally, the active systems within military organizations typically focus on the application of coercive power, which can be the actual display of power or the projection of power (deterrent capability).

This work employs an evolutionary view of SAC. Organizations are not static entities; they evolve in response to internal and external factors. Sociologists embracing the evolutionary view argue that organizations experience various stages of evolution either sequentially or simultaneously. These stages are variation (changes in organizational form), selection (differential elimination of certain types of variations), retention (preservation of selected variations), and struggle (competition for scarce resources).[10] Strategic Air Command began in one environment but had to adapt as it responded to the changing internal and external environmental conditions of the Cold War. SAC did not begin in response to the Cold War; rather, it was the airmen's belief in the promise of centralized strategic bombing and their collective history in World War II that laid the foundation for SAC. Nevertheless, the organization's mission, resources, and strength became tied to the Cold War. As the Cold War evolved, so did SAC. The external environment included more than SAC's role in the Cold War. The changes in presidential administrations and their policies played an equally important role in SAC's evolution.

When the nation needed a strategy to implement the policy of containment, it decided upon deterrence by building a strategic bombing force "in being" and gave that mission to SAC. Fearful of overspending in the 1940s and 1950s, the United States built a strategic bombing force armed with nuclear weapons because the price tag was lower than that of a large conventional armed force. By 1948, Air Force leadership earned a leading role for the organization in the nation's defense, but then mismanagement by SAC's leadership threatened to unravel these gains. SAC's first command team trained crews in a manner reminiscent of pre–World War II conflicts, when U.S. planning assumptions allowed the military time to mobilize for war. In 1948 and 1949, the Berlin airlift, the coup in Czechoslovakia, and the Soviet detonation of an atomic bomb served notice that the United States would no longer have months to prepare for possible military action. Military necessity therefore demanded a change in SAC's organizational leadership and thinking. As soon as he took command of SAC, Curtis LeMay placed the organization on a war footing. SAC was not training for war; SAC considered itself already at war. As the Cold War took shape, so did the "SAC mentality" (the term used by those inside and outside the organization when referring to SAC thinking and behavior).

The organization embodied the belief that a highly specialized strategic bombardment force was essential to national defense, but more than ideology contributed to the formation of SAC culture. SAC, like other organizations, was a social unit comprising individuals who managed uncertainties to create some degree of order in their social life. Organizational researchers argue that as people struggle together to make sense of and cope with their world, organizational cultures begin to develop.

Another important factor in the development of organizational culture is the history shared by its members, which greatly influences the character of that culture.[11] Almost all the Air Force and SAC leaders during the organization's inception fought in World War II and witnessed the struggle for a response to Pearl Harbor. Furthermore, a majority participated in strategic bombing campaigns in the European and/or Pacific theaters. These collective experiences, along with the history shared among SAC's leaders, greatly influenced the organization's early policies, routines, and organizational structure.

SAC culture did not develop quickly, nor did it remain constant throughout the organization's existence. Like most organizations, SAC culture evolved as it adjusted to internal and external forces. The importance of culture is that it typically provides its members with accepted ways of expressing and affirming their beliefs, values, and norms, and it shapes the way people operate, perform, and act.[12] Furthermore, culture exhibits itself in the symbols, rituals, routines, and even the myths a particular social group embraces.

The purpose of this book is to define those elements that constituted SAC's organizational culture and explore the circumstances that brought them to fruition. Those who specialize in organizational culture agree that there are at least two general categories of culture: the invisible (ideational) and the visible (material).[13] The ideational school—the unseen aspect of culture—defines organizational culture as "a set of important understandings (often stated) that members of a community share in common." Ideationalists look at the basic assumptions and beliefs that drive organizational behaviors and operations. Materialists stress the subjective nature of organizational culture and look at the material conditions under which the employees work. They focus on the embodiment of values and beliefs in symbols, objects, and ritualized practices. This book examines both aspects of organizational culture in SAC during its formative period from 1946 to 1962: what SAC leadership thought about strategic bombing and how that affected organizational culture, and how symbols and rituals within SAC both defined and reflected the organization's culture.

Culture formation can take several paths. The theory adopted for this work posits that culture begins with assumptions, which constitute the dominant thinking about the preferred solution among several alternatives for solving problems. These assumptions then become espoused values reflected in organizational policies and strategies. Finally, culture takes form in the way of artifacts, which can include rituals, organizational stories, jargon, humor, and physical arrangements including architecture, interior décor, and dress codes.[14] While anthropological approaches recognize this process, the theory also acknowledges the possibility that culture can form in the opposite direction when an artifact becomes embraced and eventually becomes part of the organization's cultural assumptions. All of this occurred in SAC. Therefore, it became necessary to develop a methodology that uncovered in SAC both the seen (material) and the unseen (ideational or ideological) culture.

Finding Revealed Culture

Culture can manifest itself in many material forms. Four categories of forms recognized by those who study organizational culture are symbols, language, narratives, and practices. Symbols, the first category, are considered the most basic and the smallest units of expression, manifest in objects, natural and manufactured settings, performers, and functionaries. In SAC, unique institutions created by the organization also served as a cultural symbol.

The second category of cultural expression, language, is a shared system of vocal sounds, written signs, and gestures used by members of a culture to convey meanings. Organizations use many forms of language to create certain cultural images. Language consists of jargon, sayings, gestures, signals, signs, songs, humor, jokes, gossip, rumors, metaphors, proverbs, and slogans.[15]

Narratives, the third category, use both language and symbols. Members of organizations can use several kinds of narratives to make sense of their experiences and to express their feelings and beliefs. The final category of expression is practices. These forms include specific activities and behaviors that express cultural meanings. The smallest and simplest unit of cultural practice is the ritual (or routine): standardized and detailed sets of techniques and behaviors that the culture prescribes. Other forms of practices are rites and ceremonies, the most complex and elaborate of the cultural forms because they typically consolidate several discrete cultural forms into one event or series of events.[16] Exploring these various aspects of culture for a disbanded organization, or one that existed long ago, requires an unconventional methodology.

Discovering Hidden Assumptions

Cultural forms are analogous to the tip of the iceberg, the part that can be seen above the water. Underlying assumptions and values form the bottom of the iceberg, the part that is much larger than the visible area and that is more difficult to navigate. Uncovering symbols, myths, and rituals requires talking to those who were members of an organization. Most sociologists would advocate talking to members while observing their work environment. This project, however, is a historical study about an organization that no longer exists. Therefore, interviews and oral histories were conducted with former SAC members who attended military reunions throughout 2006. These included meetings of the SAC Airborne Command and Control Association, the SAC Association, the B-52 Association, the B-47 Association, the Air Force Missileers Association, and the Airlift Tanker Association.

This data, while highly enlightening, has limitations. The sample was not a stratified random sample and therefore is not statistically representative. Furthermore, members who attended these reunions were typically those who had a positive experience with their particular organization and desired to maintain that association. Length of service was not a determining factor in attendance. Some attendees served in the organization for as little as a few years, while others belonged to SAC throughout their entire service in the Air Force.

Qualitative analysis of responses to informal questionnaires distributed to reunion attendees provided valuable insights into the culture of SAC. These perspectives from those on the front lines also showed how policy made at the elite level of the organization affected and, at times, disrupted the lives of those required to implement these decisions. In addition to the collected survey data, stories and memoirs, published and unpublished, helped construct a fuller picture of SAC culture from the perspective of those who exhibited and lived it on a daily basis. Those who went "on the record" are credited in the footnotes. Some comments, myths, and ideas expressed at these reunions are not attributed to any individual but were merely picked up through random conversation. These cultural artifacts are referenced by the particular event where they were overheard (for example, B-47 reunion, B-52 reunion, etc.). While this information proved invaluable to the construction of this narrative, determining the underlying assumptions and beliefs of the organization formed a critical part of painting the full picture of SAC culture.

The Role of Leadership in Organizational Culture

Organizational sociologists differ over the role of leadership in forming organizational culture. Those subscribing to the functionalist school emphasize the role of leaders and managers in the creation of organizational culture. Functionalist studies tend to show that a "strong" culture will lead to outcomes most top executives desire to maximize, such as productivity and profitability. Having members of the organization explain to newcomers the acceptable routines and practices is an example of the functionalist approach. This approach stands in contrast to the symbolic approach, which sees cultural forms as a lens into the organization and views leaders as more symbolic than influential.[17] This book argues that leaders do matter. Leadership played an important and defining role in forming SAC culture; therefore, functionalism provides a method of investigation with respect to SAC.

In addition to the functionalist approach, this work assumes an integration perspective when approaching SAC culture. Joanne Martin identified three perspectives on organizational culture. Her integration perspective focused on those interpretations of culture that were mutually consistent. The culture of an organization from this perspective is clear, with little ambiguity. Although subcultures exist within the organization, the dominant culture overrides subcultures to the point that deviations from the dominant culture are seen as problematic. This perspective becomes clearer when comparing the pilots' experiences in the Army Air Corps with the missileers' experiences under SAC.

The second perspective, differentiation, uncovers cultural manifestations that have inconsistent interpretations. An example of this perspective would be when top executives announce a policy and then behave in a manner inconsistent with that policy. Differentiation studies would argue that subcultures dominate the organization, overriding the dominant culture posited by management. The final perspective, fragmentation, sees very little consistency or clarity in organizational culture at all.[18] Given the nature of SAC's leaders and their collective history, the integration perspective seemed to best fit with the facts. It should be noted, though, that the Air Force writ large exhibited a differentiation perspective, as other organizations (those with fighter pilots or airlift pilots) tried to maintain their identity in an Air Force initially dominated by "bomber generals."

Since this work contends that leaders and their values play an important role in organizational culture, the work of Edgar Schein greatly influenced this project. Schein looked to leaders as the source of culture, saying, "Cultures begin with leaders who impose their own values and assumptions on a group." Using an anthropological methodology, Schein outlined why he believed a particular culture persists in an organization. If leadership is successful and the assumptions come to be taken for granted, then "we have a culture that will define for later generations of members what kinds of leadership are acceptable."[19] He defined organizational culture as "a pattern of shared basic assumptions that was learned by a group as it solved its problems of external adaptation and internal integration, which has worked well enough to be considered valid and, therefore, to be taught to new members as the correct way to perceive, think, and feel in relation to those problems."[20] Leaders at the lower levels of an organization constrain behavior rather than play a role in culture development. Accordingly, Schein posited, "leadership creates and changes culture, while managers and administration act within a culture."[21] In a hierarchical organization, especially a military organization like SAC, the views, assumptions, and values that leaders espoused matter. This meant developing a methodology to uncover these historical beliefs.

Various sources were consulted to uncover the basic assumptions and espoused beliefs that played an instrumental role in forming SAC culture. The personal papers of SAC leaders housed at the Library of Congress and the Air Force Historical Research Agency (AFHRA) revealed Air Force and SAC leaders' beliefs and what they tried to accomplish. Most organizational researchers would suggest interviewing those in leadership positions; however, as this is a historical study, the passage of time prevented that from occurring. Air Force historians conducted and continue to accomplish oral interviews with

leaders of the organization. These interviews, collected as part of the
Air Force's oral history program, are stored at AFHRA and reveal considerable details about how Air Force and SAC leaders thought about
strategic bombing and SAC operations.

Some sociologists may view leaders and managers more symboli-
cally in other organizations, but the mission and structural form of
military organizations rely on strong hierarchical command, top-
down control, and high competency developed by extreme training
and education for those who manage these organizations. Following World War II, sociologists began exploring the changing aspects
of military organizations and their role in society. The following
summary of their findings provides the rationale for why this work
adopted the functional and integration perspective with respect to the
formulation of SAC culture.

Military Sociology and the Distinctiveness
of Military Organizations

Military sociologists conducting research in the post–World War II
environment highlighted where military organizations differed from
organizations of other populations. Sociologists studying the military
focused on those permanent structures that are indispensable to the
conduct of organized warfare. This field also examined the characteristics of military men as a social type—the way military institutions
operate and maintain themselves as well as their role in domestic politics.[22] While pointing out where military organizations were distinct
from civilian organizations, sociologists also observed that technology was creating a closer identity among military members with their
civilian counterparts. Since a military organization and its members
are central to this project, it is necessary to highlight some generally
accepted characteristics about military structures and the people who
work within them.

Military organizations, like all organizations, are goal oriented.
The military, however, manages and orients its resources differently,
since military organizations have different types of goals. National
defense and mission accomplishment serve as the organizational goals,
rather than, for example, the profit motive of entrepreneurial organizations. This organizational outlook necessitates a different structure

than civilian organizations. The active systems within military organizations are more concerned with turning men and machines into coercive power—either the actual application or the projection of power. Sociologists have observed that the military authority structure is geared toward one overriding requirement: the uniform direction of troops in battle, whether on land, at sea, in the air, or even in space, to gain victory over an adversary. A commander's ability to reach quick decisions under external pressure is critical to organizational success. Therefore, hierarchy rather than equality provides the basis for unity in battle. Speed and mobility play equally important roles in operational decisions. Commanders try to array their troops so that they arrive at the decisive point with the most force in the least amount of time and at the critical moment.[23]

The hierarchical structure of the military is populated by officers with ascending levels of rank to distinguish those in charge. Academic research has revealed important trends about those who hold positions within the chain of command. Military officers view their job as more than an occupation; it is a profession and a calling. Samuel Huntington's groundbreaking work on civil-military relations labeled these professional officers the "managers of violence."[24] The interesting aspect of their work is that they rarely practice their craft. Unlike doctors or lawyers, who daily practice their given professions, military officers can go their entire career without experiencing combat. Those who do experience battle and perform well under fire are typically rewarded for their deeds and viewed as "heroic leaders"—military leaders whom the larger population normally associates with victory in battle (George Patton, Ulysses S. Grant, Dwight Eisenhower, etc.). During the post–World War II period, however, a shift took place as heroic leaders became less prevalent and military managers and military technologists replaced them.[25]

Morris Janowitz's seminal sociological study of the military following World War II uncovered several trends in the larger military society that were a direct result of its growing dependence on technology. Although some technologies—for example, the airplane and the tank—made their debut in World War I, by World War II and beyond, technological advantage became the hallmark of the U.S. military. The atomic bomb, the strategic bomber, the intercontinental ballistic missile, and the computer networks needed to control them were all part of SAC and served as signs of the nation's technological prowess. The growing reliance of the military on technology, however, brought changes in the way military members viewed themselves and the way military leaders were able to lead.

Technology, in Janowitz's view, led members of the military to identify more with their civilian counterparts than with the military at large. For example, an Air Force pilot may think he has more in common with a commercial airline pilot than with the larger Air Force population. This shift could also occur when a computer network operator identifies more with a civilian computer technician than with his own service. Janowitz and others noticed that as technology increased the automation and destructiveness of war, it was simultaneously civilizing military thought. As the destructive potential of weapons increased, Janowitz argued, deterring conflict became more of the central focus than actually preparing for war.[26] Especially during the Cold War, building a credible deterrent, rather than the actual application of force, became the goal. The civilizing of military thought would eventually alter how military leaders viewed the application of force. Janowitz's pre-Vietnam study suggested that a change was occurring among military leaders. He predicted that the absolutist view—those committed to the traditional view of the military application of force where overwhelming power brings victory—would be replaced by the pragmatic view, the holders of which considered the moral and political consequences when considering the application of military force.[27] Heroic leaders were more likely to be absolutist, while the new emerging military manager was more apt to be a pragmatist.

Technology caused a civilizing of military thought in the way leaders approached the use of force and in the way military members self-identified. These changes brought about, in Janowitz's view, a modification in military leadership styles. The nature of advancing technology shifted leadership from authoritarian domination to a greater reliance on manipulation, persuasion, and group consensus. Technology, especially artifacts that emphasized greater mobility and range, severely reduced the commander's ability to directly control operations. Mechanized troop carriers and tanks, airplanes, and submarines moved military forces physically farther from the commander.

The farther troops got from the commander, the less direct control the higher echelons could exercise over them. Janowitz concluded that no longer would "one commands—one obeys" describe military organization.[28] The trend toward greater range and mobility would place more innovation and autonomy in the hands of troops at the lower levels of the organization. In an organization bent on uniform direction of troops, more autonomy and innovation in the lower echelons served a contradictory purpose. Authoritarian leadership styles, Janowitz and others predicted, would give way to more managerial approaches to leading troops, which would require persuasion and manipulation. Heroic leaders, those identified with prowess in battle and an authoritarian style, would eventually give way to pragmatic military managers and military technologists. One interesting theme of this work is how SAC tried to battle this trend by instituting more levels of control throughout the organization.

Along with an increase in autonomy and innovation, technology brought with it an increase in specialization. This trend would play out in the Air Force as SAC evolved. In the Army Air Corps, the forerunner to the Air Force, it was common for pilots to serve in other crew positions on an airplane. Furthermore, pilots typically flew multiple aircraft and were not limited to one particular type of plane. This changed as technology progressed. Crew positions became more specialized, and pilots typically focused on one type of aircraft (for example, bomber, fighter, or airlift). Sociologists Janowitz and Roger Little predicted that increased specialization would make teamwork a vital characteristic of America's new military; weapons required cooperation rather than independence, which brought with it new forms of organization, replacement, and assignment practices.[29] In terms of identity, increased specialization caused military members to associate themselves more with a particular weapons system and, conversely, that system became part of their character. In the Air Force, for example, a distinction would develop between those who flew a bomber and those who flew a fighter.

But one technological innovation would reverse the trend toward autonomy and innovation: atomic weapons. Whereas the general trend was toward civilianizing military thought and identity, nuclear weapons created a sharp distinction between military and civilian spheres.[30]

The destructive power atomic weapons displayed at the end of World War II made them a force to be reckoned with but, in the view of political leaders, also one that required strict civilian authority. In the post–World War II environment, nuclear weapons were seen as a resource too destructive to be left in the hands of the military, so politicians created political and physical boundaries.

Since SAC eventually became an organization identified with nuclear weapons, it is important to realize how those weapons altered the notion of weapon identity. Nuclear weapons offer a unique contradiction to the prevailing trends of the time since atomic weapons derive their chief military utility from their mere existence rather than their use. The result was a general movement to a "force in being," where the mere threat of use was strong enough to prevent the escalation of conflict.[31]

Placing nuclear weapons in the hands of the military created a dilemma. Technological advances were giving peripheral members of the military greater autonomy coupled with a demand for greater innovation. Nuclear weapons, however, required strict compliance with procedures and centralized command and control lest their inadvertent use lead to the type of general conflagration that their existence was designed to prevent. If military forces were indeed becoming more diffuse with an increased emphasis on range and reach, what role would military culture play? Increased innovation and autonomy in the lower echelons meant organizational culture and operational routines became increasingly important. For example, SAC's intercontinental bombers and missiles demonstrated such reach and power that SAC leaders had to enact specific measures to keep command and control of their operations. Organizational theorists hypothesize that organizational structure, routine, and culture enabled leaders to command and control complicated, technologically driven organizations. High-reliability theorists, realizing the frailty of human beings, argue that a strong organizational structure and routine can compensate for the imperfections of individuals. Accordingly, their research emphasizes the structure of the organization, organizational training, cultural norms, and the level of decentralized authority.[32] Although decentralized decision making at the lowest levels of an organization could run contrary to effective organizational control, theorists posit that a strong organizational culture creates a common set of premises and assumptions upon which members of the organization base their decisions.

Military Culture

Military culture, much like military organizations, focuses on effectiveness. As one study of military culture concluded, "Culture . . . the bedrock of military effectiveness . . . can help explain the motivation, aspirations, norms, and rules of conduct."[33] Because of the organization's orientation to the battlefield, military culture tends to be driven by ideology. Ideology—especially with regard to strategy and the employment of troops—forms the basic assumptions of military culture. Ideology, however, tends to be more all-inclusive. According to a historical study of military culture, "Ideology is bigger, more systematic, and more all-encompassing. Ideology is a highly structured belief system, a political cosmology that tries to bring conceptual order to a world in which questions of power are debated."[34]

As this narrative argues, ideology and organizational assumptions played a significant role in the formulation of SAC's distinctive culture. Assumptions and ideology influence culture development, and culture can explain behavior. As one study of Canadian military culture noted, "One way of explaining the impact of culture on the military is to use organizational culture as a construct which can explain how the beliefs, norms, values, and premises of members of the military govern their conduct."[35] Similar studies of military culture have produced comparable results with respect to the role military culture plays in explaining an organization's actions. For example, Isabel Hull's study of the German imperial army noted that "actual behavior, habitual practices, and powerful, motivating expectations are the results of military culture. Military culture bequeaths practices, habits of action, ways of behaving that were far more robust than flat and lifeless ideas like anti-Semitism."[36] While military culture may be heavily influenced by assumptions and ideology, it is a mistake to assume that all branches of the military are monolithic. Just as military organizations differ from civilian organizations, separate organizations within a military service have their own distinctions.

Uniqueness of Air Force Culture

The U.S. military contains four armed services: the Army, the Navy, the Air Force, and the Marines. Carl Builder's study of the services revealed that although individual leaders change with regularity, these institutions have distinct and enduring personalities of their own that shape their behavior.[37] As an institution, the Air Force owed its existence to the development of the airplane and therefore, Builder argued, "could be said to worship at the altar of technology." The emphasis on advanced technology in the Air Force led Builder to conclude that "there is a circle of faith here: if the Air Force fosters technology, the net inexhaustible fountain of technology will ensure an open-ended future for flight; that, in turn, will ensure the future of the Air Force."[38] Dependence and reliance on technology meant that the Air Force always measured itself by its aeronautical performance and the technological qualities of its aircraft.[39] Armies and navies have been in existence since ancient times, but organized airpower is a twentieth-century phenomenon. Perhaps because of its newness, the Air Force promotes itself as the most technological of the armed services.[40]

The airplane provided humanity the means to take to the air, but it was those who flew the craft who had the vision of weaponizing this invention and then organizing themselves for battle. Pilots have a culture unto themselves. They are the "technical experts" who skillfully maneuver airframes. Initially, flying was a one-person show. Other than during initial instruction, pilots often took to the skies alone. Even in current Air Force pilot training, the most celebrated event among pilots is their first "solo." In part because pilots initially saw themselves as an exclusive group, they developed a distinct mentality.

Since this work examines an organization founded and led by pilots, how pilots operated and thought is central to understanding the Air Force and SAC in the initial decades of the Cold War. As technical experts in the art of flying, pilots tended to view the world in the same way they flew. A study of Air Force culture concluded that "pilots have very different needs when it comes to seeking out information and advice from others, as compared to ground force officers. In the Air Force, the brotherhood of pilots is necessarily somewhat separated from the experience of others by virtue of the specialized nature of the task: pilots simply don't need advice from

non-pilots on how to fly."[41] In the Army, for example, the new pla-
toon leader tends to seek out the advice of the senior enlisted person
on matters of command and operation. The same is not true in the
Air Force; only another pilot can tell a pilot how to properly operate
a machine. Pilots themselves drew distinctions between the Army and
the Air Force with respect to the roles of enlisted people and officers. In the Army, enlisted members tend to be the frontline fighters,
whereas in the Air Force, officers have, over time, been the bulk of
the combat personnel. Enlisted personnel in the Air Force primarily served maintenance, logistic, and support operations. Operating
under these circumstances, Builder observed, created a division in the
Air Force between pilots and all others. Janowitz's prediction about
increased specialization in the military with increasing technological development was especially true in an organization wedded to
technology. Meanwhile, Builder's study found that pilots were more
likely to find solidarity with other pilots than with other officers, and
they tended to identify themselves with a specific model of aircraft.
Associating with a specific airplane created, in Builder's view, an Air
Force with a weaker sense of community.[42]

Pilots often displayed the same skills and techniques required to
fly an airplane in their management of operations. In the cockpit,
information flow has been technology dependent, highly structured,
and highly controllable. Pilots became adept at shutting out sources
of distraction in moments of crisis in order to properly and safely
employ their aircraft. Furthermore, aircraft commanders have always
reigned as the final authority regarding their airplane; their word has
always been ultimate, immediate, and unquestionable, and has formed
the bedrock element of Air Force leadership culture. Pilots, some have
argued, tended to incorporate these same habits, attitudes, and behaviors into their management styles. As one author argued, in "the areas
of information gathering, problem solving, decision making, some Air
Force officers appeared to him to behave in the war room as they are
taught to behave in the cockpit."[43] How Air Force officers interpreted
the Cold War and managed SAC's mission constituted perhaps the
greatest influence on the development of SAC's organizational culture.

No review of Air Force culture would be complete without a
brief discussion of how Air Force pilots viewed their role in national

defense. The narrative begins with a review of airpower theory and
how SAC became the embodiment of decades of strategic bombing
advocacy. Interestingly, the Air Force mentality stands in stark contrast
to that of the Army. Builder noted that the Army branches of infantry,
artillery, and armor each have seen themselves as inextricably dependent upon the other branches if they are to wage war effectively, leading to a "combined arms" mentality. Conversely, Builder observed that
pilots believed they could win wars largely on their own.[44] This view
forms another theme that runs throughout this book. The validity of
the Air Force's arguments regarding strategic bombing has certainly
provoked bitter controversy, from the birth of airpower to today. This
work considers how Air Force assumptions about strategic bombing influenced the formulation of SAC culture. The role of technology, the symbolism of that technology, and Air Force views regarding
advanced technology—especially missiles—played a significant part in
bringing SAC culture from the ideational realm to the material form.

Overview

This book presents its historical argument in seven chapters arranged
in a chronological narrative. Chapter one traces the beginnings of
airpower and the strategic bombardment doctrine. America's first
pilots constituted a subculture of the Army. They held certain beliefs
and embraced certain doctrines and technology, which led them to
want to be free from the Army's control and dominant culture. Chapter two focuses on the shared experiences of the future SAC leaders
in World War II, especially during the strategic bombing campaigns
in the European and Pacific theaters. The narrative does not recount
these campaigns but rather explores the views, thoughts, actions, and
interpretations of those who participated. Chapter three looks at the
internal and external factors that led to the formation of SAC. The Air
Force's beliefs about how to build a strategic bombing organization
and the emerging Cold War created an environment that allowed SAC
to emerge. This chapter also examines why the Air Force replaced the
first SAC commander. Chapter four begins with the appointment of
Curtis LeMay as the commander of SAC and the initial policies that
LeMay instituted to take SAC from a "hollow threat" to a credible

deterrent.[45] Chapter five discusses how the Korean War expanded both the U.S. nuclear arsenal and SAC's forces. This expansion provided SAC with the ability to create distinctive institutions and command relationships. Chapter six examines how SAC culture found expression in other cultural forms—routines, rituals, and myths—in the daily lives of its members. Chapter seven looks at what happened when SAC integrated missiles into its command structure and the effect of the missile era on SAC's operations. Missiles became a subculture of the organization. Their indoctrination into SAC culture stands in stark contrast to early pilots' experience in the Army. The book concludes with an epilogue highlighting how the "SAC mentality" served the organization well during the Cuban Missile Crisis. With the John F. Kennedy administration, however, the nation had a new approach to national security—flexible response—and a new conflict to fight in Vietnam. Although SAC's organizational approach served it well in North Korea, years of being steeled in SAC culture did not serve it in the skies over North Vietnam.

1

"A Different Breed of Cat"
The Foundations of Pilot Culture

It is probable that future wars will be conducted by a special class, the air force, as it was by the armored knights in the Middle Ages.

—WILLIAM "BILLY" MITCHELL

Strategic Air Command began as an organization in 1946. Its founders, however, formulated the ideas, concepts, and beliefs that led to its creation decades earlier. Since the beginning of organized American airpower, whether the Air Service (1918), the Air Corps (1926), the Army Air Forces (1941), or eventually the Air Force (1947), pilots led these organizations and initially made up a majority of the organization's officer population. Organized flying began as a subculture of the Army, serving first as part of the Army Signal Corps before becoming a separate branch dedicated to flying. Collectively, pilots shared a perspective different from that of their Army brethren with regard to their occupation and the role of aircraft in war. The job of pilots—to fly—made them a "functional" subculture of the Army, meaning their subculture status derived from the technology and occupational culture of the group. Other subcultures can form within organizations due to geography or division of labor; pilot subculture came about because of technology—the airplane.[1]

21

Subcultures typically have two responses to the dominant culture: they can enhance the culture of the larger group by espousing parallel assumptions, values, and beliefs, or they can become countercultures because they oppose the organization's core beliefs.[2] Although they were members of the Army, pilots viewed themselves as something separate from the dominant culture. They developed a counterculture, which argued that flying was not just another branch of the Army but something that could change the nature of war. Their occupation and function differed from other Army branches. The barriers to entry, pay, organization, and method of evaluating one another gave pilots their distinctiveness. This chapter examines the beginnings of pilot culture in the United States from the early days of flying until the nation's entrance into World War II. The experiences are primarily of those who would play an active role in establishing or leading Strategic Air Command.

America entered World War I with a rudimentary understanding of the airplane and its capabilities. As a military, the United States lacked a coherent doctrine that could fully exploit the potential of the airplane. During the interwar years, airmen concentrated on developing a doctrine focused primarily on strategic bombing. Strategic bombing came to express the shared values of most pilots and served as a means for this Army subculture to break from the dominant culture, gain independence, and form an organization that expressed its own values.

A Special Breed
On a hill in North Carolina's Outer Banks near the town of Kitty Hawk, Orville and Wilbur Wright set out to prove that humans could take to the skies in a heavier-than-air machine. Battling gusty wind conditions and frustrated by previous delays, each of the brothers finally made two successful flights on December 17, 1903, proving that machines could take people into the air for controlled flight.[3] The U.S. armed forces, however, initially rejected the Wright brothers' attempts in 1905 to sell them an airplane for military purposes, claiming the invention had yet to prove itself. Not until 1909 did the Army agree to purchase a limited number of airplanes. The Army assigned responsibility for development and application of the airplane

to the Signal Corps.[4] The military struggled to find a purpose for the airplane in war, believing the machine served best in a combat support role by conducting reconnaissance of the battle area, reporting on troop movements, and helping direct artillery fire. Although the Army did not believe the airplane would radically alter the conduct of warfare, those who initially flew viewed the airplane and themselves as capable of changing its nature.

America's early pilots considered their job as something extraordinary. Carl "Tooey" Spaatz entered aviation training in 1916 following his graduation from West Point and subsequent assignment to the infantry. Spaatz, who would become the first chief of staff of the Air Force (CSAF), voiced his belief about the exclusivity of pilots: "I guess we considered ourselves a different breed of cat, right in the beginning. We flew through the air and the other people walked on the ground; it was as simple as that."[5] Flying was the physical demonstration that pilots could do something almost supernatural. Pilots possessed a unique freedom: the ability to duplicate the flight of birds. Pilots not only rose into the heavens and maneuvered in three dimensions; they also had, at last, broken the earthly shackles that held humanity down. Now humans could go anywhere.[6] The trouble was attracting people, initially men, to undertake such an adventure.

The military struggled to find servicemembers interested in slipping the bonds of Earth. Danger ranked among the top reasons potential recruits avoided the Signal Corps flying branch. Of the nineteen pilots qualified for flight in 1913, five left the service. Included among those who opted out of flying was Henry "Hap" Arnold, who returned to the infantry since he was about to be married. Arnold would reenter flying in 1917 and rise through the ranks during the interwar years. During World War II, Arnold would serve on the general staff in Washington, D.C., as commanding general of the Army Air Forces and would lead U.S. airpower in the conflict despite suffering numerous heart attacks.[7] Frank Andrews, a future general and the first commander of the General Headquarters (GHQ) Air Force, the precursor to an independent Air Force, also put off entering the Air Service so he could marry. Realizing the risk involved in flying and the lack of volunteers, Congress authorized pilots to receive flight pay in 1913. This measure gave pilots about 50 percent more pay than their counterparts who labored on the ground. The effort paid off—marginally. In 1914 the Army trained enough pilots to replace those who had left flying or had died in accidents.[8]

For the most part, flying became a young, single man's venture. Only those under the age of thirty-five were considered fit for aviation duty.[9] A rising prospect in the Army, William "Billy" Mitchell, became the youngest officer at that time to serve on the general staff. He developed an interest in aviation but by the time he secured an assignment to the Signal Corps in 1916, Mitchell was thirty-eight and too old for flight training. This did not sour his enthusiasm for flying. Using his own money, Mitchell paid for civilian training and became a pilot.[10]

For most, like Mitchell, the extra pay did not attract recruits to flying; some simply sought the excitement of flight. Eugene Beebe entered flight training in 1929 right before the Great Depression. Beebe, however, viewed the extra money more as a testament to his acumen than his bravery: "I never considered my pay was for hazard. I knew the hazard was there, but I thought it was because I was a little better educated and had a little more to offer."[11] Flight pay may not have been their incentive, but the extra money symbolized pilots' distinctiveness and their willingness to face the hazards of flight.

Pilots serving in the early Air Service (which later became a separate combat branch with the creation of the Air Corps in 1926) did not sense much resentment for their special pay from their contemporaries, but some officers' wives expressed bitterness. To Spaatz, the friction was not as great among bachelor officers as it was among married officers because of what he termed "the female element."[12] The wives of officers in other branches were envious of the disparate pay pilots received. Additionally, the Army's "old guard," as some termed it, looked upon "flyboys" with skepticism. Hunter Harris noticed the resentment among the Army's officer teachers while attending West Point. While at the military academy until his graduation in 1932, Harris felt that his instructors viewed the Air Corps pilots as upstarts, men too glamorous for the extra 50 percent they were making. After all, these officers contended, the Air Corps was just a supporting element of ground combat operations. These officers did not deserve anything special, especially since ground power still won wars.[13] Those in the dominant culture saw no reason to reward this subgroup; it existed simply to support the main forces.

Extra pay meant an increased budget for Air Corps personnel, which led the Army to cap the number of officers that could enter that branch of service. This was the perception of Horace Wade, who entered the service through his local National Guard in 1934. The only officers in flight training were the West Point graduates who earned their commission upon graduation or were the top graduates of the Reserve Officer Training Corps (ROTC) programs who received a commission as a reward for their performance. Wade entered flight training as an aviation cadet knowing that a commission would come with his wings. He spent a whole year waiting to go to flight school because "in those days the military just didn't have the money to pay for officers."[14] Wade felt the Army held down the number of flyboys because the additional pay for pilots made their branch more expensive to man. Since the Army limited the number of pilot billets, those who made it through considered themselves "the best of the best."

In the interwar period, budgetary constraints kept the number of airplanes, and consequently, the number of pilots, limited. In flight training, aviation cadets (recruits from commissioning sources other than West Point) and West Point officers competed for the coveted wings. West Point provided the most direct route to pilot training. Most officers, however, had to overcome insurmountable odds to complete flight training. When Earl Barnes graduated from West Point in 1925, forty-three officers applied for the Air Service. His recollection was that the Air Service ranked pretty low on the assignment popularity list, below engineering, cavalry, coastal artillery, and even the infantry. Despite an assignment to the Air Service, West Point graduates were only temporarily assigned to the air branch and had to select a backup option because of the high failure rate. Of the forty-three aviation cadets who began flight training, less than a quarter survived. Barnes recalled that if "you didn't make your wings—you didn't stay."[15] Neither brains nor brawn was a predictor of success. Among the first trainees eliminated from Hunter Harris' class was fellow West Pointer Julian D. "Jude" Abell, an intelligent engineer and a great athlete.[16] Instructors and trainees alike viewed flying as an inherent skill—either you had it or you didn't.

Aspiring pilots who did not graduate from West Point had to go through a screening process, which included written and physical exams. Curtis LeMay enrolled in ROTC while attending the Ohio State University. As a young child, LeMay remembered the aerial demonstration he observed at the Panama–Pacific International Exposition held in San Francisco during 1915. Lincoln Beachey dazzled the crowd with his mystifying acrobatic maneuvers over the Golden Gate Bridge. Rumor had it that Beachey received $1,000 a week for his show. The money, however, did not attract LeMay. "It was the sight of the plane," LeMay said. "The appealing gush of its engine . . . was enough to set your spine a-tingling."[17] Upon completing four years of ROTC training and earning the distinction of being an honor graduate, LeMay applied for the Air Corps in the 1928 fall semester even though he still lacked fourteen credits for his undergraduate degree. LeMay took a written examination geared toward the college education he had received thus far. Before registering to complete the degree, the future SAC commander received notification of his acceptance into the Air Corps.[18]

Genetic Selection: The Eyes Have It

In addition to the academic requirement, prospective pilots had to pass a physical examination. The eyesight requirement created a barrier to entry in the pilot subculture. It was something left to genetics; passing the eye exam became critical to gaining entrance into the world of flying. As Horace Wade remembered, this was usually more difficult than the written exam. The Air Service expected pilots to have perfect vision. Wade lived in Magnolia, Arkansas, and had to travel eighty-five miles to Barksdale Army Air Field for his eye examination. Rising at four o'clock in the morning, Wade drove four hours on dust and gravel roads to his Louisiana destination. When he appeared for his examination, the redness in his eyes suggested that Wade had a cold. The flight surgeon told him to return in two weeks. On the next visit, Wade had a similar experience and was told to return at a later date. For Wade, the fifth time was a charm. The flight surgeon finally figured out that Wade's drive in the dust was affecting his eyes and told him to sit in the hall. After sitting for about four hours in the basement of the Barksdale hospital, Wade took the eye exam and passed.[19]

The type of flight training emphasized during this period drove the requirement for perfect vision. A majority of the flying conducted until the late 1930s was visual or "contact" flying, meaning pilots typically flew with a visible horizon and eye contact with the ground. Technological advances that enabled "blind" or "under the hood" flying based solely on references to the instruments in the cockpit would become more important in the years leading to World War II.

Barnes remembered how his first instructor tested his capacity for flying. During a training flight, the instructor ordered the trainee to fly into a cloud and fly out again. Knowing he would become disoriented, Barnes declined. Immediately following the ride, the instructor put Barnes up for a washout check. If he passed, he continued; if he failed, he was gone. Luckily, Barnes found a thin cloud to fly through on the next flight and passed the ride. Instructors expected pilots to be able to fly by the seat of their pants—to have an innate ability to sense how the plane moved in three dimensions and the reflexes and coordination to respond accordingly. This was the true measure of a pilot.[20]

The stress of training took its toll on a pilot's health. Curtis LeMay had never picked up a cigarette before coming to flight school. Tobacco, though, seemed to calm his nerves as well as those of his fellow pilots. Despite his increased pay, LeMay had to send money home to his family. He chose to smoke a pipe since it was a cheaper habit to fund. During his tour as a bomber commander in the Pacific, he found that Guam's high humidity caused his pipes to develop mildew overnight. LeMay switched to cigars, which became one of his signature features.[21]

Despite the high failure rate, West Point cadets increasingly sought the challenge of a flying assignment. Jacob Smart, a future general in the Air Force, graduated from West Point in 1931. He would serve in World War II as a bomber pilot and would spend time as a prisoner of war. Ninety-three of his classmates went into the Air Corps, and slightly less than half, forty-two, graduated from flight training by 1932. Although a greater number completed the course, flying remained a hazardous duty. Within a decade, before the outbreak of

World War II, nine members of his pilot class—close to 20 percent—
had died.[22] When Hunter Harris graduated from West Point the
following year, 79 cadets of the 262 graduates chose the Air Corps
as their first branch.[23] Eight cadets passed the strict vision test at West
Point but elected to go into the engineering corps instead of entering
aviation training.

Despite its increased popularity, one thing remained consistent
throughout the lean years of the Air Corps—the reason for wash-
ing out. When asked to identify the number-one reason his fellow
cadets did not graduate pilot training, Hunter Harris said they lacked
the inherent ability to fly—the hand-eye coordination required to
maneuver in three dimensions.[24] John B. Montgomery, who would
direct LeMay's bombing operations in the Pacific and later serve as his
initial director of operations in SAC, felt the same way. Those who did
not succeed as pilots were unable to take in all the inputs around them
and process them in a timely manner. A trainee who focused on one
thing too long simply could not fly formation or do instrument flying,
which required a pilot to "cross-check" several cockpit instruments
that provided feedback on the airplane's performance.[25] If a prospective pilot was predisposed to good eyesight, could handle his craft, and
could do it while processing and understanding his environment, he
could gain entry into this Army subculture, which viewed itself differently from the rest of the Army.

A Different Form of Combat
The Army's senior officers looked upon the Air Corps as something
equal in stature to other Army branches, but this first generation of
flying officers felt they had something others did not. Only the best
survived pilot training and earned their wings—they had "the gift."
Their paychecks proved they had something extra and were compen-
sated for it. Perhaps more importantly, pilots organized themselves
differently for combat than other Army branches. William Sherman,
a 1910 graduate of West Point, instructed at the Air Corps Tactical
School (ACTS), a branch school initially dedicated to teaching young
officers in the Air Corps tactical knowledge on the employment of the
airplane.[26] Sherman drafted the curriculum and the initial textbook
on war in the air. His text highlighted the distinctions between air, sea,

and ground forces: "A most important difference between the fighting forces of the air and those of the land and sea lies in the functions of officer and enlisted man." Sherman further explained the difference between organized air forces and the rest of the Army. In the infantry, Sherman argued, "it is the enlisted man who is the wielder of arms. The corps of officers exists only for the purpose of directing and coordinating the blows of many thousands of enlisted men to a common end. They strike no blows themselves." This was not the case with those who fight in the air, Sherman contended: "The officer is the wielder of arms—not the enlisted man. The latter is not a combatant at all. His duties are those of a mechanic. He is not called upon ... to follow his officer forward in the charge, through the heated atmosphere of danger and earth." Since officers led the charge in the air, Sherman finished, the air leader was a leader among leaders. Enlisted forces in the air branch mastered the "shop," not the battlefield.[27]

Sherman's text further explained how the role of the officer was different in the Army's air branch. Here, officers actually were first into battle. While Sherman may have argued that this was a new development, the parallels between pilots and the knights of the medieval period were obvious.[28] A new, nobler class of fighter-warrior was emerging with the airplane, while enlisted personnel were serving as pseudo men-at-arms, supplying these noble fighters.[29] This perception was not lost on the American public. Air war seemed purer than ground war; it recalled the days when battle seemed valorous and chivalric. Dogfights—aerial duels in the air—pitted one man against another, much like medieval jousts.[30] Pilots saw themselves as the new noble class fighting a new form of warfare.

Internal Evaluations
The perceived differences between pilots and other Army officers extended beyond how they viewed officer and enlisted roles. Pilots developed their own internal methods for measuring the aptitude of their comrades. Earning merit within this subculture came not by leadership attributes, intellect, or physical strength, but by one's performance in flight. Those who excelled at flying—the "good sticks"—earned the respect of their peers. The earliest planes were controlled by a pole, or stick, that rose from the floor that the pilot used

to maneuver the plane in the three dimensions of flight. Haywood Hansell, who served as a bomber commander in the Pacific during World War II, remembered the reputation Hoyt S. Vandenberg had developed by the time he arrived at ACTS to teach. Hansell taught bombing tactics, while Vandenberg, an exceptional pilot, lectured on pursuit aviation. The lecturer also performed aerial demonstrations that displayed his flying acumen. "Vandenberg was a legend in his own time as a pilot," Hansell recalled. "Everything General Vandenberg did was quite exceptional."[31] It was not uncommon for pilots to draw parallels between how a pilot handled his machine and how he handled command. While on temporary assignment in England during World War II, James Edmundson ran into an old acquaintance who was serving as a squadron commander under Curtis LeMay, then commanding the 305th Bombardment Group. Edmundson remembered his friend telling him: "[LeMay] was going to be Chief of the Air Force someday—if we ever have an Air Force—if he lived through the war." According to Edmundson, his friend found LeMay's willingness to lead the tough missions most impressive and an indicator of LeMay's possible future.[32] When an interviewer asked Russell Dougherty, a World War II veteran and future SAC commander (1974–77), to evaluate his friend and colleague David C. Jones—a future chairman of the Joint Chiefs of Staff—one of the first things he identified was Jones' flying ability. "I hate to think as a pilot," Dougherty said, "that he's better than I am." But Dougherty noticed something extraordinary in Jones: "He did everything well. You know, if he took it under himself to fly an airplane, he flew it well or better than anybody else."[33]

Before World War II, pilots found other means to demonstrate their piloting skills. The best way to build "airmindedness" in the American public was to show them airplanes in action. Airmindedness meant enthusiasm for airplanes—believing in their potential to better human life and support aviation development.[34] When Alfred Thayer Mahan urged the United States to become a naval power in the late nineteenth century, he highlighted national character as an important determinant of naval power. Those countries whose populations historically developed an enthusiasm for seafaring, Mahan argued, became great sea powers.[35] In a similar manner, pilots wanted to win over the hearts and minds of the American people. To do this, the Air Corps formed demonstration teams to perform for local audiences and endeavored to set or break world records. They were determined to fly longer, higher, and faster. Curtis LeMay explained why the Air Corps felt the need to continually conduct operations for publicity. "We were an Air Corps, part of the Army. . . . We were getting nothing in the way of appropriations for new equipment. It was a matter of educating the people and the country to the potential of air power."[36] Furthermore, each new record or first in aviation confirmed the miracle of flight to the American people and inspired greater awe and wonder.[37] Before taking a break from flying to get married, "Hap" Arnold won the first MacKay trophy (1912) for demonstrating the ability of an airplane to find troops on the ground. On January 1, 1929, "Tooey" Spaatz, Ira Eaker, Pete Quesada, Harry Halverson, and Sgt. Roy Hooe took to the skies in an airplane named "Question Mark" and stayed airborne—through air refueling—for 150 hours (6 days), setting a new world record.[38]

Pilots Must Do It All

These first- and second-generation American pilots found their jobs rewarding but very challenging. When they weren't flying, pilots had to take care of administrative matters on the ground. Emmett "Rosie" O'Donnell Jr. graduated from West Point in 1928 and earned his wings in 1930. He led General LeMay's first fire-bombing attack on Tokyo and commanded SAC's initial deployment of bombers during the Korean War. He spent his first seven years in the Air Corps flying fighters. O'Donnell remembered those years fondly: "We just had a ball up there. We had the chance to fly our heads off—formation every day and then did the jobs on the ground to cover the whole support business of the squadron and the group." Pilots served as supply officers or even mess officers. But there were payoffs. "We were entitled to take an airplane almost any weekend to give ourselves cross-country training," O'Donnell said, "and I think of all the things that I did up there." Some of these flights were to see his sweetheart. The training paid off twofold for O'Donnell. His sweetheart became his wife, and the flights gave him self-reliance and assurance. "Going across the mountains," O'Donnell said, "gave me more experience and confidence than I would have gotten any other way and it got me off to a good start."[39]

The development of bomber aircraft with multiple crew positions meant that pilots had to learn new duties, other than flying, as part of their training. The technology was increasing, but specialization training within the Air Corps had not reached a comparable level. When Horace Wade began his bomber training in 1938, he had to cross-train as a bombardier. "The first thing you had to do," Wade recalled, "was learn to be a bombardier. I dropped a lot of bombs." While serving as a copilot in the B-17 for two years, Wade also trained as a navigator, bombardier, and gunner on the plane.[40] Wade's experience was similar to that of John Montgomery, who was trained in all three positions: bombardier, navigator, and pilot.[41] Pilots wanting to become bomber pilots usually had to accumulate a minimum number of hours in other crew positions before they could fly in the pilot seat. Although their subculture had "special" status because they broke the bonds of Earth and moved in three dimensions, within the group pilots became generalists and held multiple positions.

Perhaps no one exemplified the Air Corps assignment of pilots to other crew positions better than Curtis LeMay. LeMay spent his first seven years of flying in pursuit aircraft. When he reached Hawaii in 1934, LeMay agreed to teach a navigation course because he figured that increased navigation skills would help earn him a coveted bomber assignment. LeMay explained his rationale: "I had gotten fighters for seven years, and even stupid people like me knew that bombers were more important in a first-class war than fighters were."[42] By this time, bomber production had received increased emphasis, and bombers had more engines—enabling them to fly faster, higher, and farther.

LeMay felt that the one-week navigation course he had previously attended was inadequate preparation for teaching his fellow pilots; therefore, LeMay spent time educating himself on the intricacies of navigation. Most navigation at the time was done by dead reckoning. Pilots would fly from one destination to the next using a magnetic heading and a precalculated time based on groundspeed. Using a map, pilots could update their course and speed with reference to visual landmarks. This technique would not work, however, when it came to navigating the longer distances made possible by new bombers,

especially over open waters. LeMay set out to master celestial navigation, a steering technique based on calculating one's position from
the observation of known stars. Although the many hours spent in
Hawaii learning navigation would pay off for LeMay, his new wife
did not share the young lieutenant's enthusiasm. Instead of spending
his honeymoon nights under the Hawaiian moon with his newlywed,
LeMay would look for stars and make his new bride hold a flashlight
while he did calculations.[43]

Understanding the Big Picture

LeMay received notification of his assignment to Langley Field,
Virginia, to fly bombers in 1936. Upon arriving at Langley, LeMay
became responsible for teaching navigation. Only the most experienced pilots earned the right to fly the newly arriving B-17 Flying
Fortresses; therefore, LeMay served as a navigator on the bomber and
earned quite the reputation for his skill.[44] It was in the 2nd Bombardment Group that LeMay would learn about preparation and operations from his commander and mentor, Lt. Col. Robert Olds. While
serving as the 49th Squadron's operations officer, Olds requested that
LeMay serve temporarily as the group operations officer since the
current officer had taken ill. From his lowly position in the Air Corps,
LeMay never understood the "big picture"—what it was the Air Corps
sought to achieve. Under Olds, LeMay received a rapid education. Olds
walked by LeMay's desk the first morning at Langley and asked the
lieutenant what the weather was like in San Antonio, Texas. "San Antonio?" the startled LeMay replied. "Your airplanes will fly down there,"
Olds informed him, "you ought to know what the weather is within
the range of your aircraft." From that day forward, LeMay reported to
work each day knowing the weather at every destination within range
of the group's flying operations. The amount of work Olds laid on his
temporary operations officer helped him understand "what we were
around for and what we ought to be doing and what could be done
and how much we didn't know about the operation of airplanes and
how important the airplane was to the country we lived in."[45]

Pilots in the Air Corps during the interwar years devoted their
time to flying and trying to understand and master their technology. They knew they had something special; they had wings on their

chests and more money in their pockets. The Army considered the
Air Corps an equal branch on par with other elements of the Army
such as artillery, engineering, and intelligence, all of which provided
support to the infantry. If war came, the Air Corps would provide
critical support to America's ground forces with intelligence, reconnaissance, and fires. While LeMay may not have realized the greater
picture from his small desk in Virginia, there were airmen fighting
arduously for an independent air force. This subculture developed a set
of values and assumptions different from the dominant culture, which
they expressed in their doctrinal development. America looked upon
the airplane as a way to bring chivalry to warfare; airmen argued that
airpower could win wars alone and make ground forces the supporting force. Their airpower doctrine would advocate not only the need
for an independent air arm but also the development of technology to
support strategic bombing. Their first experience in combat with the
airplane fueled the development of this doctrine.

The First Air War

The United States entered World War I without a complete understanding of how to employ the airplane. It represented a tremendous
leap in technology, the ability to bypass the natural and physical boundaries that constrained other forms of transportation. The airplane,
however, was no assurance of victory. Possessing the best technology
could not by itself guarantee victory. Only by developing commonly
held principles that would guide the employment of superior technology could one hope to emerge victorious in battle.[46] These principles,
sometimes referred to as doctrine, had to exploit the most advanta-
geous aspects of technology. In cultural terms, doctrine development
shows how the assumptions and values of a cultural group become
practices and policies. This was the ideology of the organization. For
American airmen, World War I would prove critical in the formulation of their values and assumptions. In the interwar years, that ideology would become doctrine.

In World War I, manned flight made its combat debut. Initially,
airplanes were used in a manner consistent with the balloons that
preceded them—reconnaissance, fire control, and communications. It
did not take long, though, before each side realized that destroying

their opponent's aircraft provided tactical advantage.[47] Warfare soon expanded to the skies. For some, the extension of combat to the third dimension was a logical progression of warfare: "Men are going to fight in the air for the same reason that they fight on the ground and under the ground and on the sea and under it, because a true soldier attacks the enemy wherever he finds him."[48]

Most "bombing" that occurred during the conflict was done in close proximity to the troops. Pilots started dropping bricks and grenades from their aircraft and eventually began carrying machine guns and rifles with them to menace opposing ground forces. "Close air support" became the term to describe aerial bombardment in support of ground forces, indicating the proximity of the airplane to troops and the battlefield. Conversely, strategic bombing focused on targets beyond the battlefield—behind enemy lines. During World War I, both sides experimented with strategic bombing, but accuracy problems plagued these early attempts. Billy Mitchell—the man who paid for his own wings—felt the offensive potential of the airplane had yet to be proven.[49] Before America's entrance into the war, Mitchell went to Europe to observe Allied aerial operations and learn about European air equipment and its use in military operations. This enabled him to prepare for air operations when the United States joined the war and units started to arrive in theater. He served in World War I as the air commander of the American Expeditionary Force (AEF) and of I Corps, and he was the first American pilot to fly over enemy lines. Mitchell gained a deep appreciation for the potential of the aircraft. Victory in warfare still relied on destruction of enemy forces. With ground forces trapped in their trenches and stalemated, Mitchell saw the airplane's ability to operate free of geographical boundaries as critical to destroying the enemy. He divided the AEF air assets into two forces: tactical, which operated close to the troops, and strategic, which acted far in front of troops and had an independent mission to destroy the enemy's means of supply, aircraft, factories, and lines of communication.[50] Although the United States used mostly Allied aircraft, Mitchell managed to orchestrate the largest air offensive of the Allied air forces in September 1918 against the salient at Saint Mihiel. With more than 1,500 aircraft, Mitchell—no longer doubting the airplane's role in warfare—helped devise one of the first air-ground offensive campaigns in history. The success of the operation earned Mitchell much acclaim and a promotion to brigadier general. The war ended, in Mitchell's estimation, before the airplane could prove its effect on changing the nature of war.[51] But Mitchell was not alone in his belief about the potential of airpower. Joining Mitchell in the skies over Europe was another future advocate of airpower, Carl Spaatz. When these aviators returned from the war, they set out to develop a theory of how airplanes could be used to the maximum effect in war.

Giulio Douhet: Airpower Prophet

The first comprehensive theory of airpower came not from an American but from an Italian. Giulio Douhet may have gained his appreciation for airpower while serving in the Italo-Turkish War (1911). While flying over enemy troops, he released a few grenades into their camp. The assault from the skies did little in terms of casualties, but it did produce mass confusion among the Turkish forces.[52] Douhet's advocacy for airpower, however, landed him in jail. Prior to Italy's entrance into World War I, Douhet recommended the purchase of several bombers to build up Italy's air force in case the country was drawn into the war. Italy's governing cabinet rejected his plan. When his country entered the war and became bogged down in trench warfare, Douhet wrote a letter to a cabinet minister criticizing the government for their bungling of Italian forces. When the letter became public, Douhet faced a court-martial and subsequent jail time for his insubordination. In October 1917 Italy lost 300,000 men at the battle of Caporetto and recalled Douhet to service to help build Italy's air force.[53] After the war ended, Douhet penned *Command of the Air* (1921) and several other works that outlined his beliefs about the employment of airplanes. His thoughts probably stemmed from Italy's geography—water on three sides and mountains to the north— and the difficulty his country had in projecting power. Perhaps more perceptive was his observation that airpower would make future wars "total," since industry and civilians would become potential targets.

Trench warfare and the tremendous loss of life in World War I affected Douhet, as it did most airpower enthusiasts. "As long as man remained tied to the surface of the earth," Douhet wrote, "his activities had to be adapted to the conditions imposed by that surface. War being an activity which necessitates wide movements of forces, the terrain upon which it was fought determined its essential features." The old assumptions of warfare, Douhet argued, no longer applied. "War is a conflict between two wills basically opposed one to the other," he observed. "The attacking force tries to advance along the lines of least resistance, or easy accessibility, towards the region he intends to occupy." Since war had to be fought on the surface of the earth, Douhet theorized, it could be waged only in movements and clashes along lines drawn on its surface. Perhaps even more perceptively, Douhet noted that previous forms of warfare drew a distinction between combatants and civilians: "Behind those lines, or beyond certain distances determined by the maxim [sic] range of surface weapons, the civilian populations of the warring nations did not directly feel the war. No enemy offensive could menace them beyond a predetermined distance, so civilian life can be carried on in safety and comparative tranquility. That situation is a thing of the past." For Douhet, all these previous assumptions about finding paths through terrain and breaking through enemy lines changed with the development of the aircraft. "The airplane has complete freedom of action and direction," Douhet wrote. "It can fly to and from any point of the compass in the shortest time. By virtue of this new weapon, the repercussions of war are no longer limited by the first artillery range of service guns, but can be directly felt for hundreds and hundreds of miles over all the lands and seas of a nation at war. There will be no distinction any longer between soldiers and civilians."[54] In the era of airpower, total war meant that the population had become a viable target.

Freedom of action in the skies, Douhet contended, gave the airplane inherently offensive characteristics. Airplanes could bypass ground enemies, operate with freedom of action and direction, and attack deep behind enemy lines, where Douhet felt the key to victory lay. Those nations that could understand the changing nature of warfare due to airplanes would prevail in war, for "victory smiles upon those who anticipate changes in the character of war—not upon those who wait to adapt themselves after the changes occur."[55] The experience of World War I weighed heavily on Douhet. Victory needed to be achieved expediently; therefore, Douhet argued that nations should build up sufficient air forces that could inflict the maximum amount of damage in the shortest possible time.[56] Nations that wanted victory had to build large forces of airplanes capable of self-defense, which he termed "battleships," that would seek out and destroy the enemy's forces on the ground. Killing planes on the ground, Douhet theorized, was much easier than trying to shoot them out of the sky. Once a commander was in a position to prevent the enemy from flying, while retaining the ability to fly oneself, he would have a command of the air.[57] With air superiority, the commander could expand the conflict to bombing a nation's civilian population. Douhet went on to argue that whereas previous conflicts kept civilians largely isolated, airplanes allowed a war to become total, to involve every aspect of a nation. He doubted the accuracy of strategic bombing—the ability to strike specific targets. Instead, he stressed its psychological effect. "Aerial bombs have only to fall on their target to accomplish their purpose," he proclaimed, as "[they] can certainly never hope to attain the accuracy of artillery fire."[58] Douhet's bombing plan would destroy the morale of the enemy's civilian population to the point where they would either petition the government to seek surrender or simply overthrow the government and pursue peace under a new administration.

Nations that hoped to be powers in the future had to embrace airpower. Douhet linked national power directly to the formation of an independent air force, arguing that "national defense can be assured only by an Independent Air Force of adequate power."[59] Airpower had to be plentiful and independent of other military forces to be properly employed. "An adequate national defense," Douhet proclaimed, "cannot be assured except by an aerial force capable in case of war of conquering the command of the air." At the same time Douhet published his theory of airpower and encouraged Italy to invest in an independent air force, Billy Mitchell presented similar ideas to America.

Billy Mitchell: Advocate for American Airpower
Billy Mitchell returned from the war with a purpose. He wanted to oversee the organization and funding of an independent air force in the United States. His flamboyance, however, drew the ire of the

Army's ranking officers. It could have been the wealth of Mitchell's family or the fact that he wore a nonregulation uniform to highlight his distinctiveness as an airman. More likely, it was Mitchell's assertion that no one should command aviation except pilots who understood the nature and potential of the airplane. He said that Army officers concerned with land warfare would not efficiently employ airpower.[60] The Army's dominant culture had no desire to lose a part of its organization to form a separate service.

Although his writings are similar to those of Douhet, Mitchell appears to have been more of an advocate and promoter of airpower than a theorist.[61] Douhet linked national power to the creation and maintenance of an independent air force. Mitchell, meanwhile, tied the development of airpower more to America's defensive posture. He posited that aircraft could successfully attack naval ships and that the coastal and aerial defense of the nation should be assigned to land-based aircraft.[62] Mitchell believed that the ability of the navy would no longer be the measure of the nation's power; airplanes, he argued, would be the future determinant. In his writings and speeches, Mitchell offered several reasons why the airplane would succeed the battleship. Battleships were limited by geography; they could only project their power from the sea. Since air covered every part of the earth, Mitchell explained, "aircraft have set aside the idea of frontiers. The whole country becomes the frontier, and in case of war, one place is just as exposed to attack as another."[63] Airpower, in Mitchell's estimation, was inherently offensive; it could travel anywhere and strike anywhere.

Mitchell decided to take public his fight for the mission of coastal defense. One way to educate the American people on the airplane's ability was through public events. In July 1921 Mitchell and his fleet of bombers coordinated an aerial exercise off the coast of Virginia with the intent of sinking the captured German dreadnought *Ostfriesland*. Many observers considered the mammoth battleship unsinkable. Using two-thousand-pound bombs, Mitchell's bombers struck the battleship twice. Within twenty minutes, the *Ostfriesland* lay on the bottom of the ocean.[64] Mitchell flew by observers on the USS *Henderson*, rocking his wings in triumph. This demonstration highlighted the vulnerability of navies, both practically and politically; the U.S. Navy complained that Mitchell violated the rules of the test by flying lower than the minimums, which would, under actual combat conditions, expose the aircraft to anti-aircraft artillery.

The aerial advocate recounted the demonstration in his 1925 book, *Winged Defense*, which argued for more than airpower in coastal defense. Like Douhet's, Mitchell's works outlined how airpower could be decisive in war. If airplanes struck the vital centers of an opposing nation, war would not require the slaughter of ground armies. Mitchell identified these centers as the cities where people lived, the areas their food and supplies were produced, and the transportation lines that carried these supplies from place to place.[65] Striking these centers at the beginning of the war with overwhelming force and intensity, Mitchell reasoned, would induce strategic paralysis, causing a breakdown in a nation's industry, communications, and transportation.[66] With the industries and transportation systems thus crippled, the frontline troops would weaken in their advance or defense, and the nation would sue for peace.

The second aspect of Mitchell's bombardment plan was that all these strategic operations would be carried out by an independent, centrally controlled air force. In order to change warfare, Mitchell believed the organization of military forces had to change as well. Strategic bombing would put distance between air forces and ground forces geographically as well as politically.[67] As a subculture that opposed the dominant culture of the Army, the aviation counterculture embraced the doctrine and technology that would provide organized airpower the justification to leave the Army.

The airpower advocate soon wore out his welcome in Washington, D.C. The Army reassigned Mitchell to a training position in San Antonio, Texas, and took away his temporary rank of brigadier general (making him a colonel). Banishment, however, did not silence him. On September 3, 1925, in southeastern Ohio, Mitchell's friend, Navy Commander Zachary Landsdowne, was piloting a dirigible when it crashed, killing the fourteen crewmembers on board. Mitchell became furious over the death of his friend and what he perceived as an apparent lack of government interest in the safety and importance of flight.[68] Two days later, Mitchell called six reporters into his office and gave them a six-thousand-word statement in which he asserted that "these accidents are the direct result of the incompetency [*sic*], criminal negligence and almost treasonable administration of the national defense by the Navy and the War Department."[69] These words drew the ire of the American military leadership, since Mitchell practically accused the leadership of criminal conduct and treason. The military levied eight charges against Colonel Mitchell under the Articles of War, ordering a court-martial. He reported to Washington, D.C., where he was arrested and confined to the limits of the city.[70] After the trial ended, the panel of officers deliberated for four hours and returned a verdict that convicted Mitchell on all charges. Only one officer, Maj. Gen. Douglas MacArthur, voted against conviction. Rather than accepting the punishment ordered by President Calvin Coolidge, Mitchell resigned from the Army on February 1, 1926.[71]

The Air Corps Tactical School

Douhet and Mitchell both put forth ideas on strategic bombing. As an American, Mitchell's "fight" for an independent air force was better known by the rank and file of the Air Corps than were the writings of Douhet. But one place where Douhet's treatise found an audience was the Air Corps Tactical School. Each of the Army's branches established schools to teach officers within a particular branch tactics specific to their operation on the battlefield. The impetus for the creation of the school was the lack of officers prepared to assume high command within the Air Service. Previously, most Air Service schools taught officers only the technical aspects of their job, but ACTS emphasized tactics—the employment of aircraft. Thomas Milling, a Billy Mitchell protégé, founded the school and tapped another Mitchell mentee, William Sherman, as one of its first instructors. These instructors envisioned a secondary purpose for the school: to educate Air Service officers in every aspect of airpower employment so that they could educate other Army officers on the full potential of the airplane. The school eventually moved to Maxwell Field, Alabama, in 1931.[72]

The school remained in existence until 1940, during which time 1,091 airmen graduated from the course. Of those graduates, 261 became general officers during World War II.[73] Although Douhet's writings began to appear at the school around the early 1930s, the cadre found some of his ideas politically unacceptable. Classroom instruction and curriculum from the mid-1920s to the 1930s revealed the evolution of the school's thinking with regard to strategic bombing. Sherman, the producer of the first textbook for the school, argued that the development of bombardment functions had clearly outstripped other forms of airpower because bombardment produced strategic effects. Airpower could affect more than the battle; it could win the war. Strategic bombing would destroy certain elements of industry, thereby crippling an enemy's war effort. Sherman lamented, however, that the importance of this type of systematic bombing had not been widely appreciated.[74] Accurate delivery of bombs was critical to its successful implementation; a text from 1931 showed that instructors favored daylight bombing since it provided the best opportunity to see the target. Even more important than accuracy was the concept of centralized control of strategic bombers. Once a "system" had been targeted for destruction, bombers had to keep striking the nodes of that system until it was destroyed before moving on to another system or another mission. By 1936 the evolution of ACTS thought had gone from airpower being able to cripple a nation to highlighting how airpower could win a war. The curriculum from that year showed that ACTS instructors continually emphasized the fact that airpower could bypass opposing armies and navies. Once airpower bypassed these forces and suppressed or eliminated the enemy's air forces, bombers could go unmolested about their business of attacking vital industries, which would not just cripple the country but win the war.[75]

Those who went through the school and eventually ended up fighting in World War II did not always look upon the school as some brain trust for theorizing about strategic bombing. Earl Barnes graduated from ACTS in 1935 and returned two years later as an instructor. The primary purpose of the school, as he saw it, was to determine the role of the aircraft in the next war.[76] Curtis LeMay thought some of the exercises at the school were improbable. During one, LeMay and his classmates fought an air battle with ground troops at the battle of Gettysburg. He remembered sending a majority of his fighters on a one-way mission knowing they would not return. It was not the scenario so much as the lack of proper resources that sent LeMay's fighters to their virtual doom.[77]

But not everyone had the same experience as LeMay. George Mundy graduated West Point in 1928 and earned his wings the following year. After serving stateside until 1945, he fought under LeMay as the commander of a bomb group in the Pacific and flew twenty-two combat missions against Japan. For him, ACTS was a very important school. "The tactical school has been credited, and rightly so, I believe," Mundy said, "in setting the course that we followed during World War II." The instructors were not just developing a concept or war plan, in Mundy's estimation; they were educating officers on airpower. "When one of the officers came to the school," Mundy recalled, "they became converts."[78] The "industrial fabric" mentality, as some labeled it, became a fixture of American airpower. Strategic bombing could precisely and systematically target vital enemy centers and destroy them without the need for a costly land invasion.[79] ACTS educated the Air Corps officers on the values, assumptions, and beliefs of the air subculture, which embraced the ideology of independence and revered the cultural artifact of the strategic bomber capable of delivering its bombs accurately.

Assumptions Become Reality

A group of former ACTS students and instructors became responsible for drafting the U.S. air war plan for defeating Germany. Under the leadership of Kenneth Walker, Harold George, Laurence Kuter, and Haywood Hansell—devotees of the industrial fabric mentality—developed Air War Planning Document 1 (AWPD-1), which outlined the U.S. plan for strategic bombing in the European theater.[80] Using American bank records, Walker's team reviewed the loans that went to German construction firms and developed a systematic, prioritized list of German targets.[81] British air forces, on the other hand, adopted a Douhetian model that deemphasized accuracy and targeted the social fabric of German society. The Air Corps' systematic approach emphasized accuracy in its planning and the procurement of bomber technology geared to the precise delivery of bombs.[82] The values of the Air Corps moved from Mitchell to the classroom to doctrine to the actual war plan for World War II. Cultural ideology had become formalized in a war plan. Executing that war plan would provide future SAC leaders the opportunity to develop additional elements that would ultimately become the SAC mentality.

Conclusion

Beginning in the twentieth century, a new type of military combatant emerged—the pilot. Members of this subculture of the Army's greater organizational culture considered themselves special and different from the organization to which they initially belonged. Although viewed as equals in the Army's eyes, pilots had a higher barrier to entry, higher pay, a different way of organizing, and something else that few people had—the inherent ability to fly. Prestige among pilots was not based on leadership, intelligence, or brawn. Potential for greatness among pilots depended on how well you mastered the technology—the artifact of this subculture. Throughout the interwar period, U.S. pilots struggled to gain funds for their service and notoriety for their feats. Creating an air-minded population led them to conduct flying demonstrations and achieve record-breaking feats.

The routines and rituals pilot candidates went through to earn their wings set them apart from the Army's other branches. To fly, pilots had to prove that they had perfect eyesight and an instinctive ability to operate an aircraft in all sorts of conditions and situations. People either had these traits or they did not. Although viewed as equals in the Army's eyes, pilots believed they possessed something special. Furthermore, pilots had a cultural symbol, flight pay, that reinforced their special status. The dangers associated with the early days of flight meant the military had to reward those willing to face the associated higher mortality rates. This subculture also evaluated one another differently from the Army's dominant culture, which valued leadership above all. Potential for greatness among pilots depended on how well one mastered the airplane.

This pilot subculture also organized itself differently from the Army. The organizational structure revealed the emerging culture of these early pilots. Officers led the charge in flying, while enlisted personnel primarily served in maintenance or logistic roles. In view of the carnage of trench warfare experienced in World War I, airmen gained a special popularity in a nation entranced with the romance of flight and the hope of a return to chivalry in warfare.[83] When pilots first entered World War I, however, they lacked a coherent doctrine for employing airplanes in war. Coming out of World War I, flyers began to espouse beliefs and values contradictory to the Army's dominant culture. Organized airpower was not just another branch of the Army that aided ground forces in their victory over the enemy. Airplanes could win wars alone and spare land forces the needless ground battle. One of the earliest pilots, Billy Mitchell, compared modern-day pilots to the noble knights of the past.

In terms of organizational culture, doctrine is the formalized expression of leaders' values and assumptions combined with their accumulated experience about how to achieve objectives in war. Although pilots had superior technology, they lacked a coherent doctrine that exploited the advantages of the airplane. Influenced by Douhet and Mitchell, the Air Corps embraced the promise and ideology of strategic bombing. The strategic bombing doctrine served two purposes: it set pilots and their planes apart because they believed they could win wars without military or naval campaigns on the surface of the earth, and it provided pilots the means to sever their ties to the Army's dominant culture. During war, bombers would systematically and precisely target the critical nodes of a country's industrial structure, thereby inducing a form of paralysis. Lacking the means to supply its forces, the theory presumed, the enemy would surrender before America had to undertake the risky prospect of a ground invasion. The only way this strategic bombing concept could work, its proponents argued, was if bombers were organized as an independent force and centrally controlled by airmen who knew how to employ airpower. The pilot counterculture had found the means to escape the Army's dominant culture. Strategic bombing would lead to independence.

American airpower began with technology, the airplane, and little in the way of doctrine. By the eve of World War II, airmen had devised a doctrine of strategic bombing but had little practical experience executing it in wartime conditions. As these airmen went about executing their doctrine against German targets, they developed training and tactics to increase the effectiveness of strategic bombing. The tactics and procedures formed in World War II would become the foundation for Strategic Air Command's culture several years later.

2

Shared Experiences
The Foundations of SAC Culture

Given time, air bombardment, if sufficient, would have made the invasion of Europe unnecessary. The mistake was not to wait for airpower to build up in Europe. By the time we used airpower in Japan we had experience and we had resources. Our campaign against Japan was more a clear-cut case of the proper use of airpower than Europe.

—CURTIS LeMAY

American U.S. airmen entered World War II determined to demonstrate that the airplane had changed the nature of warfare. Although there were many missions that airpower performed in the war, airmen believed their greatest contribution would come through strategic bombing. Accurately placing bombs on the critical nodes within a country's system, they argued, would bring about national paralysis and render land invasions unnecessary. Although the Army Air Forces (AAF) had a systematic plan, this was the first experience employing a bomber in combat for most airmen. The uncertainty and chaos of those first days in battle produced shared responses and experiences, which several of these men preserved and that became initial elements of SAC culture. This chapter focuses on the shared experiences of those men who would become leaders in SAC, because organizational culture forms as people struggle together to make sense of and cope with their world.[1] This chapter examines how SAC leaders handled the problems with the U.S. entrance into World War II and the initial phases of the Allied strategic bombing campaign. In overcoming the early problems of war, SAC's future leaders, particularly Curtis LeMay, developed solutions and responses that proved successful. These cultural forms—the rituals and routines—found their way into SAC's organizational culture.

Lack of Preparation

When the nation entered World War II, the Army Air Forces went through a rapid expansion. Previously, it had taken three thousand hours of flying time and roughly fifteen years of experience before a pilot could hope to become an aircraft commander in the B-17 Flying Fortress.[2] Curtis LeMay mastered navigation, and John B. Montgomery practiced dropping bombs while gaining the experience necessary to command one of the country's elite new airplanes. Under the stress of war, flight training produced new crewmembers every ninety days.

In 1942, Curtis LeMay, the once-struggling operations officer, became commander of the 305th Bomb Group. On paper, LeMay's group had four squadrons, but he never got the full complement of personnel to train prior to departure for England; most of them were still in school. Much to LeMay's chagrin, the entire group only had three B-17s for their training, which the group flew in shifts preparing for their deployment. The lack of airframes meant that most pilots never got to experience formation flying. Furthermore, the group received some of its navigators within two weeks of its deployment to England. For some of LeMay's group, the flight across the "pond" was only their third flight with the unit.[3] Conditions never improved for LeMay or the other commanders overseas. When asked to identify a period in the war when he received well-trained crews, LeMay replied, "That never happened."[4]

The mentality changed among Army officers and recruits with respect to the air. In the face of war, the "high ground" became a place to seek refuge from possible ground combat. West Point cadets could volunteer to spend their final summer before graduation in flight training instead of participating in the usual first-class summer program. In the summer of 1942, with the United States fully engaged in World War II, a majority of Carlos Talbott's class sought to find a haven from the mortality of infantry. Although flying had been considered a risky business before, it looked more appealing given their chances on the ground. Two hundred and fifty members of Talbott's class forewent their planned summer program for flight training.[5]

Kenneth Chidster, a B-29 pilot under LeMay's command in the Pacific, did not follow the college route to the Air Corps. Chidster, out of high school less than three years, joined the Air Corps after Pearl Harbor to avoid the draft. He desperately wanted to be a pilot, which required passing an entrance exam and the more difficult eye test. While boning up for the entrance exams, Chidster and a friend drank carrot juice and did eye exercises. After passing the entrance exams, a final physical, and ten days of grueling psychiatric exams, Chidster got his assignment to flight training. Despite the war, he remembers the washout rate among Air Corps candidates being extremely high. Chidster recalled the mentality his fellow applicants had toward being a pilot: "Everyone that I knew wanted to be a pilot so badly his teeth ached." Those who washed out during the selection process went on to navigation, bombardier, or gunnery school.[6] Combat in the air appeared more appealing for these young recruits, but they continually lacked the adequate preparation to face the air war overseas.

Despite their youth and inexperience, Horace Wade credited these young flyers with building a winning Air Force. "They were 21-, 20-year-old kids that had been through a rush course of flying school," Wade said, "and here they are with a big four engine airplane, never flown anything besides a single engine. They have a crew with all this responsibility. They responded to it well. They learned the airplane; they flew the airplane. Some of them got shot down, some of them got killed, but they made it possible to build an Air Force."[7]

In the face of this inexperience and youthfulness, those who showed promise received immediate promotions and advancement. Ralph Nutter remembers when the 305th led by Curtis LeMay deployed overseas. Nutter flew in the aircraft behind LeMay's lead bomber. As they approached the deployed base, LeMay announced over the radio that his navigator was unable to locate the group's position or lead them to the base. Nutter responded that he knew exactly where the group was and could lead them. LeMay responded: "Take the lead. We'll follow you in. We're counting on you." When Nutter followed through on his promise and led the group safely to the ground, LeMay walked over to Nutter and told him that he was now the group navigator.[8]

Training and preparation were not the only problems that plagued the initial execution of the AAF strategic bombing campaign. When LeMay brought his group into theater, he discovered that although three to four groups had already arrived and participated in operations, no one had developed a standardized procedure for conducting strategic bombing missions. "Each group commander used his own ideas on the subject and everyone was using different methods," LeMay lamented. "None of them were very successful. Not only were the targets not being destroyed, but we didn't have any record of where most of the bombs actually fell."[9] One of the reasons there was no feedback from attempted bomb runs was that crews rarely placed their weapons within view of the bomber's camera to provide a picture useful for poststrike analysis. Crews were under the impression that they had to maneuver every ten seconds on the bomb run to avoid enemy anti-aircraft artillery (AAA) fire. LeMay learned this fact from his first conversation with Col. Fred Anderson, the commander who had led the first U.S. B-17 attacks on continental Europe. LeMay doubted Anderson's conclusion. Not only did the group not need to maneuver that much to avoid AAA, but excessive maneuvering also wreaked havoc with bombing accuracy.

Horace Wade thought that the Norden bombsight, used by American B-17s to place their bombs on the correct target, "was the ultimate end of days." The only problem with it was the delicacy it required to drop bombs accurately. If the aircraft commander did not fly the programmed altitude and airspeed, the bombs missed their target. The bombardier had to calculate the right drift, synchronize the crosshairs, and above all see the target in his field of view. Executing a successful bomb run required the perfect input of all these contingencies. "You could drop it in a pickle barrel," Wade concluded, "but you had to do all of those things."[10] Troubled by his intuition, LeMay spent the night devising a new bombing procedure. Drawing on his engineering education and ROTC experience with artillery, LeMay challenged the accepted notion that a bomber flying straight and level for more than ten seconds would be shot down.[11] In fact, he calculated that German artillery would have to fire 372 rounds to hit one target the size of a B-17.[12] His calculations led him to conclude that a bomber stood a reasonably good chance of survival if it flew straight and level for seven minutes. Increasing the time bombers flew straight and level on the bomb run stabilized the aircraft and increased the probability of hitting the target. LeMay hated the idea of maneuvering unnecessarily, throwing bombs off target, and having to return to strike the same target another day.

LeMay decided to try out his procedure with his group when ordered to bomb a target near Saint Nazarie. For Ralph Nutter, sitting in the nose of LeMay's B-17, the bomb run felt a lot longer than seven minutes. He heard and saw flak exploding all around him. Although he expected the worst to happen, it never did. LeMay's group made it through the bomb run without losing a single aircraft to enemy ground fire. Additionally, LeMay's tactic improved accuracy.[13] His procedure became a standard for Eighth Air Force (8 AF). Besides developing a standardized bombing procedure, LeMay worked on formalizing the group's formation procedures. LeMay considered his most significant contribution to the development of the Air Force to be "getting a bombardment program organized in World War II when everyone was learning. There was a need for standardization, and my system was adopted for formations, techniques of bombing, etc."[14]

When LeMay was not standardizing procedures for the entire Air Force, he increased the standardization within his own unit. Successfully flying a bomber under attack, finding a target, striking it, coordinating maneuvers with the numerous gunners on board, and maintaining position within the formation required different personnel to accomplish specialized and coordinated tasks. This mentality stood in contrast to the fighter, which performed and accomplished its mission based on the skills of one person. To make sure that crews ran effectively, LeMay initially published manuals in the European theater that defined what each bomber position would do during every phase of flight.[15] Bombers relied on synchronized operations, with every person knowing what every other crewmember did at a particular moment—especially during critical phases of flight. As LeMay emphasized in his manuals, "The importance of teamwork cannot be overemphasized. The individuals who are proficient in their respective duties do not necessarily make a good crew, but these ten individuals will definitely make a good crew if they know how to work together as a team."[16] Standardized procedures among crewmembers, especially pertaining to checklists, became increasingly important in war.

John Montgomery remembered how things were before the war: "We had takeoff lists and checklists. Each man had his own checklists. They were followed, not strongly enough as they should have been. . . . I can see, looking back, that there wasn't enough pressure put, upside, on the people who operate the equipment to use that checklist. For instance, [one pilot] left it up to the copilot. If you didn't finish the checklist before we got out for takeoff that was too bad because he took off anyway."[17] In the face of battle, LeMay wanted his crews running according to his procedures, which became an organizational routine.

Another method that increased the bombing proficiency of LeMay's units was the implementation of the lead crew program. Upon arrival in theater, LeMay asked his new lead navigator, Nutter, to review the reconnaissance photos of the 305th's training bomb runs prior to their departure. Nutter noticed a significant difference between the experienced crews and those navigators and bombardiers who arrived immediately prior to their mission. LeMay thought that training command naturally assumed that if a bombardier could hit the target under pristine training conditions, then he could do it under the stress of combat. Only the most experienced crews, LeMay concluded, should lead the bombing formations until the new arrivals had time to acclimate to combat conditions. LeMay explained his rationale for initiating a "lead crew" program: "The crew did not have ample time to study the target, to plan the mission, to get familiar with the area, to navigate in properly, really be on course when they came up to the target . . . in other words, ready to do a professional job." Under his program, LeMay divided areas into segments and assigned these segments to graduates of his lead crew school. Crews would spend their spare time studying the targets in their segment.

If headquarters selected a target within their area for a mission, that crew would lead the mission.[18]

Under LeMay's instruction, Nutter and the group's lead bombardier, Charles Preston, developed a lead crew school to train bombing teams that would eventually lead the group's runs against Axis forces on continental Europe. Once a crew had ten to fifteen missions, LeMay's staff selected the best crews based on navigation, bombing, and impressions of the aircraft commander to attend the lead crew school. Crew discipline and integrity (keeping integral crews together) ranked among the highest ideals LeMay sought in his lead crews; therefore, crew substitutions were not allowed on actual bombing missions. Once LeMay had a crew formed that functioned well together, he wanted to keep it intact.[19] LeMay's continued improvements in bombing procedures impressed the leadership in the European theater and propelled him up through the ranks.[20] As LeMay struggled to develop routines that led to successful bombing, other airmen were working to gain the AAF independence and centralized control of air operations.

Move for Independence

Air Corps leaders who led the Army Air Forces in World War II fervently believed the proper use of airpower would come when the nation in general, and Congress in particular, recognized the need for a third service branch. Their efforts failed to receive congressional support during the interwar period despite their constant public demonstrations of aerial might. The move for independence received new life when U.S. forces entered World War II on the shores of North Africa.

Squabbling over control of airpower in the African theater during the first U.S. campaign in World War II, Operation Torch (1942), led to the publication of Army Field Manual (FM) 100–20, *Command and Employment of Air Power.* At the battle of Kasserine Pass, conflicting notions of how air assets should be controlled by ground commanders marred America's first battle with the Germans and provided the impetus for rewriting Army doctrine. Most Army ground commanders wanted specific aircraft assigned to their unit to be used only in support of it; there was no ability to combine air assets to achieve objectives outside of units since commanders refused to give up their dedicated air support. Keeping aircraft this close to ground forces prevented them from fulfilling the first mandate of airpower—establishing control of the air—since they could not mass to find and destroy an enemy air force. Furthermore, aircraft held this close to the ground battle precluded bomber forces from penetrating enemy lines and attacking sources of military support behind enemy lines.

In Washington, D.C., "Hap" Arnold knew he needed a way to provide operational justification to free air forces from Army ground commanders. One method to formalize airmen's assumptions about airpower was to make it doctrine. If ideology is the organization's cultural expression of assumptions and beliefs, then doctrine represents the formalization of that ideology. Publishing FM 100–20 secured, in writing, the notion that air forces should be employed with flexibility and freedom so that they could create the conditions that would enable ground forces to achieve victory.[21]

Aviation officers considered FM 100–20 the Army Air Force's "declaration of independence" because of wording AAF leaders managed to incorporate into the new doctrine. FM 100–20 recognized the need to centralize airpower under a single air commander; it also stated that "land power and airpower are co-equal and interdependent forces; neither is an auxiliary of the other." The new doctrine also drew a distinction between the mission of tactical air forces and strategic air forces. While tactical air forces provided support to ground forces engaged in battle, the aim of strategic air forces was the "the defeat of the enemy nation."[22] Finally, the document stipulated that all air forces should be put under the command of an airman who understood the employment of airpower. Arnold ordered that "every" airman receive a copy of the new doctrine.[23] Each member of the AAF now had a formal artifact articulating the values and assumptions of airmen.

Diversion of Assets from the Primary Campaign

One of the central assumptions of the strategic bombing concept was the idea that once a campaign started against a prioritized list of targets, it continued until each target was destroyed. Given an independent bombing force of sufficient magnitude, U.S. airmen felt they could defeat a country without a land invasion as long as their forces were not required to service other targets as the nature of the conflict changed. In the European theater, despite the implementation of FM 100–20, future Air Force leaders decried the constant diversion of their bomber assets from the primary objective of destroying the German war machine. Curtis LeMay felt that strategic bombing operations in Europe were diverted too often to fulfill other operations such as interdiction of supplies and troops and close air support. LeMay found fault with the theater commanders for the diversion of assets. "Airmen weren't running the air war," he remembered. "We were under the theater commander, and he determined what the first priority would be at any given time."[24]

One of the inherent characteristics of airpower stressed in FM 100–20 was its flexibility. Theater commanders capitalized on airpower's flexibility and shifted strategic resources as necessary when operational requirements required the firepower of these heavy bombers. For example, in 1944, Gen. Dwight Eisenhower, the Supreme Commander of Allied Forces, asked "Tooey" Spaatz, commander of U.S. Strategic Air Forces, to direct his bombers against railroads and roads that could have been used by German forces to bring reinforcements to the Normandy coast. This change in priorities for the Allied command took pressure off German industry and production while U.S. bombers set the conditions for the invasion. Haywood Hansell, one of the architects of America's strategic bombing plan in Europe, saw airpower's greatest strength become its Achilles' heel. "One of the great advantages as well as the greatest weaknesses of air power is responsibility," Hansell said. "It can be so easily diverted from its purpose."[25] The command structure in Europe allowed airpower to be redirected since the theater commander centrally controlled the air assets.

As the strategic bombing campaign started in the Pacific, "Hap" Arnold worked successfully to build a command structure that put control of his newest strategic bombers, the B-29s, in the hands of a commander who reported to the Joint Chiefs of Staff (JCS) rather than the theater commander. Keeping these bombers outside the chain of command of Pacific theater commanders Gen. Douglas MacArthur, USA, and Adm. Chester Nimitz, USN, prevented the diversion of air assets from the strategic bombing campaign that airmen derided in Europe. The formation of the Pacific bombing command was important because it served as a precursor to the type of organizational form SAC would advocate upon its inception. An organizational form stands as a set of rules that patterns social interaction between members, facilitates the appropriation of resources, and provides an internally and externally recognized identity for an organization.[26]

Forming an Independent Bombing Force: Twentieth Air Force

Airmen achieved their desired command relationship in the Pacific theater. General Arnold recognized the divided effort in this theater of operations. Admiral Nimitz ran the campaign in the central Pacific, and General MacArthur headed the effort in the southwest Pacific. Assigning bombers to both commands, Arnold reasoned, would divide the bombing effort. Furthermore, either commander might use the new bombers for operations other than the strategic bombardment of Japan. "Hap" asked the JCS for a different command system when B-29s began service against Japan. Although Arnold faced initial opposition from the JCS, he eventually won support for the creation of Twentieth Air Force (20 AF), which controlled bomber operations in the Pacific.[27] This command remained the only numbered air force whose operations were directly controlled from Washington, D.C., by General Arnold himself.

Strategic operations against Japan began in the China-Burma-India (CBI) theater since U.S. forces had not secured an island close enough to Japan to permit round-trip operations. In July 1944, Curtis LeMay arrived from Europe to take command of the CBI strategic bombing operation.[28] By now, LeMay had built a formidable reputation as a bomber commander. He was self-reliant, an outdoorsman, and an adventurer. He also gained a reputation for being a stern disciplinarian. His reputation, however, stemmed from his leadership philosophy, although some attributed it to his inability to smile. Before deploying for the war, LeMay learned that his high-altitude flying had triggered Bell's palsy—a partial facial paralysis that made it difficult for the commander to smile.[29] LeMay told his group navigator, "I am not supposed to be liked. I don't have the luxury of liking or disliking people."[30] LeMay believed that realistic training gave his crewmembers the best chance for survival. Tough training better prepared crews for actual combat conditions. Part of that training was adherence to standardized procedures, which LeMay himself helped develop.

Once he arrived in the Pacific, LeMay implemented the same procedures that had brought him success in Europe.[31] As it had in Europe, training became the focus. Paul Carlton, who would become LeMay's aide in SAC and achieve four stars after several commands in SAC, remembered what happened when LeMay arrived in CBI. "He stopped flying over there," Carlton said, "and started a lead crew school, trained people how to bomb and navigate. We stopped flying for almost six weeks. Built up the supplies in China. After that time period . . . we started a pretty good campaign in China."[32] LeMay standardized procedures, instituted realistic training, and emphasized lead crews. For LeMay, the Japan campaign offered a new opportunity: "Our whole goal was to try and end the war before the invasion."[33]

The move to the Pacific brought with it a new aircraft, the B-29 Superfortress. This new bomber provided aircrews with advanced technology to allow a better chance of finding targets on radar, obviating the need to visually identify the target. In line with his command philosophy, LeMay began a lead crew radar school so that the best people were always leading the bombing formations.[34] Lead crews now studied a particular area of the country—and its radar returns— so they knew every contour leading to the target. When that crew's target became the objective for a mission, it led the formation, since the crew's bombardier knew the area well. Now instead of visually studying the target, radar operators focused on predicting what the target would look like on their radar screen.

In addition to operations, LeMay brought a new direction to maintenance functions, reorganizing them for efficiency by assigning all maintenance specialists to the group level, one level up from the bomb squadron. Previously, specialists worked on their squadron planes only and got to know the crews and planes. Combining the specialists gave them an economy of scale because specialists would work on any broken plane, not just those assigned to their squadron. Crewmembers, however, complained because they did not like the idea of "strangers" working on their planes. The centralization

of maintenance proved effective and efficient. Maintenance specialists now responded to the aircraft that needed their skills instead of
remaining fixed to a particular aircraft.[35]

But achieving success against Japan proved more difficult than
expected. The B-29 could achieve higher altitudes than the B-17,
which meant that Japanese fighters had difficulty reaching and targeting the bombers. The new altitude, however, also presented challenges
for the American aircrews. Jack Catton remembers his first mission
over Japan vividly. Very few pilots had flown outside the United
States. During the campaign against Japan, bomber crews experienced
tremendous changes in weather conditions. The jet stream passed
right over Japan, which created wind shifts of one hundred miles per
hour. Catton noted, "This was the first time anybody in the United
States Army Air Forces had encountered what we know as a jet stream.
We really whistled down the bomb run. . . . The synchronization by
the bombardier on the target for the bomb release left something to
be desired. We did not do a very good job, but it was the first time we
had encountered a jet stream."[36] Crews were not prepared for the new
bombing conditions. The distance from CBI to Japan meant planning for adequate fuel was critical due to the shifting winds. LeMay's
philosophy stressed the importance of the mission—dropping bombs
on target. He told his crews that the target was the sole objective;
the inability to return was no reason to abort. One navigator under
LeMay's command said it seemed like "our job was to hit the target—
planes and crews, it seemed, were expendable."[37]

When U.S. forces seized islands close enough to Japan to launch
operations from the Pacific, Arnold created 21st Bomber Command
on the island of Guam and put Haywood Hansell in charge. One of
the first units to arrive in theater was "Rosie" O'Donnell's 72nd Wing
of B-29s. O'Donnell selected Walter "Cam" Sweeney as his deputy for
the organization. These two men would have an impact on the future
of strategic bombing and SAC. O'Donnell would become one of
LeMay's first commanders in SAC and lead the initial deployment of
bombers to the Pacific theater during the Korean War. Sweeney would
be responsible for war plans in SAC under LeMay and eventually rise
to become a four-star general and command Tactical Air Command.
When O'Donnell hired Sweeney, he told him the job came with a

condition: "Cam, there's one thing we've got to get straight. Any outfit that's going to be good has got to have a son-of-a-bitch in it and I ain't him."[38]

In Washington, D.C., Arnold did his own assessment of the condition of the Pacific strategic bombing campaign. The B-29 crews continued to struggle with equipment malfunctions and weather, which led to poor bombing results. Arnold knew Japan was the last opportunity to prove the validity of strategic bombardment. Impatient with the lack of good results, he ordered the 20 AF chief of staff, Major General Lauris Norstad, to replace Hansell with LeMay. John B. Montgomery remembered what he thought of LeMay's move to the Pacific island: "There was LeMay sitting out in the CBI area, he was an established commander with a peerless record and a great reputation for precision bombing out of England into Germany. So since the B-29s were strategically important to our future operations, LeMay was put in charge, and Hansell was fired."[39] Ordering him from the CBI, Arnold wanted LeMay to make the 21st Bomber Command produce results.

LeMay's operation in the Pacific was the ideal situation as far as the new commander was concerned. "General Arnold worked a miracle," LeMay recollected, "in getting the B-29s under a separate command outside the theaters in the Pacific. They had always been assigned to the theater commander."[40] But despite having complete operational control, LeMay had to struggle for administrative and logistical support. These functions were still under the purview of the theater commander. LeMay's reorganization of his maintenance structure led his maintenance chief to predict that 21st Bomber Command's forces could now fly 120 hours a month. Nimitz's staff did not believe him, since in Europe bombers could only manage thirty hours a month; how could LeMay's forces fly more hours in the barren surroundings of the Pacific islands? LeMay explained to Nimitz, "We have a new maintenance system and a different setup; we can do it." The Navy never believed LeMay until his command ran out of incendiary bombs after five missions, and low-altitude runs had to stop for six weeks until the Navy resupplied the command.[41] Since supply was the lifeblood of his operations, LeMay felt like he spent 20 percent of his time fighting the Japanese and the rest of his time fighting the Navy for supplies. Jack Catton, who flew missions under LeMay's command, believed in the need to establish independent bombing operations. "We had to conduct a strategic bombing operation without interference from any theater commander," Catton said. "A theater commander will always apply resources to his immediate objective rather than to something that is more abstract like the strategic bombing mission. We could never have effectively done a strategic bombing job if we were to be component forces."[42] As LeMay went about building SAC's operational construct in the 1950s, self-sufficiency and command of all aspects of the organization's operations would become goals of SAC.

As he had with his European commands, LeMay emphasized training as a top priority in the Pacific. Jack Catton remembered LeMay standing down the Pacific operations for one to two weeks while the forces went through realistic training. "We practiced formation flying," Catton recalled. "We were practicing for day visual bombing at appropriate altitudes, and at altitudes where we would have substantial fighter opposition. We *trained*; I will never forget it. We flew nearly every other day. . . . We really were in a training environment. We all got the message very, very clearly."[43] LeMay observed his crews while airborne; he believed the best leaders were those who flew. When they did return to operations, Catton stated the results were much improved because of LeMay's leadership. LeMay's staff planned bomb runs that gave crews the highest probability of target destruction, taking into account unpredictable winds and enemy defenses. This approach turned out to be the safest in the long run because, in Catton's estimation, LeMay's tactics meant crews did not have to return to the target as often.

Those who led the bombing missions, the lead crews, were considered invaluable to mission success. New crews usually found themselves in the back of the formations, the most vulnerable position in the group. Surviving the requisite ten to fifteen missions meant a chance to become a lead crew. Jack Catton came to the Pacific as a lead crew commander and kept his job after LeMay's strenuous training program. As a lead crew, Catton's crew got the best treatment. Since they had to lead the mission, lead crews flew the optimum aircraft. LeMay also believed in keeping functioning crews together. He liked the idea of "hard crews" instead of splitting up a crew to spread the experience around. Once a crew functioned together well, LeMay implemented policies to keep them together.[44]

One of the factors missing from the strategic bombing campaign against Japan was the same systematic analysis that AWPD-1 had outlined against Germany. Hansell, the initial commander of 21st Bomber Command and an architect of AWPD-1, said his first directive upon assuming command was to destroy the Japanese aircraft industry. Although Hansell had an objective, he had trouble determining the targets, since the United States lacked the kind of comprehensive analysis that bank records and tour books had provided about Germany.[45] Furthermore, Japan maintained an extremely effective security system that the United States could not penetrate. Whereas Germany even had books about their country on the open market, Hansell had to rely on reconnaissance flights to provide the type of intelligence necessary to construct a systematic U.S. strategic bombing campaign. The lack of intelligence and the time required to build a true campaign ran head on into "Hap" Arnold's need for results.

The B-29 operation struggled with difficult winds at altitude, a radar system that functioned imperfectly, and a commander in Washington who wanted results. These combined factors influenced LeMay's decision to conduct low-level bombing of Japan with incendiary bombs. Ordering planes to low altitude, in LeMay's estimation, was his second most important and difficult career decision.[46] To bolster crew confidence in their ability to fly low and at night, LeMay called his staff together and ordered Montgomery to plan a low-altitude attack of three ships flying in stream formation at fifty feet. Montgomery assigned "Rosie" O'Donnell's wing to fly the training mission. The staff expressed concerns to LeMay that the bombs at that altitude would ricochet off the ground and strike the trailing aircraft; they also doubted their crew's ability to navigate and find a target at such a low altitude. When O'Donnell received the assignment, he called Montgomery and said some numbers must have been missing on the teletype since the altitude was only fifty feet. When Montgomery confirmed the altitude, O'Donnell flew from Saipan to LeMay's headquarters to express his concern to the commander. As

O'Donnell walked in, LeMay said, "Well, Rosie?" O'Donnell replied, "I can't run that mission." LeMay simply put down his cigar and said, "By God, you will run it." According to the crews on that training mission, training bombs were bouncing up between the wings of the trailing aircraft as predicted. Rumors of the mission spread like wildfire; a daylight raid at fifty feet was going to be suicide. When LeMay made the actual plan for the first low-level raid, it was at five thousand to seven thousand feet and at night. Montgomery questioned LeMay, "General, you never intended to run that mission at fifty feet?" LeMay replied only with a smile. For Montgomery, this was the sign of a great commander; instead of a great feeling of fright, the crews went in with a tremendous sense of relief.[47] The arduous training program had more than prepared the crews for the realism of combat operations.

LeMay received support from Washington for his decision to change tactics in the Pacific. In expressing his approval, Arnold revealed the pilot mentality about bombing operations and their potential for public display. "Air operations are colorful," Arnold wrote, "and consequently the actual operation is normally the only phase of a Command's work which receives public recognition. Your recent incendiary missions were brilliantly planned and executed." Arnold assured LeMay that his efforts would receive more resources by the middle of summer. With the promise of nearly one thousand bombers, Arnold felt that LeMay could be able to "destroy whole industrial cities should that be required."[48] The bomber commander continued to pressure the industrial centers of Japan but never flew in the attacks on Japan, mainly due to his knowledge of the Manhattan Project, the U.S. effort to develop an atomic bomb.[49] The results of that program became evident in August 1945.

The strategic bombing campaign in the Pacific climaxed with the dropping of the atomic bombs on Hiroshima and Nagasaki. By this time, Arnold had grown more impatient with the results of the campaign against Japan. Despite his early praise for LeMay's success, Arnold knew of the U.S. plans for an invasion and the dwindling opportunity to prove that strategic bombing alone could cause a nation to surrender. With the war in Europe over, Arnold reorganized the entire Pacific operation. Spaatz, who had commanded the strategic forces in Europe, was sent to the Pacific to assume the same job. LeMay wore only two stars and faced considerable resistance from the higher ranking theater commanders. Furthermore, Arnold elevated LeMay to become his chief of staff and redesignated 21st Bomber Command as 20 AF. Some viewed this move as a way to save LeMay the embarrassment of being relieved of command. Nate Twining, who had recently led Fifteenth Air Force in the Mediterranean in the European theater, assumed command of Twentieth Air Force.[50] Arnold expressed his frustration in the Pacific to Twining, but to Hansell, the frustration was more with the timeline than with the commander. "I don't think General Arnold was necessarily deeply dissatisfied with General LeMay's performance. Shouldn't have been—but General Arnold was habitually impatient and dissatisfied with everybody."[51] Hansell recalled LeMay's frustration with the situation: "[LeMay] told me he was not surprised, that he realized that he could not maintain that magnitude of command in that atmosphere. It must have been a severe blow to him to have run a successful operation and then be relieved of command about the time it was reaching fruition." Although debate still swirls over the impact of the atomic bomb, strategic bombing advocates felt that with or without the atomic weapons, they would have forced Japan's surrender without an invasion.

The decision to drop the atomic bomb only confirmed what many strategic bombing enthusiasts suspected—Japan was ready to fall under the weight of America's strategic bombers. The destructive power of the nuclear devices surprised LeMay, but it did not change his opinion on their role in the defeat of Japan. "I agree with dropping it, and still believe the decision to drop the bomb correct," LeMay said in 1965. "While the war with Japan could have been won without dropping either of the two atomic bombs, I am certain in my own mind that it significantly shortened the war and, therefore, saved lives in the long run."[52] Arnold had a similar opinion. "The surrender of Japan was not entirely the result of the atomic bombs," he wrote in his memoirs. "It appeared to us that atomic bomb or no atomic bomb, the Japanese were already on the verge of collapse."[53] Although these leaders believed strategic bombing had won the war in the Pacific, official studies conducted after the war did not reach the same conclusion.

Conclusion

The shared experiences of future SAC leaders in World War II helped shape the organizational culture of SAC. Culture does not arise overnight and cannot be divorced from the history people share. As a group of people spend time together, they develop common ways to deal with uncertainty and chaos. If these ideas and practices work, and the members believe they are valid, the ideas and practices have a life of their own.[54] Although the AAF had a developed doctrine going into World War II, the actual forces lacked the preparation and training to implement that action. LeMay, among others, found no standardization in Europe in training, bombing, or formation flying. Tactics— the proven techniques used to prosecute combat operations—are a cultural routine. LeMay found his tactics—standardization, lead crews, and arduous training—paid benefits. He applied the same routines to each command he assumed throughout World War II. In the Pacific, LeMay commanded the bulk of the strategic operations against Japan. In formulating new tactics—standardization, lead crews, and repetitive training—LeMay originated cultural routines that paid dividends in actual combat.

Those who shared that experience with him—O'Donnell, Montgomery, Sweeney, Catton, and Carlton—would make a huge impact on SAC culture. In the Pacific, the United States encountered some problems when forming its strategic bombing campaign. The need for timely reconnaissance and an understanding of global weather— especially the prevailing winds—would become important aspects of SAC's organizational structure. As the war ended, the shared historical experiences of this group of bomber pilots would play a formative role in SAC culture. Interestingly, the first SAC commander, Gen. George Kenney, and his staff had not shared the same experience.

After World War II, U.S. airmen continued to lobby for an independent service because of their experiences in the war. First, bomber advocates felt that theater commanders diverted bombers from their primary mission at times in the European theater. When constructing a command to conduct the strategic bombing of Japan, General Arnold gained the approval to have it report directly to the JCS. Theater commanders in the Pacific did not have control over the new strategic bombers (B-29s) or over the campaign itself. This command relationship established a precedent for building a centralized bombing command when the war ended.

The first SAC administration did not have the same history as LeMay's bomber group and therefore took the organization in a different direction.

3

Beginnings
The Evolution of SAC

Strategic air power combined with our temporary monopoly of the atomic bomb is the best means for a military application of industrial power. This country's intercontinental bomber and the atomic bomb [are] the greatest forces for peace in the world.

—CARL "TOOEY" SPAATZ

Organizations are dynamic entities; they act like living bodies. They have a beginning and an end. In between, organizations respond and react to internal and external forces. As organizations evolve, they go through stages of development, which can occur sequentially or simultaneously. First, organizations encounter variation when they can intentionally or blindly select routines and traditions that will form the basis of their operations. In the second step, selection, the organization chooses those variations that will help it obtain resources and attain legitimacy. When organizational routines are preserved, duplicated, or reproduced, an organization enters the third stage of organizational evolution—retention. Throughout the process, organizations simultaneously go through a "struggle" for capital and legitimacy—a fourth phase—because resources are scarce and limited.[1]

Internal and external forces created SAC and influenced its development. Internally, the newly independent Air Force desired to establish an organization devoted to centralized strategic bombing. Externally, the nation struggled to develop a strategy to confront a new threat—the Soviet Union—and a new war, the Cold War. At the same time, the Air Force competed with other services for legitimacy and resources. The Air Force, the newest of the armed services, viewed itself as the most progressive and technologically advanced. To show its technological advantage and growing independence, the Air Force embraced the atomic bomb and the intercontinental bomber. The strategic bomber represented distance from Army culture; the intercontinental bomber put greater distance—physically and politically—between the Air Force and the other services. By embracing the atomic bomb and the intercontinental bomber, the Air Force created an organization that fit the prevailing external environment. Although the Soviet Union presented a threat to the United States, the Harry S. Truman administration struggled to restrain defense spending. This made resources scarce. Investment in airpower and atomic weapons saved the administration the cost of training and maintaining a conventional army.

This chapter examines the initial development of Strategic Air Command. The first part of the chapter looks at the internal forces—within the AAF and the Air Force—that influenced SAC's organizational development. The second part examines the external environment. An organization that fits the external environment can gain legitimacy and, more importantly, resources. The final part explores the administration and leadership of the first SAC commander, George Kenney. Although the Air Force created an organization out of its own internal beliefs, and that organization melded with the external environment, Kenney's routines and policies were not the right "fit" for SAC. By 1948, SAC would seek another set of "variations" to serve as the organization's operating principles.

Internal Organizational Forces: Strategic Bombing Comes Up Short

One of the underlying objectives of the AAF during World War II was to prove that strategic bombing had changed the nature of warfare and could make land warfare obsolete. On this front, the Army Air Forces achieved mixed results during the war. In the European theater, U.S. air forces had hoped to prove the soundness of strategic bombardment, which advocates believed offered an alternative to a land invasion. Before the war, U.S. airmen claimed that modern societies and economies were vulnerable to aerial bombardment.[2] Enemy air defenses and adverse weather conditions, however, plagued the wartime effort. At the end of fighting, the nation formed the United States Strategic Bombing Survey (USSBS) group to study the effects of the strategic bombing campaign. The survey group found that only 20 percent of American bombs fell within their intended target area, which was a one-thousand-foot radius.[3] Not only did U.S. bombs miss their mark, but so did the hopes of strategic bombardment advocates who wanted to prove that strategic bombing could win wars alone.

The USSBS credited U.S. airpower with helping to defeat Germany but did not give aviation overwhelming acclaim. The group's report summary concluded that "Allied air power was decisive in the war in Western Europe. Hindsight inevitability [sic] suggests that it might have been employed differently or better in some respects. Nevertheless, it was decisive."[4] The USSBS never explained how it defined "decisive," and the AAF could not claim a total victory for strategic bombardment since victory in Europe ultimately required a land invasion. In the Pacific theater, the campaign turned out differently. U.S. airpower delivered the final blows to Japan and saved the Allies the expense of a costly invasion and a long, bloody land campaign. The USSBS, however, rewarded the AAF with the same ambivalent appraisal in the Pacific version of the report. The bombing survey concluded, "Japan would have surrendered even if the atomic bombs had not been dropped."[5] Airpower leaders may have lacked official recognition for their ability to end the war in the Pacific, but as the armed forces reorganized in the aftermath of World War II, the AAF used the command relationship in that theater as a template for the creation of SAC.

Reorganization

When the war ended, the air forces reorganized along functional lines. The new Army chief of staff, Dwight Eisenhower, and the new Army

Air Forces commanding general, Carl Spaatz, agreed to create three functional commands: Tactical Air Command, Air Defense Command, and Strategic Air Command.[6] Under the AAF reorganization plan, Strategic Air Command became the sole organization responsible for conducting long-range strategic bombardment. Specifically, SAC would "provide and operate that portion of the AAF which is maintained in the United States, and in such other areas as may be designated from time to time, for the employment of air attack in any location on the globe . . . either independently or in cooperation with other components of the armed forces."[7] Whereas Tactical Air Command provided critical close-air support to ground forces, and Air Defense Command protected the United States from foreign attack, the bombing mission was inherently offensive. Therefore, SAC became the offensive air arm of the AAF (soon to become the Air Force in 1947), and eventually the number-one command charged with defending the nation through deterrence.[8]

Strategic Air Command became the physical representation of what airpower's prophets had advocated, an offensive air armada dedicated to strategic bombardment. The assumptions about airpower that American airmen had held since the days of Billy Mitchell finally found expression in the creation of this organization. Experience in World War II taught AAF leaders that strategic bombardment was too important a mission for theater commanders to direct, since they might use these bombers for tactical missions to support surface forces. Air Force "bomber" generals wanted strategic bombing centrally controlled. When the AAF created Strategic Air Command, it pushed for a similar type of relationship. The Joint Chiefs of Staff submitted their first plan for organizing the U.S. military, termed the Unified Command Plan, in 1946. It specified that the commander of Strategic Air Command report directly to the JCS, which would maintain control of all strategic assets through the SAC commander. This situation enabled SAC to become the first specified command in the United States.[9] Since SAC now received its directives and targets directly from the JCS, it became a major part of the national war plan.[10] Air Force leaders felt the lessons of World War II provided them with a better understanding of how the Air Force should organize and equip SAC for its mission as part of the national defense.

Forming SAC

Many assumptions went into the formulation of Strategic Air Command. The foremost objective in its creation was to consolidate America's bombers into a single organization to wage any future bombing campaign. The varying experiences of World War II added to some of the underlying assumptions that the organization's founders used to construct a blueprint for SAC. Although formal reports failed to provide strategic bombing the accolades its proponents sought, this fact did not stop air advocates from making the case to the American people that strategic bombing was an indispensable part of the military. As leaders of the air effort in World War II addressed the nation through multiple venues, they argued that in the post–World War II environment, a formidable strategic bombing force was central to national defense.

The compression of time and space resulting from the use of airplanes and even missiles resonated as one of the foremost arguments used by airmen to justify an increased investment in SAC. Testifying before Congress in November 1945, Spaatz outlined the new geopolitical situation created by America's victory in World War II. "America emerged from the war the only nation not shattered by bombs or devastated by battle," he said. "We are the richest nation. We have the technical and air supremacy of the world. Now, it is impossible to believe we can be top dog and still be universally loved, not until human nature has changed." Preventing a third world war, Spaatz argued before Congress, "is to lead other countries to peace through our inspired strength." Organizing for such a mission, the future Air Force chief of staff reasoned, meant a "streamlined defense, constantly on alert."[11] Among those who served during World War II, a mentality had formed that would permeate SAC. Pearl Harbor demonstrated the rapid and destructive power of the airplane. America's response came slowly because of the time needed to train and prepare forces for combat. America could not afford "another Pearl Harbor." As the new global power, Spaatz intimated, the nation could only deter future attacks by building and maintaining a strong, responsive air armada.

Having come through a devastating war, the United States looked for solutions to prevent another destructive conflict. Although strategic bombing may not have won World War II on its own, that did not stop Air Force leaders from arguing that airpower could "prevent" wars. Speaking in the Pacific Northwest, home of Boeing Aircraft—the chief supplier of Air Force bombers—Spaatz remarked, "The heavy bomber is the key to air supremacy. World War II will be distinguished from all other wars in the past, by the unique role played by heavy bombers which were developed in this area." Spaatz continued to explain why bombers were central to achieving air supremacy: "To gain control of the air it would be necessary to destroy or nullify an enemy's air forces in the air, on the ground, and in the factories." Although fighters may be able to shoot enemy fighters out of the air, Spaatz acknowledged, bombers would make the greatest contribution by destroying fighters on the ground and decimating the enemy's ability to replenish those forces.[12]

His sentiments were echoed by other leaders. Speaking before a conference at Omaha, Nebraska, future home of SAC, Maj. Gen. Elwood "Pete" Quesada—commander of the Air Force's fighter forces—stated, "Air power is peace power. . . . It is a statement of fact—irrefutable fact. In these five words we have the key to the future destiny of this country."[13] In their public discourse, air leaders expressed more than an abiding faith in strategic bombing; investment in bombers, air leaders argued, could maintain peace.

In order for SAC to present a credible deterrent force, its founders believed, bombers had to exist in sufficient numbers and maintain a constant state of readiness. Testifying before Congress again in 1948, Spaatz outlined why the pre–World War II method of training and preparation would no longer suffice. "In World War II," he told the Senate Air Force Committee, "there was a lag of one and a half to two years between the induction of untrained personnel into the Air Force and their effective employment against the enemy. This lag must be greatly reduced since in a future emergency we cannot expect strong allies to execute again the vital counter attack missions for us while we train. We must plan to hit the enemy hard in the first critical year of warfare. To do this, our Regular Air Force must be freed for combat at the first movement of an aggressor."[14] The "Pearl Harbor" mentality dictated that air forces had to be ready to respond to any aggression on a moment's notice. This was the essence of deterrence. Speaking to the Society of Automotive Engineers in October 1945, Spaatz outlined his vision of "Airpower and the Future." He warned that the nation could not be lulled into a false sense of security that powerful weapons—atomic bombs, crewless airplanes, pilotless missiles, rockets—could keep it safe. Although these weapons were indeed powerful, Spaatz argued, their success depended on one thing: maintenance of air superiority. Echoing a theme he would present before Congress, Spaatz knew that America's power was the deciding factor in the two world wars, but only because the nation had time to prepare. "But never again," Spaatz contended, "will we be given the chance to prepare behind the bulwark of friendly nations already at war." Achieving air superiority to use America's powerful weapons, he reasoned, meant maintaining an air force on alert capable of "smashing an enemy air offensive, of launching a formidable striking force, and of expanding to full war strength while time is still on our side." An air force on the alert, Spaatz concluded, "is our first line of defense and offense in the future."[15]

SAC represented more than a homogeneous command of bomber aircraft. It embodied several assumptions airmen held for decades concerning airpower. Strategic bombardment had to be centrally controlled to achieve victory in war without the necessity of a costly land invasion. The collective experience of Air Force leaders added to the internal factors that influenced SAC's formation. America, the new global power, would have to lead any future effort to confront tyranny. It could not prepare while its allies fought; it had to be ready to respond from the first indication of an attack. Airplanes and missiles would shorten the response time in future conflicts. The vision cast for SAC was to build a highly credible deterrent force ready at a moment's notice to achieve air superiority and systematically dismantle a nation using a robust strategic bombing force. Building a credible deterrent required SAC to embrace two cultural artifacts that defined SAC for decades—the atomic bomb and the intercontinental bomber. The bomb represented power and progress; the long-range bomber differentiated SAC from the other services by its ability to strike directly at an enemy across any distance and win the war single-handedly. The intercontinental range of the bomber also provided SAC the justification to argue for extending its command and control across both oceans into other commanders' theaters of operation.

Atomic Weapons: Power of Progress

The Air Force approached atomic weapons pragmatically. Following the war, Arnold charged Spaatz with "determin[ing] the effect of the atomic bomb on the employment, size, organization, and composition of the postwar Air Force."[16] In forming a board for this purpose, Spaatz enlisted the help of future Air Force chief of staff Hoyt Vandenberg and former chief of staff of the Pacific Bomber Air Force (Twentieth Air Force), Lauris Norstad. In structuring the study, Spaatz's board made two assumptions: the United States would not have time to arm after a war had begun, and the atomic bomb in its current form was primarily an offensive weapon for use against large urban and industrial targets.[17] Probably most startling was the board's finding that the weapon would be effectively and economically employed only if atomic weapons were available in sufficient quantity to accomplish the required destruction. Despite recognizing the potential force of nuclear weapons, the Spaatz board reached several conclusions that demonstrated that fundamental beliefs about strategic bombing within the Air Force had not changed: the atomic bomb did not at the time warrant a material change in the present conception of employment, size, organization, and composition of the postwar Air Force; the atomic bomb had not altered the basic concept of the strategic air offensive but had provided an additional weapon; and an adequate system of outlying strategic bases had to be established and maintained.[18] The board emphasized the last point since the bomber force still lacked the means to launch from the zone of the interior and reach targets in the Soviet Union.

Air Force leaders did not see nuclear weapons as significantly altering the bomber force's employment concept or size; in their eyes, the weapons only multiplied the amount of destructive power each bomber now possessed. During World War II, limited bomb-carrying capacity meant that the United States had to send large numbers of bombers against a single target. Nuclear weapons, however, gave the Air Force an opportunity to change strategic bombardment tactics.

Instead of flying in massive groups with limited payloads, as in World War II, U.S. bombers would now have a small signature for enemy fighters to find while at the same time possessing enough firepower in their bomb bays to destroy an entire industrial target. Reducing the number of bombers in formation made it more difficult for fighters to find the penetrating bombers.

During the summer of 1947, the Air Force conducted tests to show that new jet fighters had difficulty identifying a sole penetrating bomber.[19] Jet propulsion would soon increase the speed of bombers and fighters, increasing closure rates and giving fighters only one chance for a head-on shot at the penetrating bombers. Finding a single bomber in the sky proved difficult. Combining these factors, the Air Staff submitted a report in 1947 that highlighted how the bomber and the atomic bomb reduced the need for large conventional forces. The report concluded: "The atomic bomb and the long-range bomber will permit the delivery of devastating blows to the heart of the enemy without the necessity for the conquest of intermediate bases. . . . Assuming a plentiful supply of atomic bombs, it would be feasible to risk an all-out atomic attack at the beginning of a war in an effort to stun the enemy into submission."[20] As one Air Force officer noted, arming bombers with nuclear weapons made "the airplane at present, and its descendants in the future, the greatest offensive weapon of all times."[21]

After conducting evaluations of single penetrating bombers, the government conducted tests to evaluate the military potential of the atomic bomb. Besides the Trinity test before the Hiroshima and Naga-saki events, the government had conducted few actual tests of the atomic bomb. Although the Spaatz board concluded that the atomic bomb would not significantly alter strategic operations, the Joint Chiefs of Staff formed Joint Task Force One for the purpose of conducting two atomic tests, termed Operation Crossroads, in the summer of 1946 near the Marshall Islands. As the JCS drafted the orders for Operation Crossroads, it included its own assessment of the atomic bomb entitled "Statement of Effect of Atomic Weapons in National Security and Military Organization."[22] The JCS, like the Spaatz board, concluded that the "atomic bomb is basically an offensive weapon—a weapon of rapid attrition. With it war can be carried to the enemy's heart and vitals and there it can destroy his capacity to fight and even to live. If sufficient numbers are available and means of delivery assured, it can devastate populated centers of any nation on earth." Pragmatic in their views, the JCS realized that "immediate and complete success in efforts to abolish war cannot be expected." Realizing the growing threat from communism, the JCS decided that "it is essential, therefore, that the United States maintain forces capable of immediate retaliation for the purpose not only of reducing or eliminating the aggressor's capability of continuing the attack, but also as a deterrent to its initiation."[23] The need for responsive retaliation was something expressed throughout the military services. A credible deterrent, though, had to demonstrate that it could destroy the target when tasked. Crossroads was the first test of SAC's ability to put the bomb on target.

SAC went to great lengths to find the crew that would participate in the Crossroads test. The organization selected four crews and held a competition to determine which crew would actually earn the privilege of dropping the atomic weapon. Among those aircraft commanders selected to compete were Jack Catton and Paul Carlton. Catton considered his participation in the run-up to the Crossroads test the first true bombing competition. Flying out of Albuquerque, New Mexico, Catton's crews conducted several drops, which were meticulously measured. Following their competition in the United States, SAC sent the four crews to the actual site of the test, where the contest continued. Catton's crew scored higher than the rest and looked forward to its selection. Toward the end of the competition, however, Catton's plane developed maintenance problems. The crew had to fly an unfamiliar plane for the dress rehearsal. The lack of standardization among aircraft configurations caused problems among Catton's crew. Unfamiliarity with the plane's release switches prevented crewmembers from getting a release on a practice run. Although they had the best bomb scores, the single mistake by the crew took it out of the running for the ABLE drop.[24]

Paul Carlton competed as well, but his crew did not get selected for different reasons. Carlton's crew, like Catton's, performed well in the competition; however, Carlton's wife, Helen, was near the end of her pregnancy. She approached Carlton's group commander and voiced her opinion that Paul should not be gone at this stressful time.

The next thing Carlton knew, Maj. "Woody" Swancutt had earned the right to drop the bomb for the ABLE test.[25] On July 1, 1946, while piloting "Dave's Dream," Swancutt's crew dropped an atomic bomb on the target force of seventy-three ships that surrounded the Marshall Islands. The weapon's detonation sank five ships and damaged three others; SAC's atomic era had begun.[26]

Pursuing the Intercontinental Bomber

Just as atomic weapons increased each bomber's destructive power, nuclear weapons increased SAC's political power. As the command responsible for employing a majority of the U.S. nuclear stockpile, SAC continued to receive presidential and congressional interest. Despite this power, SAC operations still required support from the other services. The B-29 and a modification designated the B-50 did not have the range required to conduct unrefueled operations from the United States to the heartland of the most likely enemy, the Soviet Union. Therefore, SAC deployed B-29s and B-50s to forward bases in the United Kingdom, the Mediterranean, and the Arctic for possible strikes into the Soviet Union. The organization relied upon the Navy and the Army to support and protect these bases. A Soviet offensive directed against these bases, however, could overrun them and shut down the strategic air campaign in the early stages of a war.[27] Therefore, SAC sought an intercontinental bomber capable of conducting unrefueled operations from the United States. The intercontinental bomber represented more than an ability to hit the enemy from the United States; it also symbolized independent operations free of sister service support.

The B-36 offered the Air Force and SAC a means of conducting autonomous operations. The United States initially conceived of the "Peacemaker" prior to World War II as a contingent means of conducting strategic bombing in case the Allies lost the battle of the Atlantic. The B-36, however, ran into serious problems that delayed production until after the war. During its postwar acquisition, the Air Force conducted several reappraisals of the program. Gen. George C. Kenney, the first SAC commander, tried to reduce the number of B-36s because performance problems plagued the experimental models. Fighters were increasing their speed and transitioning to jet propulsion. The propeller-driven B–36 was incapable of such increased speeds, leaving it vulnerable to interception near and over the target. Nevertheless, Air Force leadership overrode Kenney because it believed in the B–36 and its potential to make the Air Force autonomous.[28]

In August 1947, General Spaatz formed an aircraft and weapons board, which would allow senior officers to make recommendations on the weapons that would best enable the Air Force to carry out its mission. The board concluded that the next five to seven years were the most vulnerable for the Air Force. Senior officers knew the new medium-range B–50 bombers would soon be obsolete. The first jet bomber, the B–47, did not have the unrefueled range to strike the Soviet Union from the United States. Furthermore, the B–52, the next intercontinental bomber, would not start production until 1953. By that time, leaders would have already decided on which service would serve as the nation's frontline defense against the Soviet Union. If the Air Force wanted that role, it had to accept, improve, and modify the B–36.[29] The B–36 not only represented a desire by Air Force leaders for greater autonomy in conducting strategic bombing, it also meant a premier role for the service in the strategic mission of the United States. The JCS had previously stated that an effective deterrent required suitable delivery vehicles. The B–36 could carry the oversized atomic bombs and deliver them from the United States without support from other services. The Air Force achieved independence and decided that the number-one priority for the newest branch of the armed forces was the development and procurement of an intercontinental bomber. Out of all the aircraft variations possible, the Air Force chose the bomber as its top priority.

According to the evolutionary model of organizations, no organization can evolve strictly based on internal conditions and assumptions. SAC, like all organizations, interacted with its external environment. Although the Air Force concentrated its efforts on constructing an independent, centrally controlled bombing force, the organization depended upon the government for its resources. SAC needed these resources to construct the formidable bomber force it envisioned.[30] The organization became the right fit for the external environment— particularly the mounting Cold War, which guaranteed it would be well resourced for decades.[31]

Cold War Pressures

The onset of the Cold War following World War II coupled with national politics provided the Air Force with an environment conducive to SAC's vision and mission. The United States had just emerged from four costly years of fighting tyranny abroad only to face yet another enemy. Political leaders had to find a strategy that, in their estimation, would deter Soviet aggression, but that strategy also had to win the approval of a war-weary nation. The Truman administration faced a difficult situation in the postwar years. The Soviet presence in Eastern Europe presented a threat to West Germany and the rest of the democratic Western powers in Europe. Western Europe's industrial core became a matter of grave concern to policy makers. Although the United States did not fear an immediate war with the Soviet Union, it worried that communist movements in these European countries might enable the Soviets to coopt the industrial might of this region and use it to their advantage. The control of resources, industrial infrastructure, and overseas bases became the focus in international affairs. U.S. national security policy in the early days of the Cold War concentrated on making the nation more "powerful" than the Soviet Union through industrial and economic might, thereby creating a credible deterrent.[32]

But creating government "power" required the expenditure of money. The United States in the late 1940s was trying to rein in government spending to pay down the debt incurred during World War II. The chief struggle occurred in 1948, after it had become clear that the United States faced a security threat from the Soviet Union. In that year, the process began to draft the defense budget for fiscal year 1950. The Truman administration decided to emphasize airpower and devoted a majority of the defense budget to the Air Force in general and to SAC in particular.[33] The Soviet army far outnumbered Western forces, which left U.S. policy makers with two options to protect Europe's vital industrial core. First, the United States could field an Army that could match that of the Soviet Union, man for man. This would require a dramatic increase in personnel and money. President Truman supported the idea of universal military training (UMT), which would require able-bodied seventeen- or eighteen-year-olds to attend six months of basic military training and then

serve out their remaining obligations in the organized reserves or the
National Guard. Truman argued that UMT would allow the United
States to mobilize promptly without incurring the cost of a large
standing army: "The sooner we can bring the maximum number of
trained men into service the sooner will be the victory and the less
tragic the cost." President Truman saw UMT as the way to throw the
great energy and force of the United States into battle at the outset
of any hostilities and prevent costly wars. In his lifetime, Truman
had already witnessed two horrific world wars. Many politicians in
Congress, however, feared UMT would lead to the militarization of
American society.[34]

Military leaders estimated that it would cost between $21 billion
and $23 billion to maintain adequate conventional forces in Europe
and a naval fleet in the Mediterranean to thwart Soviet aggression.
Truman, however, placed a $14.4 billion limit on defense spending
as he struggled to limit a growing federal budget and deficit. Among
the other options available was airpower. The Air Force's belief that
strategic bombing could shorten a war by attacking another nation's
warmaking capability melded with Washington's political constraints.
Creating a nuclear-armed armada would allow the United States to
strike any attacking Soviet army and the Russian homeland without
implementing UMT or forcing the nation to fund a large standing
army. Truman himself recognized the growing potential and importance of airpower. In 1947 he appointed a blue-ribbon panel, the
Air Policy Commission, to make recommendations on national policy
vis-à-vis military and civilian aviation. Thomas Finletter chaired the
commission, which became known as the Finletter board. During his
investigation, Finletter called Air Force chief of staff Spaatz to testify.
Spaatz and several other Air Force witnesses argued for a permanent
peacetime force of seventy air groups—primarily land-based bombers and fighter escorts—that could hit enemy targets at vast distance.
No other weapon system, the Air Force argued, could perform this
mission. Truman struggled to keep a ceiling on defense spending and
approved a supplemental spending bill that would bolster the Air
Force budget by $2.3 billion.[35] Although the additional funds were
not sufficient to create a seventy-group force, they increased substantially the budget of the newest service.

In 1948 Czechoslovakia fell to a communist coup and the Soviet Union blocked ground access to West Berlin, triggering the Berlin airlift in response. The United States needed a war plan in case the Soviets attacked and attempted to conquer Western Europe. The JCS presented Truman with Halfmoon, a war plan that called for an atomic air offensive to destroy 50 percent of Soviet industry and induce "immediate paralysis."[36] Truman wanted a plan that used more conventional forces. The president's philosophy about the use of nuclear weapons had matured since their first use in 1945. Initially, Truman looked at nuclear weapons as just another part of the military arsenal. During the Berlin airlift, however, Truman articulated his new perceptions about nuclear weapons: "I don't think we ought to use this thing unless we absolutely have to. It is a terrible thing to order the use of something that is so terribly destructive, destructive beyond anything we have ever had. . . . It is used to wipe out women and children and unarmed people, and not for military purposes."[37] Truman's reluctance to commit to using nuclear weapons at the outset of hostilities with the Soviet Union forced military leaders to consider other alternatives and plans to deter Soviet aggression in Europe.

A confrontation with the Soviet Union, most military leaders assumed, would take place on European soil. Command of the air was essential to victory in such a conflict. World War II had proven how air superiority gave troops on the battlefield a greater ability to maneuver and outflank their enemy. Although the war plans remained classified, General Spaatz, now retired, outlined how he felt the next war would unfold. While U.S. ground forces secured air bases across Europe and fixed attacking Soviet forces in their positions, strategic bombers would strike the industrial base supporting the enemy troops, thereby destroying their necessary supplies.[38] Western forces, enjoying air superiority, would then face a much weaker Soviet force. Although the Joint Chiefs charged the Air Force with the strategic air mission, SAC struggled to muster the resources necessary to carry out that assignment. The first secretary of defense, James Forrestal, attempted to resolve budgetary problems by building "balanced forces." Under his plan, each service's spending would be on forces that contributed to the nation's larger strategic concept. Crucial to Forrestal's strategy was the ability to "strike inland with the atomic bomb."[39] In the interest of

balance, Forrestal agreed at the 1948 Key West conference to allow the
Navy to pursue development of a super carrier while the Air Force
purchased B-36s. Budget matters, however, forced the JCS to recon-
sider what it believed were duplicative efforts. Gen. Omar Bradley,
the chairman of the JCS, considered the Navy's primary mission to be
securing lines of communication leading to raw materials and to areas
of projected military operations. Furthermore, he determined that the
United States needed strategic air operations to carry out this plan,
and those operations were the responsibility of the Air Force.[40] When
Louis Johnson succeeded Secretary Forrestal, he cancelled the super
carrier, which put the Navy's attempt to carve out a piece of the strategic mission on hold for the time being.[41]

Cold War national security policy favored strategic bombardment
over conventional forces since it was the less costly option and would
avoid measures (such as UMT) that some thought would lead to the
United States being militarized and made into a garrison state like
Russia.[42] Early war plans for confronting the Soviet Union rarely
included nuclear weapons for a variety of reasons. First, in the years
immediately following World War II, the United States had a minimal
nuclear stockpile. Second, military leaders were aware of the power
of nuclear weapons but were not convinced of their strategic impact.
Third, military planners were unsure of President Truman's guidance regarding the inclusion of nuclear weapons in war plans. Finally,
nations continued to debate an international ban on nuclear weapons.[43] By 1947 these views would begin to change. The increasing
Soviet menace coupled with the several crises of 1948 (the invasion of
Czechoslovakia, communist victories in China, and the Berlin airlift)
led to the development of JCS war plans that increasingly relied on
the atomic bomb and SAC's bombers.

By the fall of 1948, Air Force leadership had won two significant battles: independence and a premier role for strategic bombardment. The B-36 enabled SAC to conduct autonomous operations;
atomic weapons gave SAC the ability to execute its systematic strategic bombardment theory, since they could destroy industrial targets
with a single weapon. Air Force leadership had worked effectively to
elevate the status of strategic bombardment. The organizational form

of SAC worked, given the external environment. The Air Force had succeeded in securing for SAC the additional resources necessary to construct its bomber force. Within SAC, however, mismanagement of the bomber force was creating an entity that did not meet the expectations of Air Force leaders.

Finding the Right Organizational Fit: Mismanagement of SAC

In 1946 George C. Kenney seemed like a wise choice to lead the newly formed Strategic Air Command. As MacArthur's "airman in the Pacific," Kenney had run an efficient air campaign that supported MacArthur's island-hopping strategy in the South Pacific. Kenney's organizational structure acted as a forerunner of modern ideas of how to organize and control air assets from multiple services.[44] But Kenney never took part in the strategic bombing of Japan. The Twentieth Air Force, responsible for the strategic bombing campaign of Japan, reported not to Kenney but to Gen. "Hap" Arnold in Washington, D.C. Furthermore, Arnold sent Spaatz from the European theater to the Pacific, in July 1945, to command strategic air forces.[45] After retiring, Kenney was asked why he received Strategic Air Command. Kenney just quipped, "I don't know. Maybe they didn't know what else to do with me."[46] Critics would eventually use Kenney's lack of "strategic bomber" experience to explain SAC's poor performance under his command.

Despite Kenney's lack of "real" bomber experience, he accomplished the mission Spaatz, now commanding general of the AAF, initially entrusted to him in 1946. Kenney served as an excellent spokesperson for the Air Force. When Kenney assumed command, the Air Force still was not a separate service, but Spaatz believed that "what we do now, the plans we lay, and the support we gain from the American people, during this period, will firmly establish the pattern for the future of our air power." Spaatz encouraged Kenney to be seen and heard, commenting, "While you nor I have any desire for personal aggrandizement, it is part of a commander's job."[47]

Kenney enjoyed public speaking and accepted the many requests that came his way.[48] These appearances, however, drew him away from his duties as SAC commander. Therefore, he entrusted the daily operations of SAC to Gen. Clements "Cement" McMullen, a long-time confidant. McMullen, like Kenney, lacked strategic bombardment experience. While in the Pacific, McMullen provided Kenney with the logistics, supply, and maintenance needed to carry out his operations. McMullen never commanded a combat squadron but was widely recognized as an expert in organization and efficiency. "Cement" earned his nickname for his reputation of being stalwart on his command decisions and not easily swayed in his convictions.[49] This trait would be his, and Kenney's, undoing.

Kenney and McMullen inherited a difficult situation. The demobilization following World War II left SAC in a dire predicament, with shortages in several critical areas. In May 1946 AAF authorized the command to have 43,729 personnel, but SAC only had 37,426 in its ranks.[50] Furthermore, those who left the service during the drawdown were usually the highly skilled personnel, especially aircraft maintenance and repair specialists who would be able to land lucrative jobs as civilians. A large proportion of those who remained in the command, which heavily relied on new technology, were unskilled personnel. Kenney and McMullen had three problems to overcome: obtaining and training new personnel, reorganizing for efficiency, and rotating combat groups to forward bases and the Arctic.[51] Gen. Leon Johnson, a numbered air force commander under Kenney in 1947, remembered the postwar drawdown this way: "Demobilization was not demobilization—it was a rout. We just walked away and left everything." Although SAC struggled in these circumstances, Johnson felt it was not the drawdown that troubled the organization; it was the leadership. As Johnson recalled, "Kenney was not very active in running SAC; McMullen had many ideas which I don't believe were really conducive to building an effective striking force."[52] McMullen's solution to the manning problem worsened SAC's condition, to the point where it could not even perform its basic functions.

McMullen operated on a pre–World War II mindset, when pilots made up a majority of the Air Force. During those days, the AAF expected pilots to serve in multiple capacities. This versatility was no longer practical in the highly technical Air Force of the Cold War. McMullen believed in cross-training crewmembers and assigning them to multiple positions within organizations to compensate for manpower shortages. At this time, Curtis LeMay, serving as commander of the United States Air Forces in Europe (USAFE), faulted McMullen's approach. "One of the things McMullen started was cross-training," LeMay said. "He didn't have people trained in their primary specialty before he started cross-training them on something else."[53] Nevertheless, "Cement" stood firm in his convictions. The constant deployments overseas meant absent crewmembers often left staff work unfinished. More importantly, the combat readiness of the command suffered. Brigadier General Everett Holstrom, a SAC planner under LeMay and a pilot under Kenney, recalled that "everybody would do everything, and the pilots would do a navigator's job or a bombardier's job. It was cross-training completely when no one was fully trained in what we were doing."[54] The lack of specialization manifested itself in disappointing bomb scores and lower readiness rates.[55]

The questionable readiness of SAC attracted attention when Kenney and McMullen began "maximum effort" missions to simulate bombing U.S. cities as a display of SAC airpower. Holstrom remembered the lack of organization and readiness apparent in a mission to place a sizeable force over the city of New York. "We were going to fly a large number of B-29s over New York. . . . Somehow or other, the thing got screwed up and one air force got one set of orders and the other got another set of orders. I'll tell you it was a mess from the beginning. That just shows you the lack of training of the aircrews and the staff at that time."[56] Of the planned 131 aircraft, only 101 aircraft flew that day, but many still failed to make the mission due to pilot error or faulty tactics. If SAC could not conduct operations over the United States, Air Force leaders wondered how the organization would perform over enemy territory.

While McMullen directed daily operations, Kenney ventured away from the headquarters to make speeches. His public relations exploits, however, soon drew the ire of Air Force leadership. Kenney's "maximum effort" simulated raids actually demonstrated how vulnerable the "target" cities were to enemy attack. The SAC commander then followed up the exercises with calls for more fighters to defend the nation's skies.[57] The top bomber general in charge of the only offensive air arm in the country was now on record as advocating more fighters for defense. Furthermore, he was frightening the American people at a time when the issue of an independent Air Force remained unsettled. In May 1947 Spaatz asked Kenney to downplay such "stunt performances" and coordinate future news releases with headquarters.[58] The assistant secretary of war for air and soon-to-be secretary of the Air Force, W. Stuart Symington, reminded Kenney that the Air Force was in the final round of a unification fight. "If we don't win it and the war is officially declared over," Symington said, "the Air Force reverts to its previous impossible position as a minor addendum to the War Department." He further admonished Kenney that there were times when no publicity was better than "good" publicity.[59]

Kenney never seemed to grasp what Air Force leaders were trying to accomplish. When the aircraft and weapons board met in November 1947 to consider procuring more B-36s, the SAC commander was the lone dissenting vote. Kenney felt that all the B-36s should be converted to tankers because of their poor performance and used to extend the range of the B-29s. He was not on board with the move for an intercontinental bomber.[60] As Air Force leadership fought for SAC to become the primary instrument for the nation's defense, Kenney and McMullen allowed the organization's proficiency to decrease. Bomb scores grew increasingly unreliable as crews dropped their bombs farther and farther from the intended targets.[61] Additionally, crews failed to drop the number of allotted bombs, practiced in unrealistic conditions, and used visual bombing in training. Visual bombing, when bombardiers sighted their targets through bomb-sights, showed little progress in training and tactics given the lessons of World War II. The Air Force wanted to be able to deliver bombs accurately in all types of weather. Radar bombing provided SAC the means to deliver atomic weapons through adverse weather and under the cover of darkness, but Kenney and McMullen failed to provide sufficient guidance on training.

In April 1948 General Spaatz grew concerned over the number of SAC aircraft out of commission and the distance by which SAC's bombers were missing their targets.[62] Before the Air Force chief of staff retired in the summer of 1948, Spaatz had decided Kenney's future. Spaatz called his acting vice chief, Lauris Norstad, into his office and said, "Larry, I am going to have to change the SAC commander. George Kenney is a great commander, but he is making too many speeches and talking about the great blast on the horizon, and he is not running SAC. Who would you put there?" Norstad replied, "LeMay. Put him in there now so we can get ready for war."[63]

Spaatz retired in mid-1948, and Gen. Hoyt S. Vandenberg took over as chief of staff of the Air Force with Kenney still in command. SAC, however, continued to deteriorate. Norstad recalled the pressure from the Defense Department about SAC's readiness. The secretary of defense called upon Norstad almost daily concerning SAC's posture. The escalating tensions with the Soviet Union meant the president was concerned that he might have to make "costly" decisions almost any day. The reports coming in about SAC, however, left Norstad with reservations as to whether SAC was fully ready.[64] By then, Kenney had realized the declining conditions in SAC. In an effort to spark interest in bombing proficiency, Kenney held the first SAC bombing competition.[65] The exercise impressed General Vandenberg, but Secretary Forrestal insisted that Vandenberg look deeper into SAC operations to determine if it was ready for war. Following Norstad's suggestions, Vandenberg asked Charles Lindbergh to fly with SAC crews and report his findings. During the weeks of his investigation, Lindbergh flew over one hundred hours with SAC crews from six different bases.[66]

On September 14, 1948, Lindbergh delivered a blistering report to Vandenberg that ended Kenney's tenure as SAC commander. Lindbergh stated frankly that Kenney and McMullen were training crews to the standards of the past. According to his report, "It is obvious that the standards of performance, experience, and skill which were satisfactory for the 'mass' air forces of World War II are inadequate for the specialized atomic forces we have today. Since a single atomic bomber has destructive power comparable to a battle fleet, a ground army, or an air force . . . its crew should represent the best in experience, character, and skill."[67] Lindbergh found that improvements in personnel were not keeping pace with improvements in equipment. Additionally, frequent moves between SAC bases caused morale to suffer. He recommended that SAC stabilize personnel in the atomic forces, maintain crew integrity (keeping integral crews together longer), concentrate on the primary mission of atomic forces (that is, bombing), give priority in selection and assignment of personnel to atomic squadrons, and create conditions that would draw the highest quality personnel into the command.[68]

One week after receiving the report, Vandenberg notified Kenney of his transfer to Maxwell Air Force Base, Alabama, to assume command of Air University. Vandenberg also terminated the cross-training program.

Most importantly, he alerted Lt. Gen. Curtis LeMay, currently in Europe, that he was the new SAC commander.[69] Norstad said the decision took less than fifteen minutes. For the third time in his career, the Air Force would call upon Curtis LeMay to turn a bomber organization around.

Conclusion

SAC's organizational culture would reflect the values and assumptions of Air Force leaders, who believed in the promise of strategic bombardment. Since the days of Billy Mitchell, American airmen were convinced that strategic airpower alone could win wars. Although that capability was not proven in World War II, Air Force generals fought and secured a place for this mission in the national strategy to deter the Soviet Union.

In 1946 the Army Air Forces reorganized along functional lines. This move gave birth to Strategic Air Command. Decades of advocacy for the establishment of an organization devoted to the idea of centralized strategic bombing became a reality. The Air Force shortly thereafter became a separate service and broke away from the Army's dominant culture. To signal its newfound independence, the Air Force continued production of the propeller-driven intercontinental bomber (B-36) while making plans for an all-jet version. The strategic bomber put distance between the pilot subculture and the Army culture. The intercontinental bomber put distance between the Air Force and the other services. The youngest member of the defense establishment believed that it could still win wars on its own. As a demonstration of how symbols and artifacts can become part of the organization's values and assumption, the atomic bomb, built and developed outside the organization, became part of SAC culture. Given their destructive capability, nuclear weapons allowed SAC to change tactics. Formations could be smaller and harder to find in the air. Atomic weapons made the bomber an even more powerful weapon—the most powerful in the world—with the ability to destroy entire cities in a single attack. With a sufficient force and multiple smaller formations armed with nuclear weapons, Strategic Air Command believed it could overwhelm a nation's air defenses and wreak havoc on its society and its warmaking capacity. Early mismanagement of the organization, however, threatened to undermine Air Force efforts to secure a premier position for the service in the strategy to confront the Soviet Union.

Internal beliefs of the Air Force formed SAC, but the external environment provided the impetus for the organization to emerge as the answer to a national security dilemma. Externally, the nation struggled to develop a strategy to confront a new threat—the Soviet Union—and a new war, the Cold War. Although the Soviet Union presented a threat to the United States, the Truman administration struggled to keep defense spending as low as possible. This made resources scarce. Among the military options available for confronting the Soviet Union in the Cold War, the Truman administration decided to invest in strategic bombing instead of creating a large standing army. Investment in airpower provided a greater deterrent for the cost than trying to maintain a large standing army.

Air Force doctrine and beliefs gave birth to SAC, and the external environment allowed it to grow. The organization's leadership, however, was not nurturing SAC to meet the needs of the Cold War. SAC's first commander, George Kenney, failed to adjust the command's operations, tactics, and culture to the external environment. War could come at any time, Air Force leaders thought, and SAC had to be prepared. Even the Department of Defense wanted continual updates on SAC's readiness. Kenney and his staff were leading SAC in the wrong direction. They adopted policies that resembled those of the pre–World War II environment, when nations had time to prepare for war. Pilots again became generalists at a time when aircraft would only become more sophisticated and complicated. SAC needed specialists, not generalists. What hurt Kenney the most was the fact that he had not actually participated in a true strategic bombing campaign in World War II. He did not have the same shared history of strategic bombing as those who led the Air Force or those who would lead SAC in the future. Kenney's approach, Air Force leadership felt, was not a good fit for the organization.

4

"We Are at War Now"
Implementing a New Organizational Culture

My determination was to put everyone in SAC into this frame of mind: We are at war now. So that, if actually we did go to war the very next morning or even that night, we would stumble through no period in which preliminary motions would be wasted. We had to be ready to go then.

—CURTIS LeMAY

The year 1948 proved pivotal for the United States and especially for SAC. In 1947 the Truman administration drafted and Congress passed legislation that organized the U.S. national security institutions in new ways, including placing the armed services in a new national military establishment (renamed the Department of Defense in 1949) and making the Air Force independent of the Army. The concern about Soviet intentions came to fruition in 1948 as the United States confronted the Soviets over their blockade of Berlin and the communist coup that occurred in Czechoslovakia. Although the United States supplied Europe with financial resources and, through the Truman Doctrine, provided assistance to those nations fighting the growing communist threat, the nation struggled to formulate a war plan that would defeat the Soviet Union if the Cold War became "hot." Attempting to avoid creation of a large standing army, the

89

Truman administration settled on a strategy that relied on nuclear weapons as the primary means of deterring the Soviet threat. As the national military establishment began work on its budget for 1950, the Air Force received the largest share in order to build this credible deterrent.

By 1948 the Air Force had made great strides in gaining the objectives it sought coming out of World War II. Strategic Air Command, as an organization, embodied the assumptions and beliefs of Air Force leaders that bombers should be centrally controlled by an independent air force. Still embracing the notion that a well-armed strategic air force could win wars without a costly land invasion, the Air Force took the pragmatic view that nuclear weapons were only another weapon in the air arsenal to use in the destruction of key enemy nodes that would paralyze a nation. Given their destructive capability, nuclear weapons allowed the Air Force to change tactics. Formations could be smaller and harder to find in the air, at least until radar improved. With a sufficient force and multiple smaller formations armed with nuclear weapons, the Air Force believed it could overwhelm a nation's air defenses and wreak havoc on its critical internal systems.

SAC's initial cadre of leaders failed, however, to construct the type of organization that would give the nation a credible deterrent. Hampered by a postwar drawdown that drained off critical personnel and by policies that emphasized pilots as generalists instead of the specialists required to handle advancing technology, Gen. George Kenney and his staff failed to create the truly professional organization that the Air Force believed was required. Realizing the urgency of the situation, Gen. Hoyt Vandenberg, the chief of staff, made a change in leadership. To build the credible deterrent, Vandenberg looked to a man with a proven track record of bomber command success: Lt. Gen. Curtis LeMay. With a change in leadership came a change in culture. Organizational culture can originate from the beliefs and values a leader uses to help a group of people address internal and external problems. If those values and beliefs work, the leader's assumptions can become the shared assumptions of the group and define the type of behavior acceptable in the organization. SAC's organizational culture would come from the beliefs and values of LeMay and those who shared his personal history and experience. This culture first became apparent in

SAC's policies but eventually would manifest itself in the organization's institutions, routines, technology, and appearance.[1] Like most organizations, SAC culture had ideological and physical components.

SAC: The Center of the Nation

LeMay had spent nearly a year in Europe after World War II leading U.S. Air Forces on the continent, especially in the effort to keep West Berlin supplied when the Soviets cut off ground access to the city. When notified of his new assignment, LeMay returned to Washington, D.C., to assume command of SAC. In a conversation with Vandenberg, LeMay learned of the chief's objectives for the command. Vandenberg wanted LeMay to get SAC in shape to fight. He gave the new commander few details but did offer LeMay some general guidance. "He told me to use what we had," LeMay recalled, "get it ready, and get it ready as fast as possible."[2] In LeMay's eyes, Washington had finally gotten "scared" enough that it had decided to build up the nation's strategic resources again after the dramatic drawdown.

Vandenberg provided LeMay considerable latitude in transforming SAC. Since the JCS agreed with the Air Force's concept of power projection, Vandenberg needed LeMay to build an organization capable of providing a credible deterrent. Furthermore, Vandenberg wanted LeMay to make sure that if a war started, SAC could win it almost immediately.[3] Although LeMay knew how to employ bombers, his personal goal was to build an organization "that was so strong and so efficient that no one would dare attack us."[4] LeMay's time in Washington, however, would be limited, since SAC was in the process of moving its headquarters to Omaha, Nebraska, nicely situated in the middle of the United States farther from potential attackers.

The previous year, Vandenberg commissioned a study to find a new place for the command. Writing to Kenney in 1947, Vandenberg outlined his reason for the move: "It is becoming increasingly apparent that the continued pressure of commercial air activities and the increasing density of the Military, Naval, and Air population in Washington will eventually force the relocation of [SAC] headquarters at some point other than Andrews Field."[5] In the same letter, the chief proposed several locations for the new headquarters: Topeka, Kansas; Offutt Field, Nebraska; Fort Francis E. Warren, Wyoming; and

Fort George Wright, Washington. The first SAC commander argued against the move to Offutt. Kenney felt that the proximity to Washington, D.C., the accessibility to Air Force headquarters, and the availability of housing favored staying at Andrews. Furthermore, Kenney argued that Mitchell Field, New York, made a better alternative location, politically and financially, than the middle of Nebraska.[6] A move to New York would cost considerably less than a move to Nebraska, Kenney argued, and it kept SAC closer to the political center of the nation. This was not the first time that Kenney had tried to thwart moving SAC out of Washington. In 1946 then–chief of the Army Air Forces Carl Spaatz proposed relocating SAC to the interior of the nation in Colorado Springs, Colorado. After most of the staff had purchased homes in the new area, Kenney had the orders cancelled and kept SAC situated close to the nation's capital.[7]

In May 1947 Vandenberg forwarded his decision to the secretary of the Air Force, Stuart Symington. The chief's staff evaluated locations on several factors, to include availability of housing, office space, airfield facilities, and the status of the installation. Offutt Field distinguished itself from the other candidates because of two critical criteria: location near the geographical center of the United States, and proximity to a positive axis of communication.[8] The Air Force would position SAC in the middle of the United States where it could centrally control bombers all over the country. Furthermore, SAC's geographic position would enable it to surround itself with a network of bases and become the nerve center that would orchestrate the employment of strategic forces throughout the United States and the world. On June 8, 1948, General Vandenberg made the announcement that SAC would move its headquarters from Andrews Field, outside Washington, D.C., to Offutt Air Force Base, Nebraska.[9] In addition to the geographic position of Offutt, those on the Air Staff claimed air traffic in the Washington, D.C., area increased the vulnerability of SAC's headquarters to attack from abroad.[10] Major General John B. Montgomery, who would initially take over direction of SAC operations under LeMay, remarked, "We're keenly interested in the surrounding air force and national guard units because it's conceivable they might have to defend us sometime [against possible Soviet attack]."[11] The geographic position of SAC showed how the placement of resources affected the mission and culture of the organization. Tactical Air Command remained in Virginia close to the Army it supported.[12] To LeMay, Offutt Field provided a great opportunity to control his forces. "It was the center," LeMay remarked, "where we could get to our outfits which were scattered all over the country and later all over the world."[13] SAC could now construct a robust organization networked throughout the country, even the world, with SAC headquarters as the hub.

Lack of a War Plan

LeMay took command of the organization on October 19, 1948. The move to Nebraska came a few weeks later.[14] While still in Washington, the first order of business for LeMay was to review the organization's war plan. Much to his dismay, he remembered, "There was no war plan."[15] Although the Air Force had lobbied for and won funding for the newly arriving B-36 Peacemakers, current SAC plans failed to define their role should the organization have to execute its war plan. "SAC had something in the file about go and take the high ground at Gettysburg or something of that nature," LeMay remembered.[16] SAC's war plan needed specifics. It did not name explicit targets, planned timing, or the units tasked to perform the elements of the plan. Kenney's plan also failed to emphasize the priority SAC deserved in terms of resources. Jack Catton gained considerable knowledge about atomic weapons from his competition for, and participation in, the Crossroads tests. His combination of war experience and nuclear familiarity made Catton a rare commodity and garnered him a position on the SAC staff as a war planner and programmer of future requirements. For Catton, LeMay's appointment brought a new focus to the command. The resources SAC had acquired, including the new bombers, Catton observed, "had never been properly marshaled so that they could be effectively employed as a credible force of high competence to do a military job." From his staff perspective, Catton felt the Air Force had not given SAC the priority it needed: to develop a highly professional atomic striking force for this country's defense. "That was our monopoly at the time," Catton argued. "We had to take advantage of it."[17] Catton would remain on the SAC staff to help convince the Air Force and the larger military establishment that SAC had to become the nation's number-one defense priority. Other staff officers and commanders in SAC, however, would not remain part of LeMay's team.

The deeper LeMay dug into SAC's current operations, the more convinced he became the organization lacked focus and capability. He singled out one of the main reasons SAC had deteriorated so much: there were not enough of the "right people" in the units or on the staff.[18] The right people, in LeMay's estimation, were those who had shared his experiences, views, and methods of conducting strategic operations. Immediately, LeMay shook up the personnel system to get his "Pacific team" positions in SAC. "I raised heaven and earth to try and get back into SAC some people who had gone through the war and heavy bombardment," LeMay said, "particularly the people that had gone through the same experiences I had. I finally got a group of people together that had gone through the same experiences that were dedicated not to want [the lack of preparation] to happen again."[19] LeMay brought Thomas Power back from his position as air attaché to England to become the deputy SAC commander. In the Pacific, LeMay considered Power his best wing commander and charged him with leading the first B-29 bombing raid on Tokyo.[20] Andrew Kissner, who enjoyed a reputation for organization and efficiency, became SAC's new chief of staff, a position he had previously held under LeMay in Europe and the Pacific. John Montgomery assumed responsibility for operations, a position similar to his job under LeMay in the Pacific theater. To direct his war plan efforts and turn around the command's lackluster performance, LeMay sought the man O'Donnell previously selected to serve as his "SOB" in the Pacific, Walter "Cam" Sweeney. From the staff to the operational commands, SAC would have the "right people" making critical decisions.

At the time, SAC fielded two numbered air forces consisting primarily of bombers: the Eighth Air Force headquartered in Fort Worth, Texas, and the Fifteenth Air Force (15 AF) located in Colorado Springs, Colorado. To head these operational organizations, LeMay turned to proven combat leaders. General Roger Ramey, who had distinguished himself at the battle of Bismarck Sea and the attack on Rabaul in the Pacific, took command of 8 AF. LeMay considered

Ramey the most combat-proven leader in his command and rewarded him with the only command considered partially nuclear-capable at the time. The responsibility to deliver nuclear weapons was a privilege that had to be earned in SAC. General Emmett "Rosie" O'Donnell, who led the first B-29 raid against Japan, headed 15 AF.[21] Other veterans of the European theater would eventually become part of the SAC staff, but LeMay's team primarily consisted of veterans of the Pacific, where, in LeMay's estimation, bombing operations had proven the validity of strategic bombardment.

Arrival at Offutt Field

Moving SAC to Offutt presented LeMay with a chance to get the organization off to a new start. LeMay and his staff set up SAC operations in the run-down main building of the bomber plant on Offutt Field. His arrival, however, was not without controversy. A reporter asked the general, "Don't you think this will be a great thing for Omaha?" The reporter quoted LeMay as replying, "It doesn't mean a damn thing to Omaha, and it doesn't mean a damn thing to me."[22] LeMay's intent, according to him, was to convey the notion that SAC wasn't worth much, and therefore, Omaha shouldn't be too proud of the organization at this point. Within a week, LeMay had a chance to address the city's chamber of commerce and outline the importance of SAC and the necessity of a good communal relationship between the organization and the city. In describing SAC's mission, LeMay stressed to the community that "our job briefly is to be ready to launch an immediate air bombardment against any point on the globe from which may emanate a threat to the security of the United States. . . . Our basic weapon is the long-range bomber." LeMay described the purpose of the unit that had recently moved into the bomber plant as the "command post and nerve center" of the organization. Despite the fact that Air Force studies had indicated adequate housing existed in the area, LeMay stressed to community leaders that one-third of his personnel "are not satisfied with their present quarters because of high rates or other reasons." In order to assure the local community of SAC's permanence in the area and the need to commit to supporting the base's personnel, LeMay said the city should "look on us as your organization through which the city of Omaha now becomes a point of central control in a vast network of units comprising the combat striking elements of American air power."[23]

Convincing the city of SAC's importance paled in comparison with LeMay's attempt to convince the entire Air Force of the need to make SAC the service's number-one priority. General Vandenberg announced that the Air Force would hold an exercise December 6–8, 1948, in which the Air Force commanders would present the status of their forces and an overview of their war plans. Prior to that meeting, LeMay met with Vandenberg to discuss LeMay's initial impressions of SAC and his plan for the future. LeMay said that he planned to propel nuclear attack to the forefront of SAC's operations. He would establish a force in being capable of dropping 80 percent of the nation's nuclear stockpile in one mission, then exploit the atomic attack with conventional bombing. Implementing such a scheme, LeMay argued to the chief, required recognition that SAC should direct strategic forces throughout the war, which included its ability to go overseas and conduct the command's operations. Since only the B-36 could reach the Soviet Union from the United States, SAC deployed most of its bomber force to forward locations overseas in the operating area of theater commanders. Theater staffs, LeMay maintained, should not be relied upon to command strategic operations.

Two other issues ranked high on LeMay's mind. First, if SAC was to be the Air Force's priority, then the organization had to have the best personnel. Furthermore, those people selected "must remain in the priority units without fail." Finally, a majority of SAC bases suffered from a lack of housing and adequate base facilities. The SAC commander argued, "We therefore find ourselves in a position of having the highest priority mission assigned to the AF but the lowest quality in facilities for carrying out the job."[24] SAC not only had to receive the best planes and people, but it also had to have the best facilities and housing to retain those critical to SAC's success.

Exercise Dualism
The Air Force held a commanders' conference at Maxwell Air Force Base called Exercise Dualism. At the conference, each commander would outline their plan and capabilities. Catton, Montgomery, and

LeMay sat up many nights prior to the Maxwell exercise writing a script and developing a presentation to convince the Air Force about the need to make SAC the priority.[25] LeMay and Montgomery flew to Maxwell to attend the conference. The duo briefed that SAC should not gradually expend its nuclear arsenal as outlined by the Halfmoon concept. Under the latest JCS plan, SAC's bombers would ferry nuclear bombs from their Atomic Energy Commission holding sites in the United States to England. Assembly teams, few in number, would also deploy from the United States to the United Kingdom, assemble the bombs, and load them onto SAC's bombers. Halfmoon assumed SAC would begin nuclear attacks as the bombs became available, beginning about two weeks into the war. Initial plans had SAC striking twenty cities as the assembly teams completed each nuclear bomb, which in some cases could take a full day.[26] In his briefing, Montgomery laid out SAC's new priorities: "In carrying out atomic attacks, the objective in each case will be: first, the destruction or disruption of vital Soviet industrial establishments, and second, the reduction of administrative control and productivity of the populace."[27] Like bomber advocates before him, LeMay stressed targeting Russia's vulnerable warmaking capability but wanted to expend most of the nuclear arsenal in a single massive strike.[28] The selected cities within the Soviet Union were responsible for 90 percent of airframe production, 99 percent of aircraft engines, and 63 percent of petroleum production. Twenty-four million people lived within the targeted thirty-five cities, and SAC expected eight million to become fatalities and another eight million to suffer serious injuries.[29] The combined losses, in SAC's estimation, would "bring about a suspension of all worker productivity within the areas affected." Under SAC's plan, the Soviet Union would become a severely crippled nation.

Carrying out this plan, Montgomery briefed, varied radically from the concept of strategic bombardment used in the last war. SAC's atomic attack would be carried out in a matter of a few days—not weeks or months. Therefore, LeMay argued the command of the force must be outlined well in advance. Through training and exercises, SAC would ready crews for the mission. LeMay, however, wanted the Air Force's concurrence on his ideas about command and control. The matter of command of strategic air units, LeMay told his fellow generals, was "vital to national security." The only way LeMay saw its operations being a success was "to fix the responsibility for its execution clearly on one person. . . . The commander assigned this responsibility must be provided over all units directly engaged in this campaign whether they are in the Zone of the Interior or abroad."[30] The SAC commander assumed that neither U.S. nor Soviet defensive forces could be effective; his atomic offensive would get through. The Air Materiel commander added his voice to LeMay's notion that SAC should be funded even in the face of dwindling budgets: "The first priority is seeing that the wherewithal to deliver the atomic bomb will be given first priority in funds, personnel, and . . . time."[31] LeMay was following what was now becoming a consensus: SAC should be the highest priority, and only SAC should command bomber operations no matter where the airplanes were based.

Following the conference, LeMay expressed to Lieutenant General Norstad, the Air Force deputy chief of staff for operations, a desire to bring under SAC's control the additional critical assets he needed to execute his war plan. LeMay wanted more reconnaissance and military airlift airplanes, and he asked that the Air Force excuse SAC fighters from additional taskings such as continental defense or reconnaissance so they could concentrate on escorting the command's bombers. Most importantly, LeMay felt that in the future, an atomic offensive campaign would require execution in a matter of hours. Therefore, the JCS should assign responsibility for execution to one person: the SAC commander. In his letter, LeMay wrote, "The commander assigned this responsibility must be provided command over all of his units directly engaged in this campaign."[32]

Having argued that SAC's mission should be the priority of the Air Force, LeMay received a great deal of what he proposed. The Air Staff replied that the Joint Chiefs of Staff were considering assigning all reconnaissance assets, excluding weather units, to SAC. The Air Staff also assured LeMay that his fighter units would have no additional taskings. Lastly, the Joint Staff was considering the assignment of reconnaissance forces to Strategic Air Command. The Air Force's position, as articulated in a memo from the director of Air Force plans and operations, was that "all strategic air operations should be controlled by the Commanding General, Strategic Air Command." The memo added, "The importance of your mission is fully realized by the Air Staff and all plans and programs are built around the primary consideration that we shall at the outset of any future war be required, as a first charge upon our resources, to deliver within the minimum period of time the strongest atomic offensive we can possibly mount."[33]

LeMay's Tour

With his presentation behind him, LeMay began a cross-country tour of the bases in his organization. What he found out in the field bothered the new commander. LeMay quipped to a local reporter that when he arrived at SAC, he found a guard trying to protect a hangar with a ham sandwich, suggesting the lack of resources in the command.[34] With every stop on his tour, he found forces that were manned improperly; units either didn't have the people SAC needed or had people SAC didn't need or couldn't use. Although the bases had bombers assigned to them, most had not been strategic bombing bases prior to World War II. These bases tried to keep the bombers through the drawdown to keep the base from being closed. This presented two problems for SAC: base supply warehouses were stocked with shelves full of supplies that did not support bombers, and local communities would not invest in private construction of housing because they feared losing the bombers and the people that would buy or rent their properties. As LeMay landed, he tried to convince local communities that SAC was the Air Force's, if not the nation's, priority and in their community to stay. It was the same message he had communicated to Omaha in his first address.

LeMay visited mostly the same places on each base: dining halls, maintenance facilities, hangars, post exchanges (places where servicemembers could purchase items found in a typical department store as well as military uniforms and accessories), and the different base clubs (most bases had three clubs: an officers' club, a noncommissioned officers' [NCO] club, and a service club for enlisted airmen). Between December 13 and December 29, 1948, LeMay's aide recorded him visiting seven different bases.[35] Interestingly, the commander asked few questions about operations; he would find out all he needed to know about the status of his bomber force in about a month. On this tour, the commander wanted the forces to know that SAC would not only perform best, but it would also look the best, act in the best manner, and even eat the best cooking in the Air Force.

LeMay needed SAC personnel ready to deploy on a moment's notice if directed. Certain conditions affected a servicemember's eligibility to deploy. Contracting venereal disease (VD) meant not only a visit to the doctor, but also a reduction in the base's readiness level since servicemen could not deploy with the disease. At each base, LeMay asked the commander about the current VD rate. LeMay was curious why Kearney Air Force Base, in the middle of Nebraska, reported no cases of VD. "Are there no women around here?" LeMay asked sarcastically. The base commander replied that he suspected his "infected" men were seeking treatment in town and not reporting to the base doctor. The commander at Kearney knew there was a popular brothel in North Platte but had established an agreement with local law enforcement that anyone found at the "house" in uniform would be returned to the base. At Davis-Monthan Air Force Base in Tucson, Arizona, LeMay found the VD rate excessively high compared to other bases. The Davis-Monthan commander notified LeMay that he discovered some troops were using penicillin by themselves but had stopped the practice, which caused the spike in the numbers.

Cases of VD were one measure of SAC's readiness; however, it was not the only statistic that intrigued LeMay. He also queried commanders about their training and manpower utilization. At several bases, LeMay noticed maintenance people standing around doing nothing. At Castle Air Force Base in Atwater, California, LeMay found four people working and twelve people idle. LeMay informed the wing commander that he had to establish a system by which he could track what each man was doing. LeMay issued the same guidance at Carswell in Fort Worth, Texas, and Davis-Monthan, saying that each work center had to have a load chart available that outlined the men on duty and the job assigned. Each person in SAC would have a daily schedule and know the duty he was expected to perform each day.

The housing condition at every SAC base confirmed LeMay's experience at Offutt. Kearney probably had the worst conditions given its location in the middle of Nebraska. The local commander informed LeMay that 108 married men had come to Kearney without their families, although he suspected that 90 percent of them wanted their families with them. Of the 327 servicemembers housed off base, only 100 lived in satisfactory structures. Furthermore, the housing allowance provided members at best a basement apartment. In Texas, LeMay told the Carswell commander he had to get the local community to build affordable homes. Davis-Monthan faced similar conditions; the commander told LeMay that of the 1,800 families housed off base, only 50 percent had adequate living conditions. Most of them lived in poor housing for high rent. LeMay told his commanders that the important thing was to make sure the town understood that there was no need to worry: SAC was here to stay.[36]

LeMay's tour also stressed appearances. In several of the base clubs, LeMay said the places lacked the appropriate atmosphere. He wanted tables covered with cloth and told the Topeka commander to go to a local department store and hire a decorator to make the place presentable. If the clubs were messy, it was the fault of the officers in charge. "Put a broom in a captain's hand," LeMay said, "and tell him to get busy." In each club, LeMay suggested that commanders send their cooking staffs to local restaurants and hotels to learn how to prepare first-rate meals. He wanted the food so good that no one would want to eat off base.[37] Most clubs provided entertainment in the way of bingo and dancing, but the Kearney commander said the cost of a band to play in the middle of Nebraska drained his club of $240 a night, and he didn't have enough talent on base to form a band. LeMay told the commander he was considering forming a band that would travel throughout the command to provide entertainment. LeMay also wanted alcohol regulated. He did not like reports of drunk and disorderly airmen. NCOs, LeMay said, had to lay down the law among the enlisted ranks. Gambling, however, was one vice the new commander did not change. Slot machines were allowed in most clubs and LeMay did not mind their presence since they helped keep the clubs solvent.[38]

Security, or the lack thereof, was another problem LeMay wanted fixed. An organization that prepared for war each day had to maintain a high level of security. At Davis-Monthan, LeMay discovered too many leaks about upcoming exercises, especially a planned trip by his bombers around the world: "There is too much talk going on all the time. Your men must tell their wives to stop thinking and talking." Besides their jobs and their duties, LeMay reminded the officers, they were responsible for their wives, too. The new commander's visit to select bases signaled to the organization that things were going to change. The following month the entire organization would get the message.

We Are at War

The lack of a war plan at SAC headquarters and the lack of focus at the lowest levels told LeMay one thing: SAC had to change its perspective. The commander wanted a new operating philosophy to guide operations. SAC no longer prepared for war; said LeMay, "We are at war now!"[39] He remembered the time it took to train his first squadron for operations in World War II. After Pearl Harbor, the Air Corps lacked the preparedness to mount an immediate response. During World War II, LeMay lamented, "Every group I saw go into action during the war tied up its first mission something awful, complete failure, without exception."[40] The atomic age did not afford the United States the luxury of learning by failure. LeMay's leadership philosophy reflected this new paradigm: "We had to operate every day as if we were at war, so if the whistle actually blew we would be doing the same things that we were doing yesterday with the same people and the same methods."[41]

In order to change the mentality of SAC, LeMay had to show the members of the organization that their way was not working. Upon assuming command, he looked at SAC's bomb scores. They were so good, LeMay recalled, they were unbelievable.[42] SAC bombers had been conducting their bomb runs at 12,000 to 15,000 feet, an altitude substantially below that required for combat. At those altitudes, crews were not required to use the supplemental oxygen system necessary for flying at combat altitudes. Since radar sets had functioned imperfectly at combat altitudes, the crews had been practicing their runs at lower altitudes where the radar would work. Finally, crews had been running their radar bomb runs against targets with large radar reflectors out in the middle of the ocean so they could easily identify the targets or the aimpoints. In other words, SAC crews were not conducting realistic training.[43] To make his point, LeMay ordered a command-wide exercise for mid-January 1949.[44] Each bomber crew would fly at 30,000 feet and conduct a simulated radar bomb run against Wright Field in Dayton, Ohio. The Dayton exercise confirmed exactly what LeMay suspected: SAC was not ready for war. Not one airplane finished the mission as briefed. Either crews were not accustomed to flying or bombing from the higher altitudes, or the planes experienced mechanical failure before getting there. LeMay called the Dayton exercise "just about the darkest night in American aviation history."[45]

From January 1949 forward, operations changed dramatically. SAC leadership took a systematic approach to getting the organization combat-ready. They would start with one group, get it up to speed, and move on to the next. LeMay started with the 509th Bomb Group, which had bombed Hiroshima and Nagasaki, to demonstrate the command's priority: nuclear operations.[46] While it had the B-29s equipped to drop nuclear weapons, the 509th was not living up to its reputation. When LeMay passed through Carswell Air Force Base in December 1948, he met with the new 8 AF commander, Gen. Roger Ramey, whose headquarters were collocated with the unit at Carswell. LeMay informed the commander responsible for the 509th that the unit was "no damn good based on past performance."[47] New leadership cleaned the supply warehouses, stocked the parts and supplies the unit needed, and outfitted planes with the required equipment.[48]

Standardization and Evaluation: The SAC Standard

The SAC staff implemented policies that in its eyes would ensure units maintained combat readiness once the command helped them become fully capable. Standardization and constant evaluation would ensure that a unit would never regress once it achieved "combat-ready" status, since everyone operated from the same set of standards and instructions. As LeMay had believed and emphasized in his bomber organizations during World War II, standardization became the key to achieving organizational strategic bombing success. SAC headquarters enforced standardization and evaluation through technical manuals and checklists that outlined detailed procedures for each person and each task. "I wanted a book written on how you bomb right from the start to finish for the bombardier," LeMay remembered. "A bombardier couldn't go on the crew until he knew the damn thing by heart. There would be a manual for the flight engineer. Finally, we got a manual for every job in SAC."[49] Atomic weapons added another dimension to SAC operations that required perfection. Although viewed as simply another bomb, LeMay understood the political implications that came with carrying nuclear weapons. "With atomic weapons," LeMay remarked, "we could not afford unpreparedness."[50] SAC procedures were atypical and exceeded Air Force requirements. This was the SAC standard—better than the rest—and for nuclear weapons operations, perfection was the only acceptable standard.

Air Force regulations mandated that commanders develop checklists for airplanes under their command for taxi, takeoff, and landing.[51] SAC demanded checklists that outlined procedures for crewmembers during all phases of flight. SAC lacked any semblance of standardization when LeMay took over, and in his eyes, the crews' proficiency level demonstrated this flaw. In November 1948 LeMay instructed his subordinate commanders to make standardization programs a priority. He also required each wing and headquarters to appoint a standardization, or lead, crew.[52] Lead crews had become a feature of LeMay's bombing commands in the European theater in World War II, and he continued this practice in the Pacific.[53] Beginning in 1949, SAC established a lead crew school at Walker Air Force Base, New Mexico. Thirty-six B-29 crews, considered the "cream" of SAC, went through the school from June 1 to August 15, 1949, to establish proven techniques and procedures. SAC expected commanders to send their best crews to the school, where instructors evaluated them on their bombing procedures and crew discipline. The school put increased emphasis on radar bombing as a means of selection, since this procedure required greater concentration and perfection of technique. Graduates of the school returned to their units and trained the rest of the unit's bomber crews in the best techniques and procedures.[54] The message SAC wanted sent to the force was that good procedures produced good results.

After August 1949 the school relocated to Davis-Monthan Air Force Base, where eighteen B-50 crews attended the course. The more crews that went through the school, the more it paid off in terms of units' better bomb scores. This led to the establishment of a permanent combat crew standardization school at MacDill Air Force

Base, Florida. The school strove to develop checklists and standard operating procedures (SOPs) for each crewmember.[55] SAC scripted each part of crewmembers' jobs, which made evaluating performance more of a science than an art since everyone knew the standards. For example, aircraft commanders and flight engineers would complete a six-hundred-item checklist before each flight to ensure they understood and completed critical tasks such as ensuring all firefighting equipment was positioned prior to starting engines.[56] The emphasis on standardization and procedures improved SAC's bombing performance. At the beginning of 1949, crews were averaging a miss distance of 3,679 feet; by the end of the year, the miss distance for medium bombers (B-29s/B-50s) was 2,928 feet and 2,268 feet for heavy bombers (B-36s).[57] Throughout LeMay's tenure and beyond, bomb scores continued to receive emphasis. Low nuclear stockpiles meant every bomb had to hit its target. Furthermore, the command's tactics of smaller formations of penetrating bombers led to a heavy emphasis on precise bomb delivery.

Prior to LeMay taking command, SAC had experienced a 65 percent increase in accidents, an average of more than sixty accidents per 100,000 flying hours.[58] In the second month of his tenure, LeMay temporarily grounded the B-29 fleet due to repeated crashes.[59] The commander believed that not strictly adhering to the aircraft's checklist during operations was the cause of a significant number of these accidents. Standardized procedures were seen as a way to lower accident rates. Montgomery, who oversaw operations, explained later how LeMay reduced the accident rates: "LeMay did it by demanding that the flight checklist and the maintenance checklist be adhered to. There was a penalty for violation. He didn't permit carelessness— even from somebody who hadn't had any accidents."[60] If a wing commander had an accident at his base, LeMay required him to fly to Offutt to personally brief the SAC commander on the incident.[61] LeMay grew tired of hearing his wing commanders tell him that they didn't understand how their "best" pilot could have had an accident. The best pilots, LeMay believed, used checklists. LeMay stopped one wing commander in mid-sentence, saying, "For Lord's sake, don't tell me this is the best pilot you had. I'm sick and tired of that." In LeMay's estimation, too many pilots thought checklists were beneath them; his command philosophy changed that perception. SAC could not afford to lose airplanes at a time when it was trying to get war-ready and when the prospect loomed that SAC might have to expand operations in the future. After two years the effort paid off; SAC achieved the lowest accident rate in the Air Force.[62]

Realistic Training

Armed with procedures and checklists, SAC aircrew could take to the skies and prepare for their wartime mission. The Dayton exercise had proven that crews and airplanes were not prepared to fly and fight under wartime conditions. As in World War II, SAC assigned each combat crew a particular target as part of the overall war plan. Commanders expected crews to study and know their specific mission. SAC developed training aids, especially a radar trainer, so that if a bombardier's target was in Moscow, he could "bomb" that target multiple times before being asked to do it in real life. Similarly, crews flew simulated bombing missions against U.S. cities that resembled targets in the Soviet Union. LeMay estimated that San Francisco was bombed about six hundred times a year.[63]

An organization at war operated twenty-four hours a day. This was the new SAC culture. One of the first steps LeMay took after hearing of SAC's dismal bomb scores was to order all radar bomb-scoring sites to stay open around the clock. These sites scored the simulated bomb runs conducted by SAC's bombers. Bombers would approach the site on a predetermined course. The radar sites used a radio signal emanating from the bomber to determine how close the bomber would have come to destroying the planned target. Radar bombing, not World War II–era visual bombing, was the primary means of conducting a bomb release. When notified of their new schedule in December 1948, the SAC chief of staff wrote, "Current aircraft flying speeds and bombing altitudes as well as all-weather operations have made visual bombing techniques obsolete. The accomplishment of the primary mission of [SAC] combat crews depends almost entirely upon proficiency in radar bombing techniques." SAC ordered the organization responsible for operating the twelve radar bomb-scoring sites throughout the country to go from scoring one thousand runs per month to eight thousand per month.[64]

If the radar sites were open for business around the clock, then SAC would fly around the clock. Two factors drove SAC's twenty-four-hour operations. First, LeMay wanted his crews to operate as though war could start at any minute. "We intend to develop the capability to bomb in daylight or in darkness," LeMay told his fellow generals at Exercise Dualism, "in good or bad weather, by single or by large formation. These varied capabilities will provide the commander the flexibility he must have to take advantage of any weakness shown by the enemy."[65] The second reason stemmed from the operational training requirements the new SAC commander installed. William Martin joined SAC in 1950 following his graduation from the Air War College. After a brief tour as the deputy commander of the prestigious 509th Bomb Wing to familiarize himself with SAC operations, Martin took command of a new B-36 wing (6th Bomb Wing). The B-36, in his eyes, was a "struggling beast." SAC required him to put thirty airplanes in the air and fly three hundred hours a month. This was difficult because the B-36 had ten engines (six propeller and four jet), and getting all of them to start presented a significant challenge. Martin's wing operated around the clock because "getting those 10 engines to start was a struggle and once we did we flew them until practically all the engines quit."[66]

LeMay wanted his crews to be able to perform under the most extreme circumstances. Anyone could operate when the sun was shining and the weather was good; SAC culture was to perform the wartime mission when nobody wanted to or seemed able to do. The SAC mentality was that if an organization succeeded under the worst conditions, it would certainly perform well in favorable conditions. When LeMay directed Martin's B-36 command to deploy and practice its wartime mission, he did not send them to Thule, Greenland, in the summertime. Instead, Martin remembered, he sent them in February, when Thule was dark most of the time and the temperature was thirty degrees below zero. "Every year in February," Martin recalled, "I would deploy to Thule, load weapons for practice, download weapons, prepare for a simulated prestrike mission, launch on a profile mission (32 hours) that would simulate our strike mission, and post-strike at home base."[67] Operating in the harsh cold became another cultural feature of SAC.

In the early days of the Cold War, military intelligence estimated that any surprise Soviet attack would come through the polar region and a U.S. retaliatory response would likewise traverse the same Arctic region. In 1946 SAC conducted a top-secret mission to better understand the Arctic operating environment. Project Nanook involved a reconnaissance squadron of B-29s deploying to Ladd Field, Alaska, for the purpose of gaining intelligence on Soviet operations, understanding the operating requirements of the harsh environment, and practicing navigation techniques for "over-the-pole" flights. Due to the magnetic interference at the North Pole and the fact that longitudinal lines converge there, conventional navigation techniques were not suitable for polar flying. Therefore, Project Nanook perfected "grid" flying techniques, a navigation technique that uses grids of parallel lines instead of true north because of the meridian convergence. After nearly two years in the polar region, the unit returned and trained other SAC units on its findings. SAC would not only operate out of Alaska and Thule, Greenland, but also would rotate crews out of Goose Bay, Canada, as well as new permanent bases along the northern U.S. frontier.[68]

SAC Survival School: Only Bombers Go Deep

Due to its extreme operating conditions and requirements, SAC realized the need for more specialized training. SAC had already built one institution, the combat crew standardization school, which symbolized part of SAC culture. The survival school became another hallmark of the organization's culture. During the Berlin airlift crisis, LeMay had directed a member of his staff, Lt. Col. D. G. Stampados, to develop an escape and evasion plan in case crews were downed in the Soviet-controlled areas of Germany. When LeMay took over SAC, he had Stampados assigned to SAC headquarters to work on a command escape and evasion program.[69] SAC crewmembers needed survival training because they were expected to go deep into Soviet territory. While ground forces in Europe planned to slow advancing Russian forces, SAC would be striking cities inside the Soviet Union. If shot down, SAC crewmembers would have to fend for themselves behind enemy lines. LeMay built a school to teach the skills necessary for such harsh environments. SAC selected Camp Carson, Colorado, as the site for its survival school due to the land available and the fact that the surrounding terrain simulated conditions aircrews could expect if they parachuted into hostile territory.[70] On April 1, 1950, former World War II prisoners of war and those who had escaped from camps went through the course to verify the curriculum. Stampados became the commander of the 3904th Training Squadron at Camp Carson, Colorado, as it began accepting students.

After certification, LeMay ordered that every SAC crewmember attend the school. Crewmembers learned how to procure food and water in austere conditions, as well as how to "pilfer" food from local inhabitants. A farmhouse provisioned with chickens, eggs, and a flush garden provided a realistic setting for aircrews to try their hand at stealing food. In addition to survival techniques, crewmembers had to conduct a crossing through a mock Soviet border. Attendees had one day to negotiate the booby traps, electrical trip wires, barbed wire fences, and guard posts that separated them from freedom. If captured in the process, crews underwent simulated interrogations. LeMay visited the survival school May 5–7, 1950.[71] An avid hunter and outdoorsman, LeMay joined the class as it finished classroom training and was about to head to the woods for five days of evasion and survival training, a journey that would take the group through forty-nine miles of rough Colorado countryside. The commander received the items typical in the aircrew survival kit, to include sleeping bag, axe, gun, fishing equipment, and the parachute one would have if he jumped out of an airplane. In addition, crews carried with them blood chits, the World War II name given to a square piece of cloth or silk that was inscribed with the following passage in multiple languages: "I am an American Airman, my plane is destroyed, I cannot speak your language. Please nourish and protect me and take me to the nearest American embassy or Consular Post. My government will reward you." The "blood chits" had worked during the strategic bombing campaigns in World War II and were issued to SAC crewmembers. Additionally, each airman would carry gold coins to use for bribery or to buy food.[72] LeMay's visit also included observing crew procedures with SA-16 survival aircraft. Aircrews had to learn procedures for vectoring rescue aircraft in on their position for pickup once they got within range.

The school was unique to the command and served as an artifact of SAC culture. SAC people were expected to fly deep into Soviet territory. If shot down, they would have to survive on their own and find their way out of the Soviet Union. The Air Force's and SAC's assumptions about the importance of strategic bombing were formalized in the nation's war plans. SAC's survival school stood as a physical structure with its own routines and rituals that testified to the distinctiveness of SAC.[73]

Leaders Fly and Flyers Lead

LeMay's visit to the survival school highlighted another unique aspect of SAC culture: LeMay expected his top leaders to be pilots as well as leaders. He required the same of his staff officers that he expected of his aircrews. To make the point, LeMay assigned each staff officer his own crew. LeMay put it bluntly, "We can't show up at some operating base in a plush job flown by a sharp young pilot and then chew the combat people out for the way they are handling their combat planes."[74] Paul Carlton remembered his selection to become LeMay's aide-de-camp. LeMay chose Carlton, who served in the Pacific during World War II and competed for the Crossroads test, for his ability to run LeMay's personal crew. Carlton recalled, "Aiding was just strictly secondary. My number one job was to run a combat-type crew."[75] The SAC commander expected from his crew the same thing he expected from SAC members writ large: standardization. In SAC, leaders flew and flyers led.

The emphasis on establishing a "war" mentality in SAC did not keep the command from making headlines. In March 1949 a B-50, Lady Luck II, completed a nonstop around-the-world mission using aerial refueling. LeMay said the mission proved that the United States could drop an atomic bomb on "any place in the world."[76] For that mission, SAC won the coveted MacKay trophy for having the most outstanding flight within a given year. That same month, a B-36 from Carswell Air Force Base set a long-distance record by completing a 9,600-mile trip in 43 hours and 37 minutes without refueling. The demonstration led the secretary of the Air Force to comment at the end of 1949, "Existence of this strategic atomic striking force is the greatest deterrent in the world today to the start of another global war."[77]

Air Refueling: Adding a New Subculture

The Lady Luck mission succeeded because SAC had worked to develop an air-to-air refueling capability. The air refueling tanker, like the intercontinental bomber, became a known artifact of SAC culture and created a new culture within SAC: the tanker crew. During the Lady Luck mission, the SAC crew used the British style of air refueling. B-29s were modified and equipped with a hose (KB-29M was their official designation), while the B-50s had a hose themselves as the receiver. The receiver's line had a wind sock on the end, while the tanker's line had a weight. Using this technique, the tanker crossed above the receiver until the lines crossed and the tanker caught the receiver's hose, which the tanker reeled in and connected to the fuel line. The connected hoses were then slid back out into the air, and gas flowed from the tanker to the bomber using gravity feed. The trouble with this system was the complicated rendezvous process, the slow rate of transfer with gravity feed, and the lower altitudes required because of wind and pressurization problems at higher altitudes.

SAC, with the cooperation of Air Materiel Command, developed and fielded the American system for air refueling, which used a telescopic boom that extended from the rear of the tanker and passed fuel under pressure to the receiving aircraft through a port on top of the fuselage. Although the boom system held clear advantages over the British system because of SAC's mission needs, the symbolism of the two systems was not lost on Gen. Hunter Harris, who remembered that fighter pilots had preferred the flexible hose system initially fielded. SAC, however, embraced the rigid boom system symbolic of the "rigidity" of SAC operations.[78] Air refueling capability greatly extended the range of SAC's medium-range bombers and made the organization a truly global force. Tankers embodied SAC's hope for such a force; without them, B-29s/B-50s (and soon, B-47s and B-52s) could not reach their targets. In 1949 SAC began to establish entire squadrons dedicated strictly to air refueling and by the end of the year had six squadrons operational with two of them fully manned with

KB-29Ms.[79] LeMay found SAC's dependence on overseas bases troublesome. At any moment, host countries could decide to withdraw their support for the basing of nuclear bombers. Air refueling tankers could free SAC from overseas bases and bring the bombers home under SAC's control. For this reason, LeMay pushed hard to develop the Air Force's air-to-air refueling capability.

Tankers became part of the SAC organizational culture and one of the command's subcultures. Bombers were the dominant culture, especially since a bomber pilot led the organization and each of its operational commands. Furthermore, tankers—as would be the case with reconnaissance aircraft—were initially derivatives of the bomber design. Initial tankers came from modifying the B-29/50. Therefore, tankers maintained some of the physical representation of a bomber. As a subculture, the group that flew these modified bombers espoused the beliefs and values of the organization; they were not a counterculture. Eventually, SAC would develop aircraft specifically designed for the air refueling mission.

When SAC members were not putting in long hours on simulated missions or setting records, they were serving ninety-day rotations at overseas installations, sitting alert and ready for war. LeMay knew SAC could be called upon to go anywhere at a moment's notice. He wanted SAC to develop the ability to slam the lids on supply boxes loaded with necessary supplies when ordered to deploy, throw them into airplanes, and be ready to fight when they arrived at their destination. One of SAC's developments in this area was the "flyaway" kit—another unique symbol of SAC culture. These kits, which were loaded onto deploying aircraft, contained up to 44,000 separate items that could sustain operations for a fixed period of time until the logistical process caught up with the war. "As soon as we landed," LeMay said, "we were ready to go."[80]

Competition

Creating a culture in which everyone operated as though he were at war challenged LeMay. In response, he developed a unique SAC rating system that kept organizations constantly focused on their performance. If SAC members were not actually at war with the enemy, they certainly were competing with other units. LeMay explained the system this way: "We knew what it took to make a good bombing outfit. They had to be able to bomb, they had to be able to navigate, they had to be able to fly formation. It was essential they keep their airplane in commission, and that they have the proper supply setup."[81] Each category had a point system in which LeMay gave each item a certain weight depending on what he wanted to emphasize in the command. The system gave the commander flexibility so that he could achieve what he considered an honest picture of the command.

Hunter Harris served under LeMay in Europe during World War II. Following the war, he attended the Air War College in 1947 and upon graduation landed an assignment at Sandia Laboratory as the deputy commander of special weapons projects, which developed nuclear weapons for various military purposes. His experience at Sandia gave him the nuclear expertise SAC needed. LeMay brought him back to SAC in 1950 and made him the commander of the prestigious 509th Bomb Wing. From Harris' perspective, SAC's rating system kept the organization at peak performance. It was "an evaluation system on performance of people, on performance of units," Harris recalled. "Everybody wanted to be number one in training accomplishments, in bombing accuracy, navigation accuracy, and all these things."[82] The constant pressure manifested itself in the reports commanders had to generate and send to SAC daily. Every night, SAC bases sent their combat readiness reports to SAC headquarters. Each morning by eight o'clock, LeMay reviewed the number of aircraft and aircrews available should war come. Throughout LeMay's tenure, SAC headquarters required increasingly more detailed statistical reports to justify units' combat readiness. Combat readiness meant more than just bombing scores, which by 1950 had improved 500 percent since LeMay took command; it also meant lower VD rates, higher maintenance readiness, and higher retention of personnel.[83] Retaining trained people meant less turnover, less training, and increased combat readiness. Within LeMay's first year, SAC's reenlistment rate rose to 70 percent.[84]

Operational readiness inspections (ORIs) became a routine in the organization and another feature of the SAC culture. Every member

of SAC received his SOPs, tech orders, and procedures and thus knew
the expectations. Each year, LeMay had his inspectors evaluate those
standards. The one important feature of an ORI was that it almost
always occurred unannounced. LeMay saw no purpose in telling a
wing commander when the inspection would start. War could start at
any minute, and a SAC unit had to be ready to exercise its war plan
at any time.

LeMay despised the idea that commanders would know when
he would arrive to evaluate their performance. On June 11, 1950,
LeMay observed a formation from the 2nd Bomb Group and found
its tactics and performance lacking. Later that day, LeMay grew angry
that the commander of the group had been aware of his visit. The
SAC commander informed his staff of a new policy regarding alerting
units about his arrival or the inspection of units. The policy would be:
"Do not alert any agency of my arrival unless it is necessary in the
accomplishment of the mission. . . . This policy is particularly appli-
cable to units of his command which he plans to inspect either in the
air or on the ground."[85] SAC ensured that its commanders kept their
units combat-ready through surprise annual inspections. Suddenly,
an inspection team would arrive on base and insist the commander
execute his war plan while the team evaluated the organization's proficiency. The commander's career rose or fell with the results. Those
commanders who succeeded gained status; LeMay assigned those who
failed to new jobs.[86]

ORIs and daily ratings of performance were not the only rituals
designed to keep SAC competitive and war-ready. SAC held an annual
bombing competition to evaluate the best crews, best units, and best
numbered Air Forces in the command. Kenney held the first event
to spark interest in bombing. Under LeMay, winning "Bomb Comp"
became a way to identify the best in SAC and reward them with
coveted "spot promotions."

Personnel Policies
Rebuilding an organization from the ground up meant LeMay
could not afford to lose good people, and the fact that the organization was not actually at war enabled him to eliminate from SAC
those who could not perform to his standard. Since SAC was the

General LeMay briefing his staff during the World War II Pacific campaign, February 5, 1944. LeMay's approach to bombing in World War II laid the foundation for SAC's initial operating procedures. *U.S. Air Force Historical Research Agency, IRIS 1090635*

General LeMay getting a mission briefing on Guam, July 1945. The techniques and tactics developed in the Pacific campaign laid the foundation for the formation of SAC's culture. *U.S. Air Force Historical Research Agency, IRIS 1090621*

SSgt. Billy Davis stands guard outside the entrance to SAC Headquarters at Offutt Air Force Base, Nebraska, with the SAC motto proudly displayed behind him. *National Archives*

General LeMay (center) completing his water survival training at Offutt Air Force Base. SAC initiated survival training under LeMay's command. *U.S. Air Force Historical Research Agency, IRIS 1090592*

The B-36 Peacemaker bomber performing a training mission. The bomber was distinctive because of its six propeller engines and four jet engines, which earned it the moniker "six turning and four burning." *U.S. Air Force*

Members of the 11th Bombardment Wing proudly displaying the "Fairchild Trophy" in front of a B-36J. SAC awarded the trophy to the best bombing unit in the command at its annual bombing competition. *U.S. Air Force*

WORLD
SERIES
OF
BOMBING

1957 SAC BOMBING-NAVIGATION-RECONNAISSANCE COMPETITION
PINECASTLE AIR FORCE BASE
FLORIDA

Program cover for the 1957 SAC bombing competition also known as the "World Series of Bombing." SAC used bombing competition as a way to hone the skills of its deterrent force. *National Museum of the Air Force*

Program photo of a bomber crew (B-58 Hustler) participating in SAC's bombing competition. This competition pitted the best of each SAC wing against one another as a way to keep SAC's crews "at war." *National Museum of the U.S. Air Force*

Wing leadership congratulating a B-47 crew for its bombing competition. Winning the bomb competition typically meant "spot promotions" for the victors. *National Museum of the U.S. Air Force*

General LeMay working on his own car at base housing. LeMay enjoyed working on autos, and that enthusiasm led to the formation of SAC's auto hobby shops. *U.S. Historical Research Agency, IRIS 1090596*

A B-47 crew responds to an alert exercise at Offutt Air Force Base, Nebraska. The first member up the ladder displays the sidearm LeMay required all aircrew to carry. *National Archives*

B-47 Stratojet performing a jet–assisted takeoff. The extra weight of a B-47 loaded for war meant that it needed extra thrust to get airborne. *National Museum of the U.S. Air Force*

KC-97 Stratofreighter refueling a B-47 Stratojet. The B-47 had to fly just above stall speed to match the speed of the propeller-drive refueler. *U.S. Air Force*

The XB–36H/NB–36H, the test aircraft for the nuclear-powered aircraft program. The aircraft had a 3-megawatt reactor on board to see how radiation affected aircraft systems. The program was scrapped in 1961. *U.S. Air Force*

SAC crew racing to their B-52 bomber in response to alert exercise. SAC used alert responses as a way to make sure the "force-in-being" was ready for war. *U.S. Air Force*

The B-58 Hustler prototype taking off. The B-58 was the only SAC bomber capable of achieving speeds in excess of Mach 2. *National Museum of the U.S. Air Force*

General LeMay taking a break to get in some trap shooting. LeMay was a trap enthusiast, and this eventually led to the formation of SAC Rod and Gun clubs. *U.S. Air Force Historical Research Agency, IRIS 1090595*

General LeMay getting oriented with what appears to be a new aircraft for an Aero Club. Aero Clubs were initially unique to SAC. *U.S. Air Force Historical Research Agency, IRIS 1090600*

A crew at work in the SAC Airborne Command Post, which stayed airborne twenty-four hours a day. It could command the entire SAC force if the primary Command Post was attacked. *Official U.S. Air Force Photo*

An aerial view of SAC Headquarters at Offutt Air Force Base, Nebraska. What this view does not show is the three-story control center buried forty-five feet under the surface designed to survive a nuclear attack. *National Archives*

A view inside the SAC Command Post at Offutt Air Force Base, Nebraska, which served as the focal point for controlling SAC's worldwide force. *Official U.S. Air Force Photo*

A picture of the famed "red phone." The phone was inside the SAC Command Post, and once picked up, the controller could be in contact with every SAC base throughout the world. *National Archives*

Gen. Thomas Power brief-
ing inside the SAC Com-
mand Post. General Power
served as LeMay's selected
Deputy Commander and
then assumed command of
SAC when LeMay moved
to Washington, D.C., in
1957. *National Archives*

General LeMay being sworn in as USAF Chief of Staff on June 30, 1961.
Secretary of the Air Force Eugene Zuckert swears in LeMay as President
John F. Kennedy and Vice President Lyndon Johnson look on. *U.S. Air Force
Historical Research Agency, IRIS 1090588*

Rollout of B-70A Valkyrie on May 11, 1964. LeMay wanted the new bomber, but Defense Secretary Robert McNamara never funded full production. *U.S. Air Force*

Air Force's number-one priority, leadership positions in the command became something many aspiring officers sought. At a commander's conference held within six months of LeMay taking command, he announced that all graduates from professional military schools would be accepted into SAC. Furthermore, SAC had been given priority in sending officers to schools. LeMay, however, would not allow all officers who applied to attend professional military education. Those people in key positions applying for schools would be told why they could not be released. LeMay would put an efficiency report in their record explaining SAC's special circumstances so that his officers would not lose out when considered for promotion.[87]

It was not that LeMay opposed military education. He believed the best place to learn about fighting a war was on the front lines. Horace Wade served in World War II and attended the Armed Forces Staff College before joining SAC in 1949. Although a product of military education, Wade shared LeMay's views: "He thought—and I shared his feelings when I served him at Omaha—that the best school in the Air Force was that one being conducted at SAC. If anybody wanted to learn anything about fighting a war, how to fight it, and what to do, send him to SAC, and SAC would teach him."[88]

Jim Edmundson had to petition LeMay in order to find a job under the new commander. Many of Edmundson's contemporaries at the Air War College in 1949 wanted to avoid SAC because they heard of LeMay's reputation for toughness. Edmundson, however, wanted to join SAC. He received a short reply from the commander that simply said, "I can use you Jim." Following his graduation, Edmundson reported to March Field, California, where he took over the 22nd Bomb Group.[89]

Another policy unique to SAC culture was the concept of crew integrity or "hard" crews. As was the case in both his commands in World War II, LeMay wanted functioning crews to stay together—there were no substitutions on missions involving lead or select crews. SAC depended on combat readiness, and LeMay wanted successful crew combinations to fly together year after year. If these crews mastered their planes and procedures, they could avoid the threat of a desk job.[90] LeMay demanded a maximum effort from these crews, but he found the means to reward those who achieved excellence. Exacting seventy to ninety hours of rigorous training a week from SAC's aircrew would soon take a toll and decrease retention unless LeMay could devise a way to reward his warriors. Therefore, he implemented a spot promotion system to reward officers by promoting exceptional performers in rank on the spot.

In late 1949 the SAC commander petitioned the Air Force personnel center for his first allotment of spot promotions. LeMay justified his request by arguing, "I believe that by virtue of the mission of Strategic Air Command, a higher degree of dependability, flying proficiency, and individual stability under pressure is required of the combat crew member than would be required of officers of equal rank and experience elsewhere in the Air Force."[91] Within two months, he received the approval. Eventually, LeMay expanded the program to include enlisted personnel as well. According to Gen. William Martin, the 509th Bomb Wing deputy commander in 1950, the system also worked to enhance crew integrity and professionalism.[92] Entire crews could gain spot promotions for significant achievements such as winning the annual SAC bombing competition. On the other hand, entire crews could lose their temporary promotions if the crew, or even an individual member, failed to maintain high standards of performance.[93]

Security

Placing SAC on a war footing meant protecting the planes and bases required for war. The Soviet Union made deliberate attempts to penetrate America's open society and gain intelligence. After attending an Air Force commanders' conference in April 1950, former SAC commander Kenney wrote to Vandenberg about the threat of sabotage against Air Force bases in the United States. "I believe that [sabotage] constitutes a real danger that we are not paying enough attention to. The airplanes themselves and our fuel supplies are vulnerable to operations of this type unless far greater precautions are taken at present."[94] In response to these covert actions, SAC made security a top priority. SAC's inspector general issued a letter stating, "The possibility exists that prior to or immediately subsequent to a national emergency an attempt may be made to destroy or damage aircraft . . . through fifth column type activity, thus weakening or delaying employment of the force."[95] To address the perceived threat, SAC built fences around its installations and increased security controls. SAC leadership believed that the American communist party would attempt acts of sabotage against the organization in case of war.[96] To simulate sabotage on SAC installations, LeMay created special penetration teams that acted like enemy agents and tried to infiltrate various bases disguised as flight crew, civilian contractors, or even soft-drink vendors.[97] SAC security guards had to react as though every intrusion were the real thing. General Montgomery remembered an incident at Travis Air Force Base that emphasized the importance of security in the command. A security guard saw a man jump the fence and start running toward the airplanes. The guard ordered the man to halt, but he ignored the warning. The guard fired above the intruder's head but that failed to stop him. Finally, the guard shot and killed the intruder. When Montgomery explained the situation to LeMay, he asked what they should do about the incident. Following LeMay's orders, Montgomery told the guard he owed the Air Force thirty-five cents for the round he wasted.[98] The importance of SAC as the only command capable of delivering nuclear bombs made the organization a target for infiltration or sabotage. Increased security throughout the organization was the way to preserve SAC's ability to execute its war plan. Heightened security—including sabotage teams—was a hallmark of SAC operations and a part of its organizational culture. When SAC members entered their base, they passed through wired fences and intense security checks. Upon leaving, SAC required crewmembers to put down instructions on how they could be reached. LeMay instituted the "six-ring alert," which required all crewmembers to be within six rings of a telephone.[99] LeMay also required all crewmembers to carry sidearms while on duty. Guards with sidearms patrolling fenced-in bases reinforced the notion that SAC members were at war. The more fences SAC erected, the more its members became aware that they operated differently from the rest of the Air Force.

Arming officers demonstrated how SAC culture began to take physical form. It started with the underlying assumption that SAC was at war. Knowing the importance of SAC's mission, assumptions became policy: SAC had to increase security because Soviet infiltrators would try to sabotage the nation's number-one deterrent and its only nuclear delivery organization. Finally, SAC's organizational culture took physical form in artifacts and routines. Officers carried weapons, and sabotage teams constantly tested SAC's security measures.[100]

Conclusion

By the summer of 1950, SAC had made great strides in war readiness. LeMay and his staff had implemented new policies and instituted new procedures that began to shape a distinctive SAC organizational culture. At Ramey Air Force Base, Puerto Rico, General Vandenberg held another commander's conference similar to Exercise Dualism for his top generals. This time LeMay and Montgomery presented a more detailed war plan and the progress SAC had made in the last year and a half. SAC, Montgomery reported, was 100 percent manned, but the command only considered itself about 85 to 90 percent manned because of critical shortages in key specialties. Furthermore, SAC had cut in half the distance by which crews were missing their targets. Addressing the group, LeMay said: "We have our troubles; however, we can carry out our mission. I think we can carry it out very well."[101] But events during the summer of 1950 would challenge SAC as the Cold War took a new turn.

The Air Force created SAC out of the belief that bomber operations should be centrally controlled. While other services headquartered close to Washington, D.C., the Air Force sought to give SAC its own space, geographically and politically, placing it in the middle of the United States, where the command began to construct a centralized organization of its own. As the Cold War intensified, bombers equipped with nuclear weapons were seen as the way to deter Soviet aggression and preserve peace. SAC had to demonstrate that it could perform the mission assigned. A central feature of SAC culture was standardization, which grew out of leaders' beliefs that bomber operations required everyone to follow the same routines. These rituals put bombs accurately on target, lowered accident rates, and maintained combat readiness.

In those initial years of LeMay's command, more elements of SAC culture took form that would endure for decades. Security and competition resulted from the organization's need to keep its members in a warfighting mode without actually engaging in combat operations.

SAC also created new institutions that reflected the organization's culture. The lead crew school, designed to standardize crew bombing procedures, became the standardization school, which standardized all aspects of bomber flying. To demonstrate the uniqueness of their mission, SAC established the survival school. Since SAC's crews were the only forces likely to penetrate deep into the Soviet Union, they had to be prepared to survive on their own in case they could not escape the Russian air defenses.

LeMay and his team of "bomber generals" put SAC on alert; war was not months or weeks away, but hours away. SAC's daily routines reflected an organization at war. Since the Cold War could become "hot" at any moment, bomber crews had to memorize their routing and targets. In a regimented training program that simulated the real thing, crews studied target folders, flew preplanned missions following standardized procedures, and delivered simulated bombs on U.S. cities that represented Soviet targets. Crews developed cohesion and proficiency in flying and bombing, or else they received no rewards. Wing commanders ensured they knew the location of each crewmember, reported daily "numbers" to LeMay, and nervously anticipated the yearly test of their leadership. Like the crews under their command, their careers rose and fell based on the outcome. This was the life of SAC's warriors, the nation's first line of defense.

5

Taking Charge
Organizational Culture in SAC
Relationships, Institutions, and Artifacts

*We in SAC were not saber-rattlers. We were not yelling for war and action
in order to "flex the mighty muscles we had built." No stupidity of that sort.
We wanted peace as much as anyone else wanted it.*

—CURTIS LeMAY

From 1948 through the summer of 1950, the Truman administration held the line on defense spending. The Air Force
thought it might have succeeded in making the case for a larger
force. The Finletter report, the result of Truman's blue-ribbon Air
Policy Commission, had recommended seventy groups for the U.S.
Air Force.[1] Despite the commission's findings, the Truman administration maintained a forty-eight-group Air Force and restrained defense
spending in the face of domestic economic pressures, which included
growing inflation. Although Secretary of Defense James Forrestal
offered a balanced approach to defense spending by dividing funds
equally among the services, the emphasis on airpower agreed to by
most of the Joint Chiefs gave the Air Force more than its share of the
budget. Navy dissent over the Air Force receiving funding for its B-36
at the expense of the Navy's super carrier led to a revolt among some

of the Navy's top leaders and a congressional investigation into the
B-36 decision.[2]

The decision to limit the Air Force's size did not immediately
affect SAC operations. When Curtis LeMay took over in 1948, the
command, in his estimation, was not ready for war. Within two
years, he had made great strides in building a credible deterrent. The
command had almost 52,000 people and 837 aircraft at the beginning
of LeMay's tenure. By the end of 1950, the command had increased
its ranks by more than 30,000 people and 130 aircraft, to include the
newly arrived air refueling planes.[3] Although fully manned, SAC was
still in the midst of making all of its units combat-ready. The Eighth
Air Force remained the priority, given the increasing emphasis on
nuclear operations. The discovery that the Soviet Union had exploded
a nuclear bomb in 1949 brought even more focus to U.S. air operations. Once the Soviets had the ability to produce atomic weapons
and possibly deliver them with their developing fleet of intercontinental bombers, defensive measures—particularly air interceptors and
radar—became a concern. Events in 1950, however, would reempha-
size the offensive nature of American airpower.

In the summer of 1950 North Korea invaded South Korea,
confirming America's preconceived notions about communist
aggression. The Korean War sparked a mobilization of U.S. military
power. In the fall, President Truman approved the already completed
National Security Council Report 68, which provided for an expansion of America's nuclear stockpile and the means to deliver these
weapons as well as an increase in conventional forces. No longer
would the Air Force's strength be held to forty-eight groups. Supplemental spending for fiscal year 1951 and future out-year budgets
would fund a nearly 200 percent increase in Air Force strength (up
to 143 groups).[4]

SAC's expansion added new dimensions and forms to its organizational culture and reinforced its existing elements. While SAC forces
dropped conventional bombs on Korea, SAC forces at home continued to prepare for nuclear conflict with the Soviet Union. Relying on
the National Guard, reservists, and volunteers meant that SAC had to
develop the means to retain its highly trained personnel and keep the

organization war-ready while it expanded and absorbed new recruits. Other elements of SAC culture emerged throughout the expansion, displaying the organization's emphasis on becoming a modern air force at war. These cultural forms were more than ideological; culture was found in airplane designs, housing construction, and recreational outlets. Throughout the early 1950s, SAC differentiated itself from other Air Force organizations in its operations and command relationships. Within SAC, the organization created more unique institutions and routines.

An Air Force Within an Air Force

The ability to conduct worldwide visual and electronic reconnaissance became vital to SAC's operations. During World War II, the AAF gathered intelligence from open sources on Germany (including American bank records and travel books) to build its strategic bombing plan. In the Pacific, the planners had to gain intelligence on Japan's closed society through reconnaissance flights. Now the global force of SAC faced a new enemy and another closed society. Most of the information SAC had on Soviet targets came from German intelligence and films obtained after World War II.[5] Photo reconnaissance would provide updated pictures of the Soviet Union, since most crews doubted the accuracy of the outdated photos. Electronic reconnaissance enabled SAC to understand the type and frequency of radars that now guarded Soviet borders against possible hostile aircraft. Since SAC was the command assigned to attack the Soviet homeland, the organization wanted to control all facets of long-range reconnaissance.

As with tankers, most of the reconnaissance aircraft were derivatives of bomber designs. Instead of bomb-dropping equipment, the bomber's noses were filled with cameras, signals intelligence equipment, and even devices that could sample the air. The reconnaissance subculture did not see much difference between themselves and the dominant bomber subculture, since they flew the same planes. Arguably, reconnaissance had the tougher mission, since it sometimes had to penetrate enemy airspace alone.[6] The assignment of the reconnaissance mission to SAC resulted in the formation of another numbered air force, Second Air Force (2 AF), headquartered at Barksdale Air Force

Base, Louisiana.[7] SAC initially organized along functional lines, with 8 AF and 15 AF operating the organization's bomber fleet while 2 AF primarily ran reconnaissance operations. As SAC grew, LeMay felt this organizational structure lacked rationale since some units close to 15 AF, now headquartered at March Air Force Base, California, were actually under 2 AF's control. Therefore, in the spring of 1950, LeMay reorganized SAC's numbered air forces along geographical lines. Under the new organizational structure, all three air forces would be assigned a strategic reconnaissance unit that would allow it to operate independently. The Fifteenth Air Force controlled SAC forces in the western part of the United States, 8 AF oversaw the central bases, and 2 AF commanded the eastern bases.[8] LeMay spread his organization across the United States and set it apart from other Air Force commands by giving his command a spot promotion system. Not only had SAC leaders built a highly specialized and standardized organization, they also were essentially creating an air force within the Air Force.

SAC set itself apart in other recognizable ways. Besides bombers and tankers, SAC had its own mobile airlift aircraft and fighters. Part of the SAC mentality was the need for the organization to operate not only independently but also self-sufficiently. The B–36 was the only plane in the command's inventory capable of launching and recovering from the United States without air refueling. All of SAC's medium bombers had to deploy forward to perimeter bases overseas in England, North Africa, Greenland, Canada, and Japan to successfully reach their targets. Even with air refueling, some of the bomber fleet had to plan on reaching a poststrike or recovery base other than the original departure base. SAC planned to transport its personnel on its own planes to these places to perform maintenance and recovery operations. The attitude of self-sufficiency in SAC derived partly from LeMay's experience in the Pacific. When relying on theater commanders for supply, LeMay's bombers went weeks without incendiary bombs because the theater supply could not keep up with the pace of strategic bombing operations.[9] In the rapid-strike nuclear offensive LeMay was planning, he wanted total control of all aspects of the campaign. The organization adopted the same mentality when it came to fighter support. SAC directed its fighters to protect bases at home and abroad and then escort SAC's bombers to their targets. LeMay's responses during a question-and-answer session at the National War College in March 1950 provided insight into the attitude and culture that the commander instilled from the top down regarding mutual support for its operations. During that session, the college's commandant asked LeMay why SAC had its own fighters assigned. "Because I know that if we are attacked tomorrow," LeMay replied, "the only fighters I will ever get are the ones I have. We will need them over our bases when we are loading bombs." The commandant followed up by asking, "Wouldn't it be more economical for those fighter groups to train in Army cooperation?" "They can do that when they have time," LeMay responded. "How soon do you expect to launch an Army offensive? I only want those fighters for three weeks. After that we can all go to work for the Army."[10] LeMay's replies revealed the underlying assumptions that led to the development of SAC's organizational culture of self-sufficiency and independence.

Korea: SAC Goes to War

The strategic air war that took place over Korea from 1950 to 1953 has received considerable attention from scholars.[11] Nevertheless, certain features of SAC's initial response to and participation in this conflict reveal the developing aspects of the command's organizational culture. The units SAC selected for deployment, the plan initially proposed for conducting the strategic air campaign, the command relationships sought, and the way in which the organization treated its crews in wartime indicated the emerging SAC mentality.

Following the June 25, 1950, invasion of South Korea, General LeMay tightened security around SAC bases and contemplated closing them on a weekly basis to condition the base population to the idea of restricted activities.[12] SAC could be at war at any time. Shortly after July 1, 1950, Air Force chief of staff Gen. Hoyt Vandenberg ordered SAC to provide two bombardment groups to the Far East Air Force (FEAF) to join the existing bomber group in theater (19th Bombardment Group) to form FEAF Bomber Command.[13] SAC assigned the 22nd Bomb Group from March Air Force Base, California, and the 92nd from Spokane Air Force Base, Washington, to deploy to the Asian theater and conduct operations in support of United Nations forces. The units SAC selected had the lowest priority in terms of combat readiness in the organization. Jim Edmundson, commander of the 22nd Bomb Group, understood his unit's ranking in SAC. According to Edmundson, his unit had the oldest airplanes and the lowest priority when it came to SAC's effort to make units combat-ready.[14] Furthermore, both units belonged to 15 AF. The Eighth Air Force held the priority because of the nuclear mission; conventional bombing, the current mission of 15 AF, was a secondary concern. LeMay confirmed Edmundson's thinking in sending these units to Korea. The SAC commander feared that by sending his best nuclear units to Korea, he would destroy the command's capability for a true "strategic" war if such a conflict started.[15] Even Vandenberg emphasized the effect Korea was having on efforts to build a credible deterrent against the Soviet Union. "You are aware of the fact that this diversion of Strategic Air Units can be made at considerable cost to our overall air capabilities," Vandenberg wrote Lt. Gen. George Stratemeyer, commanding general of FEAF. "To insure you are getting the most return for this investment, we are making available one of our ablest and most experienced bomber commanders and a few key people to assist him."[16] SAC sent General O'Donnell, the 15 AF commander, to the Asian theater to direct FEAF Bomber Command. Although SAC did not view the Korean War as the number-one priority, it made sure one of its own would command bomber operations.

SAC's plan to make atomic units combat-ready first left conventional units lacking the resources necessary for the war unfolding on the Korean Peninsula. When he received word that his squadron was deploying to Korea, Edmundson notified his men to report immediately for duty. To find those people on leave or away from the base because of the upcoming Fourth of July holiday, Edmundson enlisted the help of the state police. Command planes were sent to pick up personnel who were away from the base, leaving wives to drive the family car back to base. Although Edmundson managed to recall his people, he still lacked enough personnel to man the thirty bombers requested by the JCS. Specifically, the low priority given to the

22nd meant it lacked combat-ready navigators and flight engineers. LeMay assured Edmundson that he would provide the unit the necessary personnel from other units.[17]

Despite their status in SAC, both units that deployed forward demonstrated the benefits that two years of LeMay's intense training had provided. The SAC mobility plan required units assigned to SAC to be "capable of being dispatched without delay to distant bases."[18] Following standardized procedures, SAC loaded the deploying B-29s with flyaway kits and sent them forward quickly to their deployed location. Despite the rapid deployment, SAC still required the support of the Military Air Transport Service's cargo planes to move the units completely to their operating locations in the Pacific. Among those deploying was David Jones, a future LeMay aide and eventual chairman of the Joint Chiefs of Staff, who recalled his first encounter with LeMay when he addressed the 22nd Bomb Group prior to its departure. The SAC commander warned the unit that the biggest danger they would face would come from accidents—not the enemy air force.[19] Despite its recent emphasis on nuclear operations, SAC did not send the units to combat unprepared. Crewmembers who deployed forward had practiced SAC's standardized bombing procedures, which emphasized radar bombing. Furthermore, quite a few crewmembers had been through survival training, and in the estimation of SAC's operations officer, that gave them self-confidence in case they went down behind enemy lines.[20] The belief that crews had to be prepared to do tomorrow in war what they were doing today in training would come through in the Korean War. SAC units began deployment actions in early July and found themselves flying their first combat mission over Korea within two weeks. LeMay and his staff remembered the time it took for them to begin operations in World War II; SAC's new operating mentality—being at war all the time—had crews effectively flying combat missions within two weeks of receiving orders.

SAC's scripted mobility plan got the crews to theater, and its standardized training plan prepared the bomber crews to conduct bombing operations. The emphasis on deterring the Soviet Union, however, meant less time dedicated to preparing for a conventional contingency elsewhere in the world. SAC's initial thoughts on the strategic airpower campaign in Korea revealed the emerging culture of the organization. The Air Force had built strategic forces, in SAC's estimation, to unleash the fury of atomic bombing and bring about a quick decision. Tactical airpower might have suffered in the short term, one SAC general admitted, but war with the Soviet Union was going to be strategic and sudden. By the time the Army's land force and the Navy's carriers arrived, SAC believed the war would be over.[21] This minor skirmish in Korea, in LeMay's estimation, could be won handily if SAC could undertake its concept of strategic air operations. Once the nation committed military force to solve a problem, overwhelming force should be used to bring about a swift decision and save valuable resources in the long run.[22] Although he did not formally announce his ideas on how SAC should be used in Korea, LeMay intimated that SAC should be turned loose with incendiaries on North Korea.[23] LeMay initially had no intention of promoting the use of nuclear weapons due to the limited numbers in the U.S. stockpile.[24] That fact did not stop him from recommending the total destruction of the North Korean industrial base, which was in line with SAC thinking, values, and assumptions.

SAC forces entered the Korean War on July 13, 1950, when B-29s from the 22nd and the 92nd hit the railroad marshaling yards in Wonsan, North Korea.[25] Despite O'Donnell's desire to take full advantage of his strategic forces, the deteriorating situation on the ground forced Gen. Douglas MacArthur, commander of United Nations forces in Korea, to delay further attacks on North Korea and focus strategic bombers on supporting the Eighth Army fighting for its life in South Korea.[26] In a letter to FEAF commander Stratemeyer, O'Donnell, commander of FEAF's bomber forces, expressed his disagreement with the new use of strategic forces: "Any directive on targets to a 'Strategic Bomber Command' which gives last priority to the destruction of industrial targets, including petroleum refineries and storage, is fundamentally wrong." O'Donnell further disagreed with how his forces were being used, saying, "The currently directed piecemeal daily individual strikes at small targets, which will many times be obscured by cloud at this time of year, will lead only to dissipation of effort with mediocre and indecisive results."[27] O'Donnell felt that his forces were not mounting the type of offensive that used a bomber command most effectively. After writing the commander of theater air forces, O'Donnell sent the SAC commander a note about command relationships in the theater. LeMay preferred the relationship he enjoyed in the Pacific during World War II and expressed concern that his bombers were now under the operational control of the theater commander.[28] O'Donnell shared LeMay's concern: "I accept with willingness and a real spirit of cooperation the role of tactical support as my primary mission for the next week or two. . . . I have made my case as strong as I can, and of course, now must accept his [Stratemeyer's] orders as I am under his operational control."[29] The problem O'Donnell had with FEAF's plan to isolate the battlefield stemmed from SAC assumptions about planning bomber missions. Prior to O'Donnell's writing, Stratemeyer's headquarters had sent down a target change at five o'clock in the morning. O'Donnell's planning staff had been up all night working on a plan; the change came in only two hours before crews were scheduled to take off. O'Donnell relayed to LeMay that he had told Stratemeyer that Bomber Command would no longer accept target changes after four o'clock in the afternoon. FEAF's staff would have to gear operations around the bomber's operating cycle.[30] The FEAF bomber commander expressed the same view to his theater chain of command, telling MacArthur: "You cannot operate B-29s like you operate a tactical air force. B-29 operations must be carefully planned in advance and well thought out."[31] Despite the different nature of the Korean War, the SAC mentality remained unchanged. Bomber operations were something unique that required carefully scripted missions; SAC leaders wanted other military operations to conform to their requirements, not the other way around.

To further strengthen the situation on the ground and to bolster strategic forces for the resumption of what SAC hoped would be a true strategic bombing campaign, the JCS sent two more bomb groups (the 98th and the 307th) to Korea by the end of the summer. With five bomb groups in theater, FEAF Bomber Command could mount a maximum effort of two bomb groups on strategic targets every third day.[32] SAC's bombers demonstrated their full power and destroyed legitimate military targets in North Korea. Despite their proximity to military targets, civilian installations showed little damage. SAC's bombers had attained a new level of precision. FEAF bombers struck their targets in good weather and bad, using non-visual radar bombing as the primary means of attack.

By the fall of 1950 FEAF Bomber Command had run out of strategic targets. In October, FEAF reduced Bomber Command's sorties by 25 percent, and by the end of the month, the first squadrons that deployed to the theater were allowed to return home.[33] The initial way SAC approached the Korean War demonstrated the elements of the emerging SAC culture: strategic bombing should be unleashed to mount a full offensive to destroy the enemy's industrial capability in the quickest possible time, and strategic operations required detailed planning, which meant theater commanders seeking bomber support had to fit within SAC's operating schedule. At a lower level, personnel policies during the Korean War provided additional insight into SAC's evolving culture.

Ironically, crews flying and fighting in Korea were not eligible for accelerated promotion because their units were not "combat-ready" when they deployed to the Pacific. Personnel considered combat-ready were pulling nuclear duty in the states or overseas at SAC's forward bases, while crews ineligible for promotion were actually flying in harm's way. To correct this situation, O'Donnell implemented a spot promotion program within FEAF Bomber Command that recognized the contribution of crews flying in Korea. According to his commander, David Jones benefited from the program and earned a spot promotion for his flying duties while in theater.[34] The FEAF spot promotion program ended in 1953, and all crewmembers holding temporary promotions lost them with the truce along the Demilitarized Zone.[35] SAC linked rank and privilege to its members' ability to maintain their combat orientation.

The Korean War served as the impetus for expanding the Air Force beyond its current limit of forty-eight groups. Strategic Air Command, already receiving the lion's share of the Air Force budget and controlling bombers, tankers, reconnaissance, and some support aircraft, received the greatest increase in resources.[36] As SAC expanded, the organization sought to gain more control over its operations and make policy changes to ensure that in future conflicts, a SAC general would control bomber employment. These steps revealed the level of control sought by the organization. Direction of its operations had long been a hallmark of bomber culture; SAC wanted control over all facets of strategic operations, from preparation through employment to include the nuclear weapons themselves. While SAC would be able to obtain control over much of its operations, control of atomic weapons would remain in civilian control—for the time being.

SAC's forward-deployed bombers serviced all strategic targets in short order. The Korean War became a limited war for the United States and soon became an air superiority fight highlighting the importance of newly developed jet fighters. As interdiction of supplies to North Korean troops and close air support of U.S. troops emerged as another priority, the fighter-bomber, F-86, took on a dominant role. The U.S. bomber force would reemerge as a dominant power toward the end of the war as dam-busting became a focus to drive the North Koreans to the bargaining table to negotiate an armistice.

SAC Reorganizes

SAC's mobilization for the Korean War highlighted some flaws in the existing command structure. Despite what SAC considered a success of its standardized mobility plan, it discovered that its wing commanders, always pilots, were too focused on the "housekeeping" tasks of running the actual base organization and not spending enough time on overseeing actual combat preparations.[37] At a commander's conference in December 1950, SAC deputy commander Gen. Thomas Power announced that LeMay would soon implement a new command structure. "We should be organized for peace time with an organization that requires a minimum change to war footing to carry out our primary mission," Power argued. "So what we want to do is change our present organization to one that requires a minimum change in time of war." During the conference, LeMay explained the reason for this change as well as other changes that would be forthcoming: "What we are talking about is control. . . . There must be control from the top man right on down to the last private. What we are interested in is how to accomplish this control."[38] To allow wing commanders the ability to focus more on combat operations, the air base group commander, sometimes referred to as simply the base commander, became responsible for managing the housekeeping functions on the base. Under the plan implemented in February 1951, the wing commander focused primarily on the combat group and the maintenance necessary to support combat aircraft. As a result, the term "bomb group" fell into disuse, to be replaced by "combat wing."[39] Although wing commanders could now focus primarily on combat, SAC would have to establish another level of leadership and bureaucracy due to its rapid growth in the 1950s.

SAC increased the number of bases during the expansion, but the organization still found it necessary at times to double the number of wings on a given base. The increased number of wings created a difficult situation for SAC's numbered air force commanders. According to Hunter Harris, who commanded a numbered air force himself, there were simply too many wings for a commander to supervise.[40] Therefore, SAC built another institution initially unique to the organization: the air division. The air division commander, with his staff of roughly seventeen people, served as the intermediate level of authority between the wing and the numbered air force.[41] Air divisions performed administrative and control functions at bases that had multiple wings to reduce the amount of oversight required by the numbered air force commander. At the multiple wing bases, air divisions served as a higher authority for the collocated wing commanders to resolve disputes over facilities and resources. The drive for standardization and control, so central to SAC culture, created the need to find additional ways to manage SAC operations.

Although the expansion program added aircraft to SAC's bomber and tanker force, tanker production failed to generate the airframes necessary to permit SAC's medium bomber force (B-29s initially, then B-47s) to conduct their Emergency War Plan mission from the United States. Horace Wade served as commander of the 301st Bomb Wing stationed at Barksdale Air Force Base, Louisiana, and explained SAC's basing and refueling problem: "We had an air-to-air refueling capability before we built bases in Morocco and Spain, but we didn't have sufficient numbers of bases to take care of the programmed force. We knew we would have to refuel the B-47 from those forward bases in order to get to some of the targets. Forward bases made it possible to reach targets that we couldn't have reached without those bases."[42]

Therefore, in 1951 SAC made plans to establish two air divisions—one in the United Kingdom and one in Morocco—that would act as forward bases for SAC's medium bomber fleet. The personnel policies and command relationships SAC created provided insight into other elements of its organizational culture.

Once SAC established air divisions overseas, the organization planned to rotate crews, bombers, and maintenance support through those locations every ninety days. Given the tensions in the Cold War and the desire to maintain a credible deterrent, another possible solution would have been to place crews permanently at those locations and avoid the disruption that came with crews constantly having to leave their homes for ninety days at a time. Horace Wade explained the rationale for the rotation policy: "LeMay wanted to maintain control. He didn't want to put them under the theater commander . . . [and] as long as they were assigned to SAC and the unit had a home assignment back in the states there was no argument about who was in command of the unit."[43] In addition to personnel policies, LeMay would seek command relationships unique to SAC to ensure the organization's control of its bombers.

Initially, LeMay decided to send Gen. Paul Cullen to the United Kingdom to assume command of 7th Air Division, which would oversee SAC units assigned on a rotational basis to the United Kingdom as well as the development of future bases in the area. While en route to his new assignment, Cullen and his staff were lost when the C-124 they were traveling on disappeared. In his place, LeMay sent Maj. Gen. Archie Old, who was the acting commander of SAC's prestigious 8 AF. Old explained why LeMay chose him for this assignment: "He thought I was the logical choice to go in and work with Leon Johnson [3rd Air Division commander under U.S. Air Forces in Europe]. That wasn't going to be easy because I had to break off most of what we would have away from Leon Johnson's command . . . he didn't give up things easily."[44] In his first report to LeMay, Old reported that Johnson had reluctantly cooperated and shared his division's assets and personnel with the new SAC headquarters. Old, however, noted that neither USAFE commander General Norstad nor General Johnson was completely sold on the organization of 7th Air Division (7 AD), especially since it was a SAC headquarters in another commander's area of responsibility.[45] Nevertheless, LeMay created the command relationship he wanted in Britain and then sent Old to establish a new SAC command in Morocco.

Prior to leaving for Morocco, Old needed to find a replacement commander for 7 AD. The way Old related the story highlighted the culture that permeated SAC in terms of loyalty and commitment to the organization. Old, Wade, and Edmundson knew the importance of being in SAC and understood that once a person was out of the organization, he was probably out for good. Wade considered turning down an assignment to one of the military's senior service schools because he figured once he left SAC, he would never be able to return. LeMay rescued Wade from the school assignment because he considered him too valuable to the organization. SAC not only enjoyed special promotions but also had more command opportunities for general officers with the creation of the air division. When LeMay asked Old for suggestions on who should replace him, Old recommended John P. McConnell, a brigadier general working in 3rd Air Division under USAFE. LeMay approved the move, and Old called McConnell to give him the good news. McConnell stated, "I don't think I will mind working in SAC. I have heard stories about that guy LeMay." At that time, McConnell informed Old that it would be a month before he could assume the duties since he and his wife were leaving in a few hours for a trip to tour Europe. "You won't be making that trip," Old told his replacement. "The hell I won't," replied McConnell. Old told the young general that if he left for that trip, he would regret it the rest of his life. "I'll just tell you this," Old said. "I am pretty sure your goddamn Air Force career is over. . . . If they don't fire you, they are probably going to tell you they want your resignation." SAC was a command at war—there was not enough time for a month of sightseeing. Old told McConnell he was going to call LeMay to relay McConnell's decision. As he was on the phone with LeMay, McConnell called back to say he had postponed his trip and he would take the immediate assignment. Serving in SAC became something few turned down.[46] McConnell eventually became chief of staff of the Air Force, replacing LeMay in 1965.

Old arrived in Morocco in the spring of 1950 to establish another SAC headquarters. This time, SAC would not share the location with

USAFE or any other Air Force command. LeMay wrote a personal letter to Old—for his eyes only—that outlined his desires in Morocco: "I think we have an excellent arrangement now in the UK with the 7th Air Division clearly assigned to Strategic Air Command and directly responsible to me. It is still our intention to press for a similar arrangement in North Africa at some time in the future."[47] In his reply, Old assured LeMay that he was establishing in Morocco a headquarters unique to SAC. "This is a SAC show completely in French Morocco," Old told LeMay. "It is obvious to myself and staff that USAFE thoroughly realizes that this is a SAC show." The 5th Air Division was headquartered in the coastal city of Rabat and manned with 2,450 permanently assigned personnel. That number paled in comparison to the number expected to rotate through North Africa every ninety days. Initial SAC plans called for two wings of bombers to rotate through the area, bringing with them 8,940 airmen.[48]

SAC's first experience in combat created the impetus for yet another command relationship unique to the bomber organization. By the time O'Donnell, who would lead the strategic bombing campaign, had arrived in theater, the plan for using SAC's bombers had already been formulated. SAC did not want theater commanders controlling its bombers when they landed in other theaters following execution of its nuclear offensive. Since SAC lacked the refueling resources to return its entire force to the states, SAC planes planned to recover at bases in foreign theaters of operations. The plan was to send the SAC commander to the theater to assume command of bomber operations once a war started.[49] These centers would also have the ability to continue strategic operations in case of an attack on SAC headquarters in the United States. To ensure continuity of command of bomber operations, LeMay appointed deputy SAC commanders in each of the operational theaters. After General McConnell took over 7 AD in England, he received a letter from LeMay announcing his appointment as SAC Zebra (deputy commander). "In case of a war emergency you will assume command of all Strategic Air Command forces in the United Kingdom," LeMay wrote, "and conduct such operations as may be directed by the Commanding General, Strategic Air Command." McConnell would oversee strategic air operations until deployment of the forward SAC team.[50] In addition to the appointment of SAC Zebra, LeMay appointed a SAC X-Ray in the Pacific theater.[51] From Offutt Air Force Base, SAC centrally controlled more than its U.S.-based force. The organization planned to orchestrate bomber operations worldwide.

Lack of Control: Nuclear Weapons

By 1952 LeMay had managed to create an impressive organization and a network of bases and command relationships that allowed SAC to direct a majority of its operations unimpeded. In addition to the bombers themselves, SAC controlled reconnaissance planes that identified possible targets, tankers that refueled SAC's bombers in the air, and fighters that protected SAC bases and bombers worldwide. But the one asset that eluded LeMay's grasp was the nuclear weapons themselves.

The armed services tried to gain control of nuclear weapons immediately following World War II, but President Truman wanted them to remain in civilian custody. This policy stemmed from Truman's evolving perceptions of nuclear weapons. Although he initially viewed atomic bombs as part of the military arsenal, their enormous destructive capacity convinced Truman that nuclear weapons should remain in civilian hands. At a press conference in March 1946, Truman laid out his rationale for civilian control: "It is a mistake to believe that only the military can guard the national security. The full responsibility for a balanced and forceful development of atomic energy looking toward the national economic good, national security, and a firm, clear position toward other nations and world peace, should rest with the civilian group directly responsible to the President."[52] The Atomic Energy Act of 1946 created the Atomic Energy Commission (AEC) that would oversee the development of peaceful uses of atomic energy and retain custody of America's nuclear stockpile.[53] The AEC stored nuclear weapons that would be released to the military upon direction of the president. Truman rejected military arguments that they needed "familiarity" with nuclear weapons and maintained civilian control.[54]

Under current operational concepts, SAC bombers would need to fly from their home base in the United States to an AEC storage site, where they would be loaded with their atomic weapons.[55] From those locations, bombers could then deploy forward to staging areas where they would sit on alert for possible strikes against the Soviet Union. As it did for many other policy changes, the Korean War served as the impetus for gradually eroding assertive control (by a civilian agency) of the nation's nuclear stockpile.[56] The war forced the president to modify his position. Truman began to transfer critical nonnuclear components to SAC bases in Europe and the Pacific.

LeMay's thoughts on the nuclear custody issue were recorded in his diary: "It takes simultaneous commands from Washington one to me and one to the custodians of the bombs before the attack can be initiated. I feel that I should be given the authority to draw bombs were such a catastrophe to occur."[57] From his pragmatic standpoint, LeMay felt that his ability to build a deterrent force required the ability to respond rapidly to a conflict anywhere in the world. Nuclear custody issues were preventing SAC from implementing its concept of operations.

The expansion of the nuclear stockpile under President Truman created the need to construct more storage sites, which in turn created new custodial arrangements. In 1951 agreements to construct these new sites gave administrative and operation control to the Air Force's Air Materiel Command. The move would facilitate the rapid transfer of atomic weapons in an emergency.[58] Given the expanding stockpile and the need for a credible and responsive atomic force, the AEC relinquished some of its control over nuclear weapons. Additionally, SAC began to train assembly teams to accomplish the mass loading of nuclear weapons required under its all-out atomic offensive war plan.[59] The AEC became the agency primarily responsible for nuclear weapon development; maintenance and design of delivery vehicles came under purview of the military.[60] Although SAC bases would house nuclear weapons, a civilian agency always maintained control of the weapons, at least on paper.

Patches, Planes, and Privacy: SAC Culture Takes Form

Throughout the first four years of his command, Curtis LeMay sought to enact policies and programs that would tie SAC to its mission of strategic bombardment. The organization created special command relationships and built institutions particular to it that gave SAC a distinctive culture. Although it took four years, SAC designed and submitted its own insignia for approval. On January 4, 1952, the U.S. Air Force Headquarters approved SAC's request for its new organizational symbol. SAC selected the design following an internal competition. The judges—LeMay, Power, and LeMay's chief of staff, Andrew Kissner—reviewed over sixty entries and selected the one submitted by Staff Sergeant R. T. Barnes. The design was a mailed fist against a sky of blue holding an olive branch and emitting three lightning bolts.

Symbols—such as the SAC patch—are the most basic and smallest form of cultural expression. They typically stand for something and convey abstract ideas. On SAC's patch, one saw the mailed fist, which harkened back to Billy Mitchell's charge that pilots would be the new knights of the air. The fist symbolized the "strength, power, and loyalty and represents the science and art of employing far-reaching advantages in securing the objectives of war." It also showed the primacy of the organization's atomic mission. The blue represented the realm of its operations. While the smaller olive branch represented SAC's mission to maintain peace, the lightning bolts signified the ability to respond rapidly with overwhelming power.[61] Those who served in the organization described the insignia as "the fist of fury," "the SAC claw," and the "SAC fist." Few members of the organization identified the patch with peace but rather with the power and the strength the insignia represented.[62]

Another symbol of SAC was the bomber, with which the command became synonymous. SAC grew out the Air Force's desire to form an organization devoted to centralized control of strategic bombing. The Air Force developed and acquired the strategic bombers, like the B-29/50, which were medium-range bombers. After World War II, the intercontinental bomber became a fixture of SAC culture. Intercontinental bombers symbolized greater independence from other services, the capacity to strike anywhere in the world, and the ability to destroy entire target complexes in one mission.

The Boeing B-47 Stratojet was the first true all-jet bomber aircraft to enter SAC's inventory. This aircraft symbolized technical progress and gave SAC a different image. Casting away the propellers of the B-36, SAC pilots looked to the B-47 as the Air Force's newest "sports car." Although the initial models did not even have ejection seats, pilots welcomed the chance to fly the plane because it "looked good."[63] With its swept-wing design, the B-47 both looked and was fast. Moreover, in General Old's estimation, "The B-47 was probably the greatest airplane ever built." The six engines gave it speed, but the swept wing design allowed it to perform more acrobatic maneuvers, something few pilots had the chance to do in previous bombers. "You could roll it or do any damn thing you wanted to with it," Old recalled.[64] The plane had a reduced crew complement, which meant less need for internal communication and more cohesion among the crew. Instead of the thirteen crewmembers it took to fly the B-36, the B-47 only required three. The crew sat in tandem configuration, one seat behind the next. The navigator—who plotted the plane's course and operated its radar—sat in the nose of the plane. The pilot (technically termed the aircraft commander) sat in the middle, and the copilot (technically termed the pilot) sat in the rear. This in-line configuration earned the B-47 a new nickname—the "three-headed monster."[65] That moniker, however, did not detract from the exhilaration of those who flew the B-47.

Under LeMay's tenure, bomber designs began to reflect values indicative of SAC culture and the leader's personal values. LeMay preferred intercontinental bombers to smaller, faster bombers. Medium bombers had a limited payload capacity and a limited range. Given the low rate of production of air refueling planes, medium bombers still had to deploy forward to reach their targets. The only way to get all the bombers back to the United States under LeMay's firm control was to reduce the need for forward basing. LeMay preferred bombers with longer range that could strike anywhere from the United States and reduce the tanker commitment. Additionally, the B-47's cockpit configuration ran counter to the cultural routines LeMay had tried to instill in SAC. In the B-47, crewmembers could not "monitor" one another's actions because of the tandem seating. The intercom served as the primary means to communicate with one another; there was very little visual communication. In the initial concepts for the B-52, the first all-jet intercontinental bomber, the manufacturer had the crew seated in the same tandem configuration as the B-47. LeMay altered this design and placed the pilots next to each other so they could observe each other's actions and visually ensure compliance with standardized procedures. Checklists for the bombers required pilots to query one another on the placement of cockpit switches. By sitting next to each other, LeMay was ensuring pilots could visually confirm adherence to prescribed procedures. The same concept applied to the navigator and radar navigator (bombardier) in the lower compartment of the aircraft.[66]

Planes, however, were not the only physical evidence of SAC culture. The living quarters of SAC personnel began to reflect a command at war. SAC distinguished itself from other organizations in the Air Force and even other military services in the way its airmen lived. When LeMay took over SAC, airmen lived in the open-bay barracks typical of most military organizations. LeMay felt this arrangement, however, did not accommodate an organization at war. SAC operated twenty-four hours a day, seven days a week. At that pace, it would be impossible for airmen to rest in their barracks given the differing schedules of the enlisted force. "Several tired men would come in, direct from their jobs," LeMay explained, "and they'd be showering or going to the toilet or trying to get to sleep. And an hour later, perhaps, other folks would be getting up. Boys and men became weary and annoyed, tempers frayed. . . . Efficiency and discipline suffered." Therefore, LeMay came up with a barracks design more conducive to SAC's operating mentality.[67] Airmen would sleep two to a room, and two rooms—four airmen—would share a common bath area.

The initial construction of the SAC barracks occurred at SAC headquarters on Offutt Air Force Base. LeMay addressed the local community in an attempt to raise funding for his new project. "We intend to pioneer the development of a new concept in the living conditions of airmen," LeMay told them. "We hope to establish a precedent that will spread throughout the Air Force to better living conditions of airmen everywhere and at the same time save the taxpayer money." LeMay further explained to the community that today's military—SAC in particular—required a highly professionalized soldier. Loafers and misfits had no place on a $5 million aircraft like the B-36. Therefore, SAC needed to treat its airmen like the professionals they were. "I have always found the best way to change military custom and tradition," LeMay continued, "is to go out and do it by positive and vigorous action without waiting." Although the Air Force provided

SAC $300,000 for construction, LeMay explained, none of the appro-
priated money could be used for furniture. Therefore, he needed the
community's help to build what he considered to be a modern building for the new modern airmen.[68] The community came through,
ensuring that when the airmen moved into their barracks, they were
not sleeping on government-issued cots. Instead, airmen found themselves surrounded by Simmons beds, genuine innerspring mattresses,
dressers, desks, table lamps, and easy chairs.[69]

The development of the SAC barracks revealed something else
about the organization: it cared about its people. General Everett
Holstrom, a commander in SAC, remembered LeMay as a champion
of trying to improve the living conditions of the airmen. The SAC goal
was to build the technologically modern Air Force a modern barracks
where people could enjoy private rooms.[70] According to Lt. Gen. John
McPherson, "[LeMay] was the greatest man the Air Force ever had
in providing for the people. The people of Omaha got together with
him and raised something like $300,000 to $500,000 to build airmen
barracks where the airmen had individual rooms."[71]

LeMay's contributions to SAC culture extended beyond building
barracks and designing airplanes; the commander created recreational
facilities unique to the organization that, like the barracks design,
became fixtures of the Air Force writ large. The expansion of SAC
under the rearmament sparked by the Korean War severely stressed
the SAC personnel system. SAC could barely keep 50 percent of its
airmen after they completed their initial enlistment. When the expansion began in earnest, the organization drew heavily on the National
Guard and Air Force Reserves. For example, in January 1951, SAC had
four months to organize four entire wings. SAC planned to go out
and screen these volunteer outfits to select people to come on active
duty.[72] Keeping volunteer airmen on active duty given the intense
requirements of the SAC mission and lifestyle proved a challenge to
LeMay. "I would stay on in the Air Force; it was the only thing I knew
how to do or wanted to do. But our reenlistment rate was pretty piti-
ful," LeMay recalled. "It seemed to me that if we fired up a new form
of off-duty recreation, that might help a bit."[73] His solution was to
establish various clubs that would appeal to the differing interests of
SAC members.

The clubs formed in SAC also reflected the values of the organization's leadership. The uniqueness of SAC's different clubs, in addition to the existing "social" clubs, was that they addressed more the interests of the commander, which may or may not have been the interests of the members. LeMay, the engineer, enjoyed tinkering with cars and planes. General Paul Carlton, LeMay's aide in the early 1950s, recalled that LeMay once tried golf but hated the sport because he figured no matter how hard he tried he could never become an expert at it. LeMay approached cars differently. LeMay's aide recalled, "He liked to drive race cars . . . he would get in the car business up to his eyeballs."[74] One of the first things LeMay envisioned was an auto hobby shop that was a do-it-yourself-type garage. Here SAC members could perform minor maintenance on their vehicles with the help of their fellow airmen. To LeMay's amazement, the auto hobby shops caught on: "People started building cars, making hot rods, sports cars, fiddling with engines, souping them up, so on." As he had with the airmen's barracks, the popular SAC general lobbied various communities to contribute machine tools and automotive repair equipment to SAC's auto hobby shops. In LeMay's estimation, "The automobile hobby shop got to be a vital thing on our bases, as much identified with SAC as the B-47."[75] Other interests of LeMay's became fixtures of the SAC culture in the way of recreational clubs. Flying clubs, where airmen could take private flying lessons or, if they were qualified, rent airplanes for personal use soon became active on SAC bases. The SAC commander also enjoyed hunting. While he couldn't hit a golf ball, LeMay proved to be a great shot when it came to skeet shooting, earning a few awards over the years.[76] The general also enjoyed fishing. Therefore, SAC established rod-and-gun clubs that brought together SAC airmen interested in outdoor activities. Every SAC base would carry variations of these clubs. They were not only part of the SAC culture but demonstrated how organizations can take on the values and interests of their leaders.[77]

Another aspect of SAC culture was the publication of a unique magazine, *Combat Crew*. Previously, SAC circulated the magazine *Professional Pilot* but liked the idea of *Combat Crew* to increase readership beyond merely the pilot force. On the cover, *Combat Crew* featured "superforts manned by the crews of Strategic Air Command," which the premier issue claimed "graphically symbolize both the mission of the command and the title of this magazine."[78] The publication's main purpose was to promote safety throughout the organization. Articles ranged from "there I was . . ." stories, in which crewmembers recounted how they found themselves in harrowing situations, to "how-to" articles, which provided SAC members the chance to offer their opinions about standardized procedures. LeMay's aide, Paul Carlton, published an article in the magazine on the use of standardized procedures during takeoffs and landings and the use of the Takeoff and Landing Data card he devised to assist crewmembers during these procedures.[79] Sections of the magazine also challenged crewmembers' knowledge of SAC regulations and flying procedures as well as offering commanders a chance to editorialize on the role of professional crewmembers in SAC.

The publication began in 1950 but ran into funding issues almost immediately. In 1953 budget cuts threatened its existence. The fervor with which LeMay fought for its continuance showed how much he thought the magazine had become part of SAC culture. On May 29, 1953, Lee White, assistant to the secretary of the Air Force, asked Walter F. Schaub of the Bureau of the Budget for approval for the continued publication of *Combat Crew*. In his response, Schaub noted that the SAC publication contained information that overlapped with other Air Force publications, including a magazine simply entitled *Flying Safety*.[80] LeMay heard rumblings that his magazine might be canceled and wrote the Air Force hierarchy to draw distinctions between his publication and those available to the rest of the Air Force. "I consider *Combat Crew* to be one of the most valuable tools we have in our flight safety program—a program which has resulted in SAC achieving, during 1951 and 1952, the greatest reduction in aircraft accidents of any major command," LeMay wrote the Air Force chief of staff.[81] A month later, as the budget battle continued, LeMay wrote another letter stressing even more distinctions concerning *Combat Crew*. "*Flying Safety* magazine has been suggested as one medium in which to present material now published in *Combat Crew*," LeMay wrote. "This is not a practical solution because much of the material contained in our publication is security information on complex aircraft operated by this command." The commanding general pointed out that SAC's magazine carried a restricted classification, which meant that the broader option, the Air Force's *Flying Safety* magazine, could not publish information vital to SAC members. LeMay went on to say that he did not think *Combat Crew* duplicated information. In fact, LeMay contended, the magazine "fosters a competitive spirit among individuals by publicizing accomplishments of pilots." Since competition was a key aspect of SAC culture, the magazine was integral to promoting this competition. "In many instances," LeMay argued, "articles are of a specific nature concerning operations peculiar to SAC's mission and particular types of aircraft in SAC. Since they are primarily of interest only to SAC personnel, a general Air Force–wide publication would not normally carry such items which are vitally important to our mission."[82] In the end, LeMay received funding to continue his publication, which ran until SAC went out of existence in 1992.

LeMay and Twining: Staying in Position

When LeMay wrote his letters about SAC's magazine in 1953, he wrote them to the new Air Force chief of staff, Nathan Twining. Prior to Twining's appointment, however, the Air Force had announced that Curtis LeMay would become the new vice chief of the Air Force, and Twining had been nominated to assume LeMay's command at SAC. President Truman forwarded LeMay's nomination to the Senate, which confirmed the appointment in April 1952. General Vandenberg, the chief of staff, took ill shortly after the approval, and the Air Force held up the switch between LeMay and Twining. Vandenberg's illness, suspected to be stomach cancer, made Twining the acting chief from the spring until the fall of 1952, when Vandenberg returned to duty. By that time, the defense establishment decided that keeping the generals in their respective positions would be in the best interest of the Air Force and SAC.[83]

The decision to leave LeMay at SAC afforded him another four years to leave his imprint on the organization. Given his four years in charge already, LeMay would become the longest-serving general in charge of a major command in U.S. military history. SAC culture would become even more idiosyncratic to its commander in the next few years, and his influence would persist long after his departure.[84]

Conclusion

During the initial years of his command, Curtis LeMay focused on making SAC an organization capable of rapidly delivering the nuclear arsenal of the United States anywhere in the world on a moment's notice. Placing SAC on a war footing allowed LeMay to emphasize standardized procedures, crew integrity, and vigilant security. The shared history of SAC's new leadership played an important role in these initial policies. The organization's rapid expansion, originating in the onset of the Cold War, provided SAC the opportunity to create new levels of control to manage its burgeoning fleet of bombers, tankers, reconnaissance aircraft, airlifters, and fighters.

Organizational culture is typically viewed in two forms: ideological and material. Ideology and policies drove the creation of SAC and its initial organizational culture. Eventually, SAC's full culture took form. By creating institutions unique to his command, LeMay helped formalize SAC culture. Whether through airplane design, the creation of air divisions, or the design of its insignia, SAC differentiated itself from other organizations in operation and function. The B-47 brought the command into the modern jet era, while new barracks designs brought its airmen into the modern age as well.

The architecture of SAC reflected its commitment to twenty-four-hour operations. LeMay had new dorm rooms constructed that afforded crewmembers more privacy and rest, enabling SAC to continue around-the-clock operations. To show SAC members that they were constantly on "duty," LeMay required his people to wear their uniforms to the social clubs on base. No matter where a person went in SAC, on duty or off, he was in uniform. The standardized procedures in SAC gave members the ability to continually monitor each other's actions. LeMay did not have a hand in the design of the B-47 cockpit, but he did take an active role in making sure pilots could see each other when designing the B-52 cockpit. The rigidity of SAC came through even in its selection of air refueling methods. SAC leaders preferred the stiff American boom design over the more flexible British hose refueling system.

By 1950 LeMay and his staff had created an organization that was capable of fulfilling its assigned mission. SAC's commander created a highly disciplined, modern organization that presented a credible deterrent to the Soviet Union. Over the next years, SAC would continue expanding its number of wings while struggling to maintain its combat readiness. LeMay tried to create living conditions and recreational opportunities that would alleviate some of the stress the organization's members experienced during these times. Nevertheless, the aura of competition, the constant rotations, and the high alertness required of SAC members created more elements of the SAC mentality. The evolving nature of the Cold War would rapidly expand SAC's ranks.

6

SAC Life
The SAC Mentality in Action

The B-36 was more than an airplane; it was a way of life.
—JAMES EDMUNDSON

In 1953 President Dwight D. Eisenhower brought a "New Look" to defense policy and national security strategy.[1] The new administration sought a way to deter the Soviet Union and prevent communist expansion while simultaneously reining in defense spending. The solution emphasized a responsive strategic air armada equipped with nuclear weapons. The nuclear strategy that evolved from the New Look policies came to be known as massive retaliation, which went beyond the containment strategy developed under the Truman administration. Under massive retaliation, the United States reserved the right to respond to an attack with disproportionate force, even nuclear weapons. In one analysis, massive retaliation restored, through airpower, the spirit of the offense in military strategy.[2]

Under the New Look, the Air Force continued its expansion. Budget limitations, however, capped the Air Force at 137 wings instead of its planned 143. Since massive retaliation relied on a responsive Air Force with nuclear weapons, Strategic Air Command continued to receive funding and resources to build its fleet of bombers and support aircraft. LeMay had put into place the policies, procedures, and command structure he believed essential to carrying out SAC's mission. These formalized aspects of SAC culture—policies and procedures—enacted at the top levels shaped and affected the lives of the 270,000 people who made up the command's strength during the 1950s.[3] SAC's organizational culture originated with the assumptions, values, and beliefs of Air Force and SAC leaders. Its organizational culture also permeated down to the lowest levels of SAC. By examining the rituals and stories of SAC members, it is possible to understand what its members were thinking, doing, and believing.[4] This chapter examines SAC life from the perspective of those who flew the long, arduous bomber missions, risked their lives penetrating Soviet airspace to take photographs, worked ceaseless hours to maintain the aircraft and make sure they took off on time, guarded SAC's base around the clock, and served multiple ninety-day tours overseas. Although these airmen served on the front lines of the Cold War, the SAC lifestyle took its toll on the home front on families and marriages. Horace Wade, a SAC commander during this time, put it this way: "Massive Retaliation developed by SAC back in those days kept us as a peaceful nation. It was a high price that we paid for some of the things that we got—but it was good insurance."[5] Some, however, paid a high premium for the nation's insurance.

Security and Competition

By its nature, the Cold War proved a paradox for SAC. The command had to build a credible deterrent to prevent war with the Soviet Union, while at the same time creating an organizational environment that kept its members on a constant war footing. The nation relied on SAC to preserve peace; SAC fulfilled that mission by keeping its members vigilant and "war-ready" using security and competition. SAC's standardization grew out of leaders' beliefs that bomber operations required everyone to follow the same routines, which put bombs accurately on target, lowered accident rates, and maintained combat readiness. These elements of SAC culture—security and competition—resulted from the organization's need to keep its members in a warfighting mode without actually engaging in combat operations.

Like other components of organizational culture, security had a visible and an invisible, or ideological, component. Beginning with LeMay's assumption of command, SAC developed standardized means to secure its bases. SAC erected fences, gates, lighted control towers, and guard towers as part of its physical security measures. The fences were seven feet high, with a steel arm at the top of each post through which ran three strands of barbed wire. Along the fences, SAC armed guards patrolled or dog handlers walked their fierce trained dogs to protect against intrusion.[6] At a minimum, SAC would fence the following critical structures on each base: the flying field, the operations area, the fuel supply, cantonment areas, and the main electrical installations.[7] At the entrance to each base, SAC people had to show identification cards to gain entry. On base, they passed through fences to get to the operations center or the wing command post and were greeted at the plane by a sentry who stood watch over their aircraft. LeMay wanted the command to know that security awareness was everyone's responsibility.

SAC forces had to be on guard against sabotage, espionage, or subversion by the enemy and SAC's own people. LeMay recruited a special kind of person to be on sabotage teams that tested bases' security measures. "Spice of danger builds a kind of romance in the minds of young men serious as the task may be," LeMay explained. "And it is exciting too, to pit your wits against the best armor of security which the Command can fasten into place." The commander took pride in the fact that men from his penetration teams tried every disguise in the book and often found themselves under the muzzles of pistols or submachine guns or wounded by the dogs. Despite the danger involved, SAC never lacked volunteers to form its sabotage teams.[8] SAC protected more than the area inside the fences; the command guarded the skies above SAC bases as well. Planes landing at SAC bases had to have prior permission before being allowed to taxi into the guarded areas. Tom Cantarano began his career in SAC in the 1950s flying KC-97s. He remembered the first time he landed at a SAC base, and there was a question about the aircraft's clearance. His plane soon found itself surrounded by a team of air police.[9] Each day, SAC's security program reminded people they were fighting on the front lines in the Cold War.

General Carlton explained the reason for SAC's implementation of heightened security measures beside the suspected sabotage efforts by Soviet agents in the United States. "[Security] oriented people toward an enemy and vigilance," Carlton recalled. According to LeMay's aide at the time, security measures were a way to keep men and flyers focused on a common enemy in day-to-day alert.[10] To reinforce this mentality of security, Curtis LeMay forced everyone to qualify in fire-arms; officers carried sidearms on their hip as a persistent reminder of SAC's operating mentality. SAC's unique rating system promoted the other aspect of day-to-day operations: competition. SAC measured and quantified multiple aspects of an organization's operations, from its ability to get the aircraft airborne to the bomb score to the VD rate on base. SAC could weight factors differently based on what it wanted to emphasize. Although LeMay claimed he designed the system to find units' weak and strong points, the end result was competition among the units to be the best.[11] Squadrons within a wing competed against each other, wings within a numbered air force competed against one another, and SAC's three numbered air forces vied for the top position. SAC members experienced some of the stresses of war without engaging in actual combat. At any time, their actions could result in a lower rating for their unit, wing, or numbered air force. One bad bomb score, and multiple people—the bombardier, the aircraft commander, and even the wing commander—could lose their jobs. Despite LeMay's attempts to mitigate some of the stresses of SAC life through recreational programs, few SAC members remembered this period in their lives as anything but stressful. A majority of those interviewed who served during the 1950s believed SAC was at war with the Soviet Union.[12]

Severe security established the operating mentality of SAC but also generated some of its most colorful myths. Myths can sometimes reveal as much about culture as the true recollections themselves. While myths recount events that never happened, people imagine they did. They do present, however, a kind of integrity and truth since they are grounded in a set of cultural beliefs. Through myths, people express emotionally laden ideas that are believable but difficult to validate or prove.[13] According to LeMay's aide, Paul Carlton, a story circulated among SAC, and among the wider reading public through *Reader's*

Digest, that one day General LeMay barged through a checkpoint to challenge the security guard. The guard reportedly shot at the car but missed. LeMay then allegedly stopped the car, got out, and ripped the stripes off the guard's uniform, saying, "That's because you missed." Carlton denied this ever happened.

Another story inflated the legend of LeMay. Purportedly, LeMay was at MacDill Air Force Base standing outside his C-97 with his characteristic cigar in mouth. A security officer approached the general and reminded him to put out his cigar or the C-97 might explode. "It wouldn't dare," LeMay declared.[14] The fables of LeMay and security became even more pronounced. Richard Purdam served in SAC for twenty-two of his twenty-nine-year career. By the time he entered SAC in 1959, LeMay had moved to Washington to be vice chief of the Air Force, but his legend remained. According to Purdam, the story was that one night LeMay's command car crossed the red line on the flight line that surrounded SAC's aircraft. The armed security guard ordered the car to stop, but the car continued, so the airman shot out the window of the general's car. When the security supervisor arrived on scene, LeMay told him to have the young airman report to him the next morning. When the airman reported in the following morning as ordered, LeMay awarded him a medal for having the courage to fire at his car. Allegedly, LeMay then ripped off one of the soldier's stripes and told him, "Now get out on the firing range so you won't miss what you are shooting at."[15]

LeMay himself dismissed a myth circulating about him and security. The myth was that a telephone repairman had begun working on the phone lines in the commander's office when LeMay grew suspicious, grabbed an automatic machine gun, and held the repairman at gunpoint until the air police arrived.[16] In these myths, LeMay's own security measures challenged the SAC commander but he emerged victorious, gaining almost legendary status. These myths revealed the seriousness of SAC's security; two myths revolved around a guard actually discharging his weapon. More importantly, they show the heroic status LeMay was gaining within the organization.

Although myths surrounded SAC's security operations, the threat was real whether it came from SAC sabotage teams or true Soviet agents. It was not uncommon for aircraft specialists and crew chiefs to find placards simply labeled "bomb" hidden around aircraft to test airmen's procedures. George Gott served as a specialist on B-47s. When some people approached Gott identifying themselves as Soviet spies, Gott followed SAC's standardized procedures and notified the base police. To his surprise, they were not part of the SAC sabotage team but were actual spies, whom the base police apprehended.[17] Whether anecdotal evidence or myth, security awareness and vigilance became important aspects of SAC culture. As the only organization considered to be standing between American democracy and Soviet oppression, LeMay made sure its operations were free of infiltrators, especially the ones trained by SAC.

SAC Flying: Day-to-Day Operations

While civilians went to their jobs and logged forty hours of work a week, SAC's mission and requirements demanded more time from its members, sometimes seventy to ninety hours a week and possibly six or even seven days a week. Rituals—the repetitive behaviors of people—are expressive and symbolic of organizational culture.[18] The work routines of SAC's people demonstrate how the emphasis on security, competition, and standardization in SAC reached down and affected the lives of airmen. Since SAC was a flying organization run by pilots, flying operations and routines exhibited the most obvious signs and stresses of the SAC mentality.

Flying missions in SAC, whether training or operational, consisted of flight profiles in excess of eight hours, sometimes twenty-four to thirty hours of flight time. Therefore, members devoted the day prior to planning the mission in detail. Edwin Ross, a B-47 crewmember, described the typical day prior to a mission for SAC's flight crews. Integral crews, crews formed by SAC and kept together for continuity, would arrive at the operations building at eight o'clock in the morning and be handed a folder by the staff, which contained all the information crews needed for their scheduled mission. Crews would find the assigned aircraft, their scheduled takeoff time, the air refueling track and time assigned, and the scheduled time over target at one of SAC's radar bomb sites. Crews spent the majority of the morning diligently planning the mission in accordance with established SAC regulations, which included constructing the appropriate maps and charts and agreeing when crewmembers would accomplish the required checklists for each portion of the mission. Furthermore, crewmembers would check celestial charts with their time in flight to identify the specific stars they would use during the celestial navigation leg planned for each mission. When crews completed their planning, they had to brief squadron leadership—the squadron commander or the operations officer—on their assigned mission and answer any and all questions before they would be cleared to fly.[19]

Those crewmembers who did not finish their planning in the allotted time had to finish the work at night, since the day made other demands on crewmembers' time. Navigators and radar operators were required to review radar images of their aimpoints leading into the target. To keep crewmembers from becoming complacent or too familiar with given bomb runs, SAC would schedule crews against new targets to test their ability to find a target they had not previously attacked.[20] Following mission planning and target study, crews went into crew rest for twelve hours, during which they were free from duties and expected to sleep at least eight hours in preparation for their mission. Since SAC operated around the clock, crews could be scheduled to take off night or day after the expiration of their crew rest.

SAC routines required crewmembers to report for their mission two and a half hours prior to scheduled takeoff. This gave them time to preview the weather along their entire route of flight, which could cover a considerable portion of the United States, international waters, and even other countries. Following a weather brief, crewmembers collected their life-support equipment—parachutes, helmets, and survival equipment—prior to heading to the aircraft. At the aircraft, the aircraft commander briefed the crew chief in accordance with the numerous items on his SAC-approved checklist, which included how the crew chief would help the aircrew with the aircraft's preflight and engine start.

On the B-47, crews proceeded through a seventy-six-item checklist that made sure aircraft switches and equipment were in proper working order. Items on the checklist usually were "challenge-and-response." The copilot would read off the item, with the pilot replying appropriately.[21] The B-47 seating prevented the copilot from visually confirming the pilot's actions; however, future SAC aircraft design would allow visual as well as verbal confirmation. Following an inspection of the cockpit, pilots conducted an exterior examination of the aircraft, making sure there were no structural problems or leaks of fuel or hydraulic fluid. The pilots would then enter the aircraft, start engines, and prepare to take off on their long-duration mission. The crew chief and his team monitored the engine start and manned fire extinguishers in case of problems when the crews started engines. Crew chiefs zealously protected their record of on-time takeoffs and made sure their jet was ready to fly when scheduled.

Making the scheduled takeoff time required a team effort. The number of on-time takeoffs became extremely important in the SAC rating system.[22] In order to maintain a responsive force, SAC had to prove it could hit targets as scheduled. Exact takeoff times were crucial to the overall mission and emphasized the meticulous, standardized, and carefully monitored operating mentality that existed in SAC at the time. Moreover, the rate percentage of on-time takeoffs was one of the metrics reported each day to headquarters and used to distinguish the best among the squadrons, wings, and numbered air forces within SAC. Crew chiefs took pride in their individual aircraft making the scheduled takeoff. Promotions could hinge on the ability of a crew chief and his team to prepare the aircraft for successful on-time take-offs. Pilots would start their engines thirty minutes prior to takeoff while maintenance trucks hurried up and down the ramps. Specialists for each major aircraft subsystem—propulsion, hydraulics, electronics, and so forth—rode in these vehicles, which also held spare parts to respond to any maintenance problems the airplanes experienced, all to ensure the on-time takeoff.[23]

James Wells served as a mechanic and technician on bombers at Carswell Air Force Base, Texas, for much of his career. His most vivid memory regarding on-time takeoffs came during a routine launch when he rode in the lap of a pilot while he taxied out to the hold line on the runway in a B-36. The pilot had tried to fix his sticking altimeter by tapping the glass, but he struck the device's face so hard he broke the glass. Wells was called to the plane to replace the altimeter. Given the importance of the on-time takeoff, Wells sat in the pilot's lap as he drove the B-36 to the runway for departure. Following his repairs, Wells slipped off the plane in time for the B-36 to make its scheduled take-off time.[24] After close to three hours prepping the plane and getting it airborne, the SAC crewmembers' day was just beginning.

A typical SAC training mission for the bomber fleet began with air refueling. SAC's all-weather mission demanded crews reach the target regardless of circumstances or the prevailing conditions. Poor visibility in flight was not a reason to abort air refueling. The command devised electronic means that allowed tankers and receivers to rendezvous with the aid of radar. Tankers had electronic beacons that radars aboard the B-47 and the B-52 could detect. Air refueling procedures demonstrated why crew coordination became an essential aspect of SAC's organizational culture. Radar operators would guide the pilot to the tanker using their scopes and position the bomber within a quarter mile of the other aircraft until the pilot could see the tanker (the B-36 had no refueling capability since it could reach the target unrefueled).[25] Bomber technology outpaced tanker technology in the earlier years of SAC's refueling practices. The B-47, with its jet engines, had different flying characteristics from the propeller-driven KC-97 air refueling planes. While the KC-97 had its throttles maxed out, the B-47 pilot flew his plane close to stalling speed just to maintain position behind the slower plane. As the pilot refueled the bomber, the copilot designated which tanks on board the bomber would receive fuel to maintain the plane's center of gravity within acceptable limits. When the B-47 took on fuel, it became heavier; therefore, it needed to accelerate to maintain flying speed. If the KC-97 could not accelerate, the tanker formation would have to "descend" while connected at a distance of twelve feet in order to make sure the bomber received the required amount of fuel while not falling out of the sky in a stall.[26] Unless the crew planned to fly a long-duration mission, the bomber took a token amount of fuel from the tanker. The refueling training prepared the bomber crew for the time when getting the gas became critical. Under war conditions, receiving the required off-load was the difference between succeeding or failing to reach the target. In 1957 air-refueling conditions improved with the arrival of the first all-jet tanker, the KC-135.[27]

Although most bomber missions began with air refueling, some missions involved training with nuclear weapons before climbing to altitude. In the late 1940s until the early 1950s, in-flight insertion (IFI) of the nuclear core served as the primary method to arm the atomic weapons. After takeoff, the bomber would fly below 10,000 feet since the plane had to remain depressurized while the bomb commander made his way through the fuselage to insert the nuclear core into the weapon. Given the cramped nature of the crawl spaces, the weapons officer did not wear a parachute even though his duties placed him inside the bomb bay.[28] Training for this position required an extensive security background check and intense training at the Sandia Laboratory in Albuquerque, New Mexico.

David Jones cleared the extensive security protocols and remembered the environment that characterized the training in New Mexico. Jones passed his time playing golf while his security checks went through. After perfecting their golf game at Kirtland Air Force Base, Jones and his fellow prospective bomb commanders gained entry into Sandia's Atomic Energy Course. The primitive safety devices on these initial nuclear weapons made his job very difficult and stressful. "You would insert the coil into the weapon and check it out different ways," Jones recalled. "If you made a series of very bad mistakes, you could blow the whole thing up. In the simulator, students were blowing up. It would give a big boom, instead of anything blowing." Mastering bomb insertion required memorization of procedures and understanding weapons design and function. Jones, a bomber pilot, likened his atomic duties to flying an airplane "It was kind of like an emergency procedure in an airplane. If you did the wrong thing, the airplane might blow up or catch fire, and you might have to bail out."[29] The nuclear safety features could prevent a nuclear yield during an accident, but that differed from the possibility of detonating the high-explosive material that surrounded the nuclear core. An accident in 1958 demonstrated the dangers of these procedures. While performing the IFI over Florence, South Carolina, the officer accidently grabbed the emergency bomb release and jettisoned the bomb. When the weapon hit the ground, the high-explosive material destroyed a house and injured the family of five, in addition to leaving a crater seventy-five feet wide and thirty-five feet deep, but the nuclear material never exploded. This was the first time a nuclear weapon had been dropped inside the United States outside of testing.[30] Completing the IFI was only half the exercise; before landing after completion of a mission carrying nuclear weapons, the bomb commander would have to remove the nuclear core.[31] By the early 1960s weapons design and electromechanical technology would allow for arming of nuclear weapons from the cockpit.

The most important aspect of SAC's training missions came when bombers approached their preplanned target, which could be many hours away, and accomplished simulated bomb runs. For SAC bomber crews, bomb scores were an important measure of merit used to separate "select" from regular crews. Placing the bomb on target required perfect coordination among the crewmembers. While the radar operator found radar images in his scope to refine the ship's navigation system and place bombs on target, the copilot (in a B-47) or electronic warfare officer (in a B-52) jammed electronic signals generated by the bomb sight to resemble the frequency of real Soviet air defensive systems. After completion of the bomb run, the crew awaited the verdict on their attempts. Sigmund Alexander was a self-described "triple-headed monster." Although at times this referred to the configuration of the B-47, the endearing term also included the officer in the nose of a B-47 responsible for navigation, radar operations, and bombing. Alexander recalled the endless wait they endured as crews stood by to receive their scores. "Shack" or "right down the smokestack" meant the crew had a perfect score. The opposite of a shack was a score of "99999," meaning the simulated run had resulted in a bomb that was incapable of being scored; the crew had missed the target.[32] On at least one occasion, more good news came from the radar site than simply bomb scores. SAC's war footing made few allowances for tending to pregnant wives. When Fred Wendt's crews passed over the bomb-scoring site in Oklahoma City in 1956, the site operator said, "Tell [Wendt] he is the father of a baby girl, and mother and daughter are doing fine. On your next run, drop cigars."[33]

Bomb scores were a serious matter nonetheless. Dropping a bad bomb could land the aircraft commander and his radar operator or bombardier in front of the wing commander. When one radar operator went before the wing commander following a bad bomb run, he was asked what happened to his bomb. The officer simply replied, "It is still falling."[34] Failure during bombing produced serious consequences;

for example, it could result in a demotion from "select" crew status, which meant a reduction in rank, privileges, and pay. If a crew had a bad bomb run during a bombing competition or, more importantly, during the wing's yearly readiness inspection, the crew, the squadron commander, and even the wing commander could find themselves out of a job. On the other hand, crews could elevate their status by their performance during a critical mission. Don Shea joined the Air Force in 1944 and served in SAC from its inception until his retirement in 1974, flying most of the bombers in the SAC inventory (B-29, B-47, B-52, and FB-111). His crew went from a regular to select crew, and they all received spot promotions because of the outstanding bomb scores their crew achieved during an ORI while stationed at Platts-burgh, New York, in 1957.[35]

As if the stress of the flying operations were not enough, SAC crewmembers relished the idea of flying simply as a crew, with no one looking over their shoulders. Andrew Labosky also served as a B-47 "triple-headed monster" and recalled the number of check flights each crewmember had to undergo annually. Crewmembers were subjected to supervision of their performance by evaluators from the squadron, wing, numbered air force, and even SAC headquarters. The combat evaluation group would often show up unannounced and fly with crews to make sure they followed standardized procedures and remained sharp. Since crew compartment design on the B-47 provided little room for extra observers, crewmembers were usually evaluated one at a time. This meant it could take two or three flights to evaluate all positions in a B-47. Given the number of evaluation teams from the different command levels in SAC, Labosky remem-bered, "It seemed that someone was evaluating every other flight." Much like bomb scores, flight evaluations could determine promo-tions and pay. Standardization teams not only assessed flying capa-bility and adherence to standard operating procedures, but they also checked crewmembers' publications to ensure that their checklists and technical orders had the most current information. "Missing an important page [in the checklists or the multiple tech orders kept in binders]," Labosky remembered, "could be a failure."[36] Finally, evalu-ators would administer written tests that required crewmembers to recall critical emergency procedures (EP) by memory. Failure during a critical portion of the flight or on an EP test made the crewmember non–mission ready, which meant that if he was on a select crew, he had just cost his crew their spot promotion. Select crews only retained their spot promotions as long as everyone assigned to the select crew remained mission ready. SAC used the policy to promote teamwork and cooperation among the crews, as well as perfection.

While en route to the bombing portion of their mission, bombers kept in constant contact with SAC, issuing in–flight status reports so that the organization could account for its bombers at any moment. The nickname of the B-36, "six churning and four burning," was the standard response B-36 crews radioed if the mission was going as planned. B-36 crews felt a sense of pride, since no one else in SAC, or the military for that matter, could make such a claim.[37] Although SAC's bombers flew extremely long missions, the cockpits were not designed for crew comfort. The B-36 design provided for a lot of windows in the crew compartment area to increase pilot visibility. For the pilots, however, the exposure to the sun's rays on long flights created a greenhouse effect. The B-47 allowed for little movement in the crew compartment given the tandem configuration and sleek, fighter-like design. Conditions like these forced SAC to develop physical conditioning programs that would meet crewmembers' physical needs after landing.

The demands of SAC flying duty required the organization to pay great attention to physical fitness. The creation of the SAC survival school and an assessment of SAC crewmembers' performance in the Korean War revealed a need to revamp the organization's physical conditioning program. Part of LeMay's plan involved adding judo training to the survival school's curriculum so crewmembers could become proficient in hand-to-hand combat, which might help them avoid capture in certain circumstances. Additionally, LeMay introduced exercises into the program that would emphasize correct posture and stronger abdominal muscles to help overcome the effects of sitting in the cockpit for long-duration missions. As part of the program, LeMay also wanted to emphasize group competitive sports over mass calisthenics. This move seemed more in line with the organization's desire to foster competitiveness and cohesion among groups that directly related to a mission-specific need. One final aspect of the program was the installation of steam rooms and massage tables. LeMay wanted the program to focus on "building up a resistance to fatigue and combating nervous tension, while at the same time, improving the physical capabilities of the individual." By 1952 SAC had nineteen "conditioning rooms" operating at SAC bases.[38] After long flights, SAC crewmembers entered these "Scandinavian" rooms to receive rubdowns and steam baths. Exposure to the high-altitude environment for the long-duration missions SAC flew—sometimes thirty hours—created, in SAC's estimation, nervous tension as well as physical and mental exhaustion. As the only military command regularly placing these types of demands on its members, SAC used Scandinavian rooms as a way to help crews unwind after operating in the stressful environment.[39] Given the conditions of SAC life away from the flying, SAC crewmembers welcomed the relief from stress.

For some SAC crewmembers, the realistic training did not end with landing. Although crewmembers had been to formal survival training, units did not want its airmen to forget what they had learned; therefore, they established a program to continually evaluate their members' ability to survive. After each mission, crews faced the possibility of being randomly selected to "survive" with what they had on them for a few days in a remote location near their base. Once members boarded the bus after a mission, they didn't know if it would take them to the hangar for debriefing or to the survival area. In addition to their in-flight rations, crewmembers made certain someone in their group had a portable hand-cranked generator to establish radio contact with the base and schedule their "rescue," which would come within four to five days. While SAC crewmembers recalled the program itself, their recollections tended to highlight the exceptions rather than the rule. At one SAC base, the location of the "random" training survival site became common knowledge. When the base notified one SAC wife that her husband would not be home for a few days, she took the family boat loaded with supplies to the survival area, much to the delight of the "survivors." After that episode, locations were then randomly selected. On another subsequent survival exercise, the base dropped the crewmembers off in a cotton field a few miles outside a small Texas town. Given the coldness of the February night, the crew decided to seek shelter in the nearby town. Although the crew was short of cash, the owner of the hotel had a son in the Air Force and was sympathetic to the crewmembers' plight. For a nominal fee, the patron rented out the entire second floor to the "survivalists." Crewmembers could not inform the townspeople why they were in the neighborhood, but that fact did not stop them from checking out the local restaurants and cinemas. Some local townspeople even took the crewmembers out skeet shooting. When it came time for the "rescue," local farmers offered up their pickup trucks to haul the crew and their gear to the rendezvous point.[40] Those not selected for the survival exercise after their long-duration mission usually experienced the preferable "physical conditioning" reserved for SAC's crewmembers.

Reconnaissance and Realism

The emphasis on realistic training drove bomber mission profiles; however, the "spy" version of the bomber mission actually experienced hair-raising situations more like combat than any ORI mission profile SAC could generate. Reconnaissance planes were initially stripped-down bombers. James Edmundson explained how the Air Force developed the RB-36, a recon version of the bomber: "In the RB-36, the forward bomb bay had been pressurized and converted to a compartment for photographers and ECM [electronic countermeasures] ferrets."[41] In order to man the various photographic and electronic collection equipment on board, reconnaissance planes typically had larger crews than normal bombers. Bombers had fighter support for some of their missions, but a recon crew "goes in alone, penetrates deep, and comes home alone. Unlike bomber formations that depend upon their concentrated firepower for protection, the RB-36 must protect itself."[42] Bombers flew training missions in preparation for their wartime mission, but recon crews flew profiles that came as close to combat as anyone during the Cold War. Obtaining intelligence from a closed society before the invention of space satellites required penetrating Soviet airspace and sometimes challenging the air defense system. Harold Austin remembered one fateful day, May 8, 1954, when SAC tasked his RB-47 crew to take pictures of nine different Soviet airfields in search of the new Russian fighter, the MiG-17. During their mission, Austin's crew found the MiG-17s, but not on the ground. A flight of four MiG-17s jumped their

RB-47, making several firing passes. Luckily, none of the fighters' guns found their target. The crew privately received medals for their mission. Despite risking their lives, the crewmembers could not view the photographs they took because they did not have a high enough security clearance.[43]

Recon crews did not enjoy public recognition of their work. Their rewards were handed out in private. One crewmember recalled the "Recon Tac doctrine": if asked by the press about his activities, he was simply to reply, "We do not discuss reconnaissance activities," and refer the reporter to the SAC public affairs officer on base.[44] The difficulty of the bomber mission and the recon mission was one reason they received special recognition. Recon crews were considered just a special form of bomber crews and, therefore, eligible for spot promotions.

Spot Promotions and Crew Integrity

Probably no program exemplified the unique quality of SAC more than the spot promotion program. Initially, SAC used it to reward airmen for exceptional performance and to enhance retention. By the early 1950s, SAC adjusted the program to promote two essential elements of its organizational culture—crew integrity and competition. In early 1951 Horace Wade converted the unit he commanded to SAC's newest bomber, the B-47. SAC gave Wade six months to complete the transformation and assign emergency war plan (EWP) targets to his lead and select crews. While the unit converted to B-47s, they were unable to fulfill their wartime mission; therefore, crews that had spot promotions lost them. A crew had to be assigned a target and certify their mission to the wing commander before they could gain back their mission-ready status. Wade remembered that the entire conversion took only five months because earning back their spot promotions gave the crews extra incentive to complete the task quickly.[45]

Constant evaluation ensured that spot promotions went to the deserving crews. Each quarter, wing commanders would determine the rank ordering of their crews. Based on bomb scores, testing, and in-flight evaluations, among other factors, commanders would list their crews from top to bottom. The top 15 percent of the crews for any given wing were eligible for spot promotions. If selected by SAC, that crew either maintained the promotion; if it was a new crew, they received their spot promotion usually at the expense of some other crew. Keeping members on the same crew became a central feature of the spot promotion program. If a navigator accidently broke his leg, the crew went non–mission ready, and everyone on the crew lost his promotion.[46] Two primary causes, therefore, existed for losing a spot promotion: either a member went non–mission ready, or he became deficient in the performance of his duties. In 1951 forty-three officers and sixty-three enlisted personnel lost their promotions.[47] Although a small number lost their spot promotion each year, the perception of the frequency was something totally different. One SAC member reflected humorously on the effect of the program on SAC uniforms: "Flight suit and uniform shoulders became frayed with cloth insignia repeatedly being cut-off and sewn-on again."[48]

Spot promotions served as one means of bringing crews together; training accomplishment served as another. Previous combat experience formed the impression LeMay and SAC leadership had regarding crew integrity. LeMay liked keeping good teams together, much as he had in World War II. During the Cold War, pressure mounted to get crews combat-ready and keep them at peak performance. The expansion of the Cold War and SAC placed further pressure on the organization to keep people who functioned well together. It was not unusual for crews to serve several years together. Andrew Labosky served as the navigator on the same B-47 crew for more than five years. In fact, he and his crew moved together from one base to the next and continued to fly as a crew at their new location. Labosky recalled that his crew grew so accustomed to each other that they would know what the other was about to say on the interphone before they even spoke.[49]

Don Shea had a similar experience. After earning their spot promotion, Shea's crew flew together for six years until he and his navigator transferred to a new base and began flying the B-52. When Shea took over command of a B-52 crew, he asked the commander to assign him his old radar navigator. Given the previous performance of the two, the commander obliged.[50]

Each year, crews had a specific number of sorties they had to accomplish to maintain proficiency. If more than one crewmember was sick or unable to fly, the crew would not receive credit for the sortie. On a crew of three people, this might not have caused much of a stir, but on a fifteen-person B-36 crew, it became more critical to make sure the aircraft commander accounted for each person. Crew integrity extended beyond flying operations; crews were the central social group in SAC. Like flying, their recreation and rest were collectively scheduled. One tanker navigator recalled of his crew during the 1950s that they flew together, fished together, and even partied together.[51] Given the limited number of substitutions and requirements for training and readiness, SAC required crews all to take leave at the same time. This was not a big deal unless the interests of the crew differed. Lower-ranking crewmembers could be assigned to an aircraft commander who liked to hunt, which meant leave during the hunting season whether the other crewmembers liked it or not.[52] Crews did, however, meet at the base's social clubs or have parties together to foster and maintain that sense of unity required of a SAC crew.

Going to the officers' club, or the social clubs for enlisted people, never really served as a break from the demands of the SAC lifestyle. LeMay required uniforms to be worn in the clubs during the evening hours. Crews could frequent the clubs in flight suits until dinner but had to show up in their dress uniform in order to eat. SAC worked around the clock, and keeping personnel in uniforms even during their off-duty activities seemed to reinforce the idea.

Officers could not escape the mandatory nature of SAC social life; joining the officers' club was another requirement and reportable metric. Ed Fields remembers the air division commander who addressed the crews at Homestead Air Force Base, Florida. The commander told the crowd that he expected every officer to become a member of the officers' club; he would personally review the squadron membership rolls and name those who failed to join. Although single officers found Miami more conducive to their off-duty pursuits, they still had to join the officers' club.[53]

SAC insistence on keeping proficient crews together threatened the career advancement of its officers. An officer who remained in the

cockpit and assigned to a crew could jeopardize his promotion opportunities. LeMay and his leadership already limited the number of officers it would send to professional military education since they were
needed in leadership positions or in command of aircrews. Although
SAC considered itself a command at war, there were no "wartime"
promotions for its members. In 1951, SAC succeeded in having the
maximum rank crewmembers could attain through spot promotions
elevated to lieutenant colonel. Congress, however, imposed limitations on the number of officers the military could have in 1953
under the New Look initiatives. SAC continued to grow; therefore,
allowances were made for the command. In fiscal year 1953 SAC
received additional allotments of 142 lieutenant colonels, 289 majors,
and 6 captains. As SAC increased its forces and the number of targets
assigned under its EWP, the number of spot promotions correspond-
ingly increased. Two years later, SAC had increased spot promotion
allotments to 185 lieutenant colonels, 525 majors, and 56 captains. The
one group that saw a decrease in spot promotions, however, was the
enlisted force. During the 1950s SAC converted from the B-29 and
B-36 with six enlisted positions apiece to the B-47, with no enlisted
positions, and the B-52, which only had one enlisted crewmember.[54]
Most of the decrease came at the expense of gunners. Jet engines
increased the performance of bombers, and SAC tactics assumed most
fighter attacks would come from behind. In the B-47, the copilot
doubled as the gunner manning the aft gun. For the B-52, the gunner
targeted rear attacks using nothing but radar, which guided his four
rear-facing guns; there was no visual sighting. Like the radar navigators
on the lower deck, the gunner came to rely on the radar screen for his
information instead of his own eyes.

While SAC typically rewarded "select" crews, the organization
held back certain promotions for bombing competition winners and
reconnaissance crews—which, like bomber crews, earned their spot
promotions for maintaining combat readiness. SAC set aside spot
promotions for those who flew riskier missions.[55] Of the primary
flying subgroups in SAC—bombers, reconnaissance, and tankers—
only air refueling crews were ineligible for spot promotions. Bomber
crews planned to fly into hostile territory, and recon crews at times
entered enemy airspace; these were the combat-ready forces in SAC

that deserved special consideration and promotion. Belonging to a tanker crew meant never planning to enter enemy territory, which removed the crews from consideration for spot promotions. Don Shea remembered when he earned the 1,500 flying hours necessary to apply for air observer bombardment school. Shea became eligible to move from his KB-29 tanker to the B-47, where he eventually earned his spot promotion.[56] Flying a bomber or bomber derivative in an organization dedicated to strategic bombing was the path to advancement and leadership. Other subcultures not derivative of the bomber were essential to the mission but not "select."

The Toll of SAC Life

When SAC members left work to return home, they found little escape from the stress and intensity that permeated SAC life. One of the main problems for families was the lack of adequate housing. Curtis LeMay, during his initial tour in 1948, found the housing situation at most SAC bases extremely troubling. There were not enough quality houses to handle the number of people assigned, and local communities had not invested in building affordable housing that SAC members could purchase or rent on their government allotment. Much like his approach to combat readiness, LeMay devised an idea for handling the housing situation. "We would build these houses with a down payment," LeMay explained, "erect them on the base, connect up the base sewer system and water supply and all other utilities. Everyone on base, in [their] spare time, would turn out to put those houses up along with some technical help from the manufacturer." Like squadrons in SAC, each base would target one house before moving on to the next. The member whose house was up for construction would spend his leave working full time on the house; everyone else would spend his spare time on the house until it was time to construct the next house. Although the program would promote unity and solve SAC's housing crisis, it would also perpetuate the notion of an organization continually at work.[57]

LeMay initially tried to secure appropriated money for SAC's housing, but his early attempts failed in the face of budgetary hurdles. At that point, LeMay decided, "To hell with it—we will build our own." SAC decided to purchase prefabricated homes from a reputable builder, lease the land from the government, and implement the program. The final aspect of the plan was that each member would contribute his monthly housing allotment to a general fund that would pay off the houses. There would be no distinction in rank; everyone contributed his entire monthly allotment. LeMay's plan would have had the houses paid off within five years. He even had $27 million lined up through the Federal Housing Administration for the contractor. At this point, the bureaucracy stepped in and stopped SAC's program. The Air Force comptroller general made SAC aware of the fact that airmen living on base would not be entitled to housing allowances since they were on government property. Only personnel living off base could receive a housing allowance. The lack of allowances for airmen on base quickly killed the SAC program.[58]

The housing problem received an infusion of help from Nebraska Senator Kenneth Wherry. When LeMay explained the deplorable housing situation, Wherry managed to get a bill passed that funded military housing, but the conditions of the contract were completely different from SAC's original plan. Instead of the military forming the company, as LeMay desired, civilians formed the company, leased the land from the government, and were paid back over a period of thirty years. The result soured LeMay's impression of Washington politics. Whereas he had developed a plan that would pay off SAC's houses in less than five years, Washington devised a plan that provided the contractors income for thirty years. Furthermore, the contractor decided upon was not as reputable as the one SAC had contracted.[59] Although termed "Wherry" housing, one SAC member described the living conditions as "Weary" housing.[60]

LeMay knew the importance of providing for SAC families. An article that ran in *Air Force Magazine* during 1951, at the beginning of SAC's expansion, cited housing as the number-one reason members were leaving the Air Force after their initial enlistment.[61] Without adequate housing, SAC's skilled specialists were seeking employment outside the military. Jet engines, radar equipment, and nuclear weapons all required highly technically trained individuals. Failure to keep these personnel threatened SAC's readiness. Although SAC secured federal funding for housing through the Wherry bill, living conditions depended primarily on geography. Those families living in the south, where access to labor and materials was plentiful, typically got more home for the amount allotted. People stationed in the north, especially in the more remote areas, received less square footage. Bringing the materials into the isolated regions of the northern tier and properly insulating the homes forced builders to reduce the size of the house they could construct on the allotment. Not only did those people stationed along the northern tier feel the full brunt of Mother Nature's fury, but they also lived in cramped quarters. General William Martin served as an air division commander on Loring Air Force Base, Maine. He personally found Wherry housing less than suitable for the northern environment.[62] Living in the cold, isolated northern areas of the United States closer to Soviet targets was essential to SAC's mission, but the housing conditions, coupled with the weather, made an assignment up north even more intolerable.

The Cold War drew distinctions between Soviet and American life that even revolved around kitchen design.[63] As contractors drew up plans for Air Force housing, the kitchen became a key feature. Airmen were serving in a modern, technical organization; therefore, the Air Force assumed that wives would appreciate a similarly technical kitchen. *Air Force Magazine* boasted that each new house would have a modern kitchen, saying, "Star of the new housing show is the kitchen. . . . After all, this is Mrs. Airmen's workshop and service wives deserve a break."[64] SAC leadership knew that trying to keep wives content was a major organizational goal. General Montgomery explained it this way: "If their wives are miserable all day . . . raising hell when [airmen] get home . . . they are going to get a job somewhere else."[65]

Despite LeMay's attempts to make SAC a family-friendly organization, the mission always took priority. It put stress on family ties, sometimes breaking them. In the 1940s airmen had to seek the permission of their commander to marry. Enlisted airmen serving in the late 1940s recalled that "most enlisted people didn't marry. . . . I don't remember a corporal or a buck sergeant getting married in 1948." In fact, another airman remembered, "Marriage was discouraged."[66] This perpetuated the myth that if the Air Force wanted a person to be married, they would have issued that person a spouse. But military life was changing. Instead of the traditional single man living in a barracks, nearly 50 percent of airmen were married in the 1950s.[67] SAC had grown by over 200 percent in 1955.[68] As SAC increased its number of bases, the housing problem that plagued the organization in the early years only became more acute. In addition to finding shelter for their family, airmen were called away to serve alert overseas on ninety-day rotations. Even when home, the demands of SAC's operating tempo made the husband and father typically just a breadwinner and often absent from the family.

A study conducted through the early years of SAC's expansion outlined how the organization's demands were affecting the wives and children of its members. The study selected at random twenty-five officers' wives and twenty-five airmen's wives to participate in an exploratory exposition on marriage and family life in SAC. The findings illustrated the strain on marriages. Of the participants inter-viewed, forty "expressed marked dissatisfaction with the effects of SAC requirements on married life."[69] Wives worried about how the frequent moves were affecting their families. In addition to education concerns, constant moves prevented families from establishing ties within the community. Furthermore, the excessive temporary duty (TDY) assignments and changing schedules prevented families from planning travel.[70]

A majority of the wives in the group had not furthered their educa-tion beyond high school and found their employment opportunities limited because they had married early and soon found themselves tied down with children. SAC demands even forced some husbands to leave the altar shortly after the vows were taken; many missed honeymoons. No sooner had they been married than some of the wives found themselves immediately thrust into the domestic role. Homes were not something couples built together. SAC airmen opted to rent furnished apartments or homes since "frequent and unpredictable military trans-fers made it necessary to be able to move on a few hours' notice with only their wearing apparel which could be carried with them."[71] Train-ing at different locations for their SAC duties and constant TDYs kept many husbands from the home. Some wives gave up on the idea of trying to truly build a home and simply went to live with parents until the husband returned. When husbands did return, there was the chance to conceive the first child, but there was no guarantee a SAC airman would be present for the birth of his child. The absence of a father for months, sometimes even years, created family stress because children had difficulty adjusting to his presence when he returned. The overall synergistic effect of these factors typically led women to build a maternalistic household in SAC communities. Husbands rarely contributed to making family goals or long-range plans. Their main contribution simply turned out to be the monthly paycheck.

The security and competition that helped define SAC's organizational culture on the job affected the home life as well. The constant secrecy prevented wives from engaging in conversation about their husbands' activities; therefore, wives developed the ability to interpret their husbands' actions. "I've learned never to ask questions," a wife confessed, "but only to observe my husband's behavior. It is easy to tell when he is worried or when he's on edge." Another wife complained about the atmosphere of competition that surrounded the organization. "So many of the problems which the men face seem to me to be due to SAC policies and practices over which the top command has control. We wives may be only women but we do see some of the outcomes when competition is the keynote in all of the work relationships." Wives felt the competition bred by SAC culture made developing cooperation, the central principle of home life, more difficult. One wife summed up the overall effect of SAC life: "The kind of family life that SAC makes possible is a poor substitute for what we believe life in families should be."[72]

The survey found that "loneliness" was the word most wives used to describe the disadvantage of SAC life. Some wives found little motivation to maintain their house or their personal appearance. "Why bother," one wife complained, "when there is no one coming home for dinner and no social affair in the evening." Although the wives were reluctant, a few admitted to sexual frustration as well. "Physical love is important to me," a participant confessed, "There are nights when I ache . . . I can tell you this that during TDYs wives get relief by masturbation and by promiscuity. They take cold baths and douches to bring relief."[73] Marriage, among some women, was rarely seen as something permanent. Given the isolation and separation, promiscuity or adultery by one or both partners threatened marriages.

The demands of SAC left families with few options. By 1955, 75 percent of SAC's highly technical enlisted force were in the first term of enlistment.[74] Some airmen simply chose to leave the command after their initial commitment. Other couples sought divorce. By 1954 SAC had the highest divorce rate in the entire Air Force.[75] The problems at home, however, could not drive mission needs. Horace Wade explained the SAC commander's dilemma: "There was no way that General LeMay was going to reduce [SAC's] capability as if he were walking away from a commitment. The wives suffered. The crewmembers suffered. It's true that this brought on some divorces, but it was patched up within a period of time." One solution wives sought was to join their husbands overseas. Some wives obtained passports and traveled to England, where their husbands were sitting alert. Other women took to writing their congressmen.[76] As he had in the past, LeMay did not wait for Washington to act; he developed his own program.

The Wives' Clubs
LeMay thought families should pull together to help one another through difficult times. One of the programs that provided help to the organization's families was the Dependents Assistance Program. While Curtis LeMay ran the most powerful bomber force in the world, he left organization of the wives to his wife, Helen. In an article for a magazine dedicated to service wives, Mrs. LeMay outlined the SAC program. The Dependents Assistance Program organized volunteer wives to provide support to wives in need. Volunteers could work in the program after they went through specialized training, much like their husbands did in SAC. Volunteers would help families find homes, provide emergency babysitting services, and even do grocery shopping for wives who could not get to the store. Each SAC base had a Dependents Assistance Center, and by 1956 nearly 14,000 officer and enlisted wives had completed the requisite training. Mrs. LeMay credited the program for increasing the organization's retention rate, saying, "General LeMay and I have received many letters citing the Dependent Assistance Program as the reason for reenlistment, for greater family happiness and security, for better understanding and peace of mind."[77] Perhaps more revealing than the details about SAC's program was how the article referred to officers'

wives. The article never mentioned Mrs. LeMay's first name or the first names of the other wives. They were always identified in the article by their husband's name, as though they carried the rank of their husband. Although never official, this highlighted a feature of SAC wives' associations confirmed by other members. The privilege of the husbands' rank usually followed wives when they joined these volunteer associations.[78]

In addition to the care program, SAC created an aid society that provided emergency relief to families. General Holstrom remembered how his wife and other commanders' wives volunteered in the aid society to take care of the younger airmen's wives. These programs were just beginning when he took over command and sometimes lacked resources since funding came primarily through donations. The downside of voluntary donations was that like many activities in SAC, it became a metric reported to command and a competition among units.[79]

LeMay found another way to bolster the aid fund using the organization's recreational activities. The SAC commander's enthusiasm for building sports cars led to a partnership between his command and the Sports Car Club of America (SCCA). SAC bases would close their runways and hold car races, in association with the SCCA, to raise money for SAC's nonprofits. Joining the SCCA and participating in sports car events, LeMay felt, was a suitable sport for Air Force people since it required a "fast eye, steady nerves and mechanical skill coupled with the thrill of speed and competition."[80] Sports car events, LeMay felt, would be indicative of Air Force pilot culture, much like polo had seemed to fit the Army when the cavalry rode horses. The main concern with SAC participation in these events was the chance for injury. LeMay sought an Air Force judge advocate general interpretation on whether injuries or death resulting from competition in these races would be ruled outside the "line of duty," which could mean a loss of medical coverage and survivor benefits. On May 19, 1952, Lt. Gen. Laurence Kuter, deputy chief of staff for personnel, expressed to LeMay his concern about SAC plans for sports car races and indicated that SAC "could not be assured that injuries or death resulting from this type of activity would be ruled 'in the line of duty.'"[81] Three weeks later, however, LeMay learned that the chief of staff of the Air Force could authorize airman participation in SCCA events under Air Force regulations, which would still give them "line of duty" status.[82]

LeMay began races on SAC bases, but the venture was short lived as several problems arose. The General Accounting Office launched an investigation into what it considered "irregularities" in the financial conduct of SAC's car races. Controversy revolved around whether the government was reimbursed for materials and personnel used to put on the races.[83] Furthermore, there was concern over whether the money raised was taxable, although LeMay claimed it was for nonprofit organizations. Despite the coming congressional inquiry, the SCCA events on SAC bases gained a lot of support. Offutt's race in 1954 drew close to 25,000 people.[84] In the face of controversy, however, the chief of staff asked LeMay to suspend the races after 1954.[85] In November 1954 SAC held one of its last races at March Air Force Base, California. The crowd numbered 30,000 but the total proceeds for SAC charities was only $23,000. "I believe that SAC-wide we have milked the sports car race program of all the reasonable profits we can expect," Maj. Gen. Walter "Cam" Sweeney wrote. "Since the position had been taken by the Air Staff that there are to be no more sports car races, I recommend that you do nothing to reverse this decision."[86]

Ending the races did not, however, curb LeMay's enthusiasm. Sports cars become a notable expression of what LeMay considered pilot culture; the new knights rode in fast sports cars, not on horses. In 1954 LeMay hired Lt. Gen. Francis Griswold as SAC deputy to replace Thomas Power, who had assumed command of Air Research and Development Command. Griswold shared LeMay's enthusiasm for cars, and the two built a car powered by a jet engine. David Jones, LeMay's aide, remembered red flames that would come from the side of the car when they fired it up. More importantly, this vehicle was used as the pace car at the Indianapolis Speedway.[87] The races at SAC bases ended in 1954, and so did the extra money for the aid society. That same year, however, plans were already in the works to reduce airmen absences and burdens by bringing more of SAC's assets back to the United States.

The "Full House" Concept

In 1953 LeMay's aide, Paul Carlton, went to work for Cam Sweeney at 15 AF and eventually became its director of plans. Sweeney had Carlton work on a plan to return a majority of SAC's operations to the United States. In 1955 SAC accepted delivery of its first B-52. Two years later, SAC gained its first all-jet air refueling tanker, the KC-135. Given the rapidly expanding bomber and tanker fleet, SAC foresaw a time when bombers could take off from bases within the United States and strike their targets in the Soviet Union. This would allow the command to have most of its crews continually flying out of the United States, closer to SAC headquarters and not in another theater commander's area of responsibility. It was also, according to Carlton, a political move. Spain and Morocco were growing increasingly uneasy about the presence of nuclear weapons on their territories. Therefore, LeMay and the SAC staff decided to get "the bombs further away from the forward area." After a year of work on the war plan, Carlton briefed LeMay on his work. The plan was then briefed to the Air Staff to gain final approval.

Bringing SAC home increased the number of aircraft on bases and created other strategic problems. The high density of aircraft per base made SAC bases lucrative targets for Soviet attack. As General Carlton explained it, some bases had wings with forty-five B-47s and thirty tankers. If the base housed a double wing, that meant ninety bombers and sixty tankers trying to take off all at once.[88] Therefore, SAC implemented dispersal, another concept that became characteristic of its operations. By dispersing assets to smaller bases, SAC made targeting of its bomber and tanker fleets more difficult. In 1956 SAC announced plans to activate eleven additional bases as part of its dispersal plans.[89] Several lay along the northern U.S. border at locations from which tankers could provide bombers enough fuel to strike targets inside the Soviet Union. Places such as Goose Bay, Canada, and Thule, Greenland, eventually fell into disuse, as did the notion of ninety-day rotations. While husbands might have been away less frequently under SAC's new EWP, the organization's new basing structure placed entire families in harsher environments. Instead of men braving the cold weather away from home and hearth, entire families, crammed into

"Weary housing," would now reside in the coldest parts of the nation in order to maintain the peace.[90]

SAC Goes Hollywood

The SAC commander believed there were three essentials to operationalizing deterrence: "Deterrence of aggression is composed of three basic elements—forces in being, public understanding of this force, and national determination to use the force if necessary. These are three elements that make our force credible to our friends and to our enemies. If any of them is missing, credibility suffers proportionately."[91] To date, LeMay had spent considerable time honing his force in being. National will, he knew, was something he had little control over. In the mid-1950s he turned his attention to educating the American public on the mission and purpose of his organization.

In 1955 a movie titled *Strategic Air Command* hit the big screen. Curtis LeMay had approached Beirne Lay Jr. about the possibility of making a movie about SAC.[92] Lay, a veteran of the 8 AF bombing campaign in Europe where he got to know LeMay, had written the screenplay for *Twelve O'Clock High*, an Academy award–nominated picture about the early strategic bombing of 8 AF in Europe. Through the big screen, LeMay hoped to conduct his education of American.

For *Strategic Air Command*, Beirne Lay wrote a script that featured "Dutch" Holland, a big-league baseball player and Air Force reservist, as the central character. Holland, on reserve status for over six years since the end of World War II, was recalled to active duty to fly bombers for SAC. Jimmy Stewart, an Air Force reservist and veteran of twenty bombing missions in World War II, played the title role.[93] Stewart accepted the role because "the drama inherent in the SAC story made me think that here was a unique opportunity to combine some needed public education with a lot of entertainment."[94] The movie featured many elements of SAC culture: bombers, air refueling, long days, select crews, no-notice security checks, and most importantly, the notion that SAC was a command at war. "We tried to tell the story of these people," Stewart explained, "and the sacrifices they are making every day to make your bed and mine a safe place in which to sleep."[95] The theme that ran throughout the movie was that every day, SAC was maintaining vigilance for those in the audience.

The moviegoers' two-hour education emphasized that there was a command at war in the 1950s—SAC.

Before the opening frame, a banner scrolled across the SAC patch that said, "America today is watching her skies with grave concern. For in these skies of peace, the nation is building its defenses." The movie opens with Stewart's character, Dutch, playing baseball when a war buddy, General "Rusty" Castle, informs Dutch that he has some important news: Dutch is being recalled to SAC because the organization has too many young people and needs the experience of the older men who flew in combat. "Where is the fire? I just don't see the necessity," exclaims Stewart's character, echoing what many in the audience probably thought at one time. As if taken directly from LeMay's playbook, General Castle replies, "You would if you were in my shoes. Do you realize we are the only thing that is keeping the peace? By staying combat ready, we can prevent a war." When Dutch informs his wife Sally (played by June Allyson) about the recall, she says supportively, "If you go, then we both go on active duty." Stewart's character reports to Carswell Air Force Base in civilian clothes and encounters another symbol of SAC culture: security. Dutch cannot get onto base because he does not have a military identification card. The security officer informs Dutch that recently the air police let a person on base who had a monkey for an identification picture and the general "had [them] on the carpet for that one."[96] Obviously, the stories of LeMay's countersecurity efforts had reached Beirne Lay's typewriter.

About twenty minutes into the picture, "General Hawkes" makes an appearance. Played by Frank Lovejoy, the Hawkes character, rarely seen without a cigar, clearly resembled LeMay. A plane simulating an emergency malfunction lands at the base and taxis close to the base's bombers. Since the plane's landing was unscheduled, it is instantly greeted by the base's security police, but not before the plane's door opens and members of SAC's sabotage team rush onto the taxiway where they are surrounded by security. General Hawkes then emerges from the jet holding a cigar and berates the security officer for the slow response. Indicating the level of training in SAC, the officer replies, "I don't have enough experienced people." "Don't tell me your little problems, son," Hawkes replies, "I only want results." When

Dutch reports to his squadron to assume his desk job, the commander tells him he will need to fly. Emphasizing the SAC mentality, the commander says, "All my pilots are pilots first and desk jockeys second."[97] The scene epitomizes LeMay's emphasis on readiness and an "at war" mentality.

It is on Dutch's first flight that members of the audience begin to understand the stress and strain of the SAC life through the character's conversation with the supporting cast. At the aircraft, he meets a flight engineer buddy from World War II (played by Harry Morgan). This crew, Dutch learns, is a "select" crew, which the crew commander describes as "sharp tools." As the crew prepares the aircraft for take-off, the audience witnesses the extreme detail with which SAC crews accomplish checklists to get the ten-engine bomber airborne. Once airborne, Dutch's old friend introduces him to the crew. Through these introductions, the movie reveals the different mentalities that existed in SAC.

The first person Dutch meets is Sergeant Jones, the radio opera-tor, who is leaving SAC because his enlistment is over. The sergeant explains his reason for leaving: "No more high-pressure stuff for me; fella likes to see his wife and kids." The Jones character goes on to say that constant overseas rotations, long nights at work, and maintenance duty on the weekends had taken its toll on him and his family; he is leaving. Dutch also meets the disgruntled radar navigator whom SAC recalled, just as it had recalled him. This character complains because he had to give up his new television business because of SAC's needs. Only Dutch's friend seems content with his duties, explaining that SAC is still "an aircraft and a crew working together to get the bomb on target." "But there isn't a war on," Dutch replies. As if taken directly from a LeMay speech, the character responds, "Every day is a war, colonel. We may never know when the other fellow may start something. We have to be ready twenty-four hours a day, seven days a week." Dutch's indoctrination into SAC culture is complete as he realizes the importance of his recall. But this does not stop Dutch from asking how SAC can manage to keep operating at such a high tempo. The "select" crewmember replies, "It is the competition; keeps them in there pitchin'," again highlighting a crucial element of LeMay's philosophy.[98]

Dutch returns home to his wife after just another day in SAC: a flight from Texas to Alaska and back. He informs Sally that he has to start flying again, explaining that "you can't tell an aircraft commander what to do unless you can do it yourself. . . . In SAC, everybody flies from General Hawkes on down." After Dutch becomes combat-ready, he is sent on a ninety-day rotation. To add drama to the movie, Dutch's plane develops engine trouble during a routine flight, and the crew must bail out. After being rescued, Dutch must face General Hawkes over the accident—just like every SAC aircraft commander who crashed had to one day face LeMay. Despite Dutch's explanations, General Hawkes, sounding too much like LeMay, says, "Accidents don't just happen. There is always a reason. As the aircraft commander you are completely responsible." Coincidently, it is on his rotation that Dutch finds out he is going to be a father.[99]

General Hawkes takes Dutch into a secret hangar that contains SAC's newest bomber, the all-jet B-47. Dutch admires the plane, saying, "She's the most beautiful thing I've ever seen. I sure would like to get my hands on one of these." During a training mission, Dutch's B-47 passes over a radar bomb-scoring site on a practice run. Below the clouds, the radar site is being pounded by rain. The camera focuses on the radar site tracking the plane's path and scoring its simulated release. An observer inside the radar site comments that the crew "just wiped out a city in a storm by a bomber they didn't see or hear." Another character replies, "With radar, weather is no problem. This happens every night all over America, only people never know it."[100]

As the climax of the movie approaches, Dutch must decide if he will stay with SAC or return to baseball. Predictably, he decides to stay in SAC. Sally is obviously upset by Dutch's decision and asks why she was not consulted. "There are times when you are given certain responsibilities," Dutch replies. "You can't ignore them." When Sally tells Dutch he has served his time and there is no war going on, Dutch looks deeply into Sally's innocent eyes and says, "But there is a war on. A kind of war. We've got to stay ready to fight without fighting." The movie ends as Dutch suffers an injury that takes him off flying status, which means he can't command an operational squadron. When given the choice of a desk job or getting out of SAC, Dutch selects the latter. The movie closes with Sally clutched in Dutch's protective arms observing an entire wing of B-47s pass overhead. SAC is keeping them—as well as those in the audience—safe.[101]

Conclusion

In 1956 SAC celebrated its tenth anniversary. At the celebration, LeMay used Billy Mitchell's sword to cut the cake.[102] More than three decades after the court-martial of Mitchell, SAC now immortalized the first American advocate for strategic bombing during the commemoration of its first decade in existence. Curtis LeMay had commanded the organization for nearly eight of its ten years in operation. Mitchell probably could not have imagined the organization LeMay built, a command devoted to the idea of centralized strategic air operations. SAC had made great strides throughout its first decade. By the end of 1956, SAC had two types of all-jet bombers and soon acquired an all-jet tanker. The command had accepted nearly two thousand B-47s and had thirty-nine bomber wings, six recon wings, six fighter wings, forty air refueling squadrons, and four support squadrons equipped with cargo airplanes.[103] The total capitalization of SAC, including its more than fifty air bases, totaled $7.7 billion, roughly one and a half times that of General Motors (the largest U.S. corporation at the time).[104]

In the process of building a credible deterrent, SAC came to rely on competition and security as ways of maintaining vigilance and combat readiness. The routines and rituals demanded of SAC's members created a culture of competition because of the rewards—rank and pay—associated with being the best. Each year, the best from each unit gathered at SAC's annual bombing competition, which it referred to as the "World Series of Bombing," to determine the ultimate champion. Even recreational activities involved competition, as SAC members took to their race cars to prove who was the best on the ground as well as in the air. Competition and the demands of SAC life, however, took their toll. SAC members found themselves constantly pitted against one another in competition. Those assigned to support SAC's flying mission competed for bomb scores and on-time takeoff records; air police found themselves pointing—and even firing—their weapons at members of their own organization. Technology and politics combined to bring SAC's forces home, but mission requirements ended up placing SAC families in some of the harshest environments in the United States. Although SAC pitted its members against each other, the organization did foster an idea of cooperation. Isolated by fences and living in some of the most barren places in the United States created within the organization cohesion and a culture of teamwork. Some raced cars at events to raise money, others gave donations, and wives donated their time to make sure SAC took care of its own.

Although SAC tried to build a family-friendly command, its atmosphere of competition ran counter to the cooperation needed at home to create a family. By the mid-1950s a majority of the organization members had wives and families, and leaving them behind became a ritual in SAC. Even when crewmembers were home, the organizational demands of SAC hurt family life. "Combat crewmembers at times found themselves overwhelmed," one SAC crewmember remembered, "with the constant training, standardization, checklists, tactical doctrine, command and control procedures [instructions for employing nuclear weapons], and weapon system proficiency."[105] Families probably suffered the most as SAC trained its forces and kept them constantly vigilant. A lack of adequate housing and long absences also hurt morale. Some airmen left the Air Force to preserve their marriages; some wives left their husbands.

Seventy-hour workweeks were the norm in SAC. Most of America did not realize the sacrifices SAC was making each day to keep America safe. Therefore, the organization encouraged Hollywood to produce *Strategic Air Command*, featuring World War II bomber pilot and movie star Jimmy Stewart. The production educated the American people that around the clock, while they slept, there was a command at war practicing overhead to keep them safe.

Throughout its existence, SAC made changes to its cultural rituals as the organization evolved from an independent strategic bombing force to a nuclear-armed deterrent force. Members of the organization knew why they were being worked so hard, but leadership and members continued to work out the how and why of deterrent operations. In 1957 the circumstances of the Cold War would change even more dramatically and add new elements—ideological and physical—to SAC culture. The organization would see an entire new focus in operations as the strategic environment changed forever.

7

Living in the Missile Age
Fear and SAC Culture

Our task is very simple in concept but infinitely complex in execution. We must be strong and so immediately ready to counter any aggressor, that no sane world power would dare run the risk of starting another war.

—THOMAS POWER

During the 1957 Christmas season, SAC headquarters came up with a campaign to promote reenlistment. The staff erected a fifty-foot Christmas tree in front of the headquarters building. SAC commanders could light a Christmas light by enlisting a certain number of first-term airmen. The painter hired to construct a sign to promote the reenlistment campaign, which SAC called "Maintaining Peace Is Our Profession," could not fit the entire slogan on the sign. Therefore, Lt. Col. Edward Martin and Chief Warrant Officer Ben Kohot, project officers for the campaign, had the painter shorten the slogan to simply "Peace Is Our Profession." When Col. Charles Van Vliet, 8 AF director of information, visited SAC headquarters and saw the sign, he liked the slogan; Van Vliet convinced the 8 AF commander, Maj. Gen. Walter Sweeney, to place a sign with the slogan outside the front gate. By 1958 the slogan had become the motto of the entire command.[1] Those in SAC viewed the motto as something more than a simple slogan for retention. Horace Wade, a SAC commander, described how the motto reflected SAC's mission. "If you are strong, then you maintain peace," Wade said, "If you are weak, you get run over."[2] The realism reflected in U.S. foreign policy became culturally embedded in the motto adopted by Strategic Air Command. Bases, publications, and even stationery carried the reminder that peace came by strength.

Throughout the mid-1950s SAC operated a formidable and credible deterrent based on a ready and responsive strategic bombing force armed with nuclear weapons. At the same time, both sides in the Cold War were pursuing technologically advanced weapons—ballistic missiles—that threatened most of the planning assumptions in SAC's EWP. The Soviet development of a long-range bomber compelled SAC to consider measures that would protect its airplanes in case of a surprise attack. A 1953 RAND study calculated that within one year, the Russians would possess two hundred to four hundred more bombers than American forces. Furthermore, the study predicted that the Soviet Union would develop a surface-to-surface missile capability in the 1958–62 time frame.[3] The continued development of Soviet offensive capabilities caused SAC to alter its operating assumptions and basing strategy. By 1957 SAC implemented plans to have its forces back on U.S. soil and eliminate the need for ninety-day alert rotations overseas. This move coincided with LeMay's desire to have all his forces under his control. Crewmembers, however, would still need to deploy to forward operating locations to improve the U.S. ability to respond rapidly in case of war. Additionally, SAC developed a dispersal plan to move its aircraft to more bases to reduce the chances that a few well-placed nuclear weapons could destroy America's retaliatory capability. Events in 1957 would add another dimension to SAC culture: fear.

This chapter examines how the development of ICBMs, provoked in part by the unexpected launch of Sputnik, brought an element of fear into SAC culture. In 1957 SAC crews began sitting alert, ready to launch against the Soviet Union within fifteen minutes. Additionally, the threat of nuclear attack from ballistic missiles would drive SAC's operations underground. New leadership would add to the anxiety already permeating the organization as SAC's most recognizable leader, Curtis LeMay, moved from the nation's geographic center to its political center and became vice chief of staff of the Air Force. Finally, the development of "push-button" warfare—through the launching of nuclear missiles—signaled a decline in the airplane's role in nuclear warfare. SAC pilots did not fully embrace the development of the missile because of early operating reliability and accuracy. At the same time, bomber generals wanted to make sure no other service would control technology that threatened their dominance in the military establishment. Missileers, "push-button" pilots who launched missiles from the comfort of their silos, formed a new subculture in SAC. Their integration into SAC culture presented an interesting study of the dominant pilot culture creating and then absorbing a subculture that operated with a different mentality. When pilots were the subculture of the Army, they became a counterculture and sought their independence. Missiles were more than an extension of long-range strategic bombing; they were pilotless. SAC took active measures to make sure this new subculture espoused the same values and beliefs as the organization. Missileers would, therefore, be indoctrinated into the SAC mentality.

The Emergency War Plan: Changing the Assumptions
Understanding how the missile age impacted SAC's EWP in particular and the nation's war plans in general requires a look at the assumptions and plans that were in effect prior to 1957. On March 14, 1954, Gen. Archie Old, then the SAC director of plans, briefed Navy officers on SAC's EWP. The briefing notes taken by Navy Capt. William B. Moore provide insight into the planning assumptions, strategy, and objectives of SAC's war plans. Old's briefing focused on the organization's proposed plan for the 1956 fiscal year. Organizational planning began from inputs SAC received from the Joint Strategic Capabilities Plan, which outlined "the disposition, operations, and support of all existing American armed forces in the event of an outbreak of war within a given fiscal year, and set wartime tasks and objectives for those forces, including SAC." Planners took the forces assigned by the JCS and developed the command's war plan. In his briefing,

Old outlined the objectives for the different JCS code names used in the war plan: BRAVO targets were selected to ensure a blunting of Soviet capability to deliver an atomic offensive against the United States and its allies; DELTA targets, which had been the primary focus of U.S. planning estimates as far back as 1945, provided for the disruption of the vital elements of the Soviet warmaking capacity; and the ROMEO branch plan outlined how U.S. and North Atlantic Treaty Organization (NATO) forces would retard Soviet advances into Western Europe.[4] SAC's plans focused on the DELTA list of targets. Actual targets in war plans remain classified even today; however, the DELTA objective fell in line with the SAC idea of launching a massive nuclear armada to destroy the Soviet Union's air defenses, industry, and production in a matter of hours. The ROMEO plan was the retardation of Soviet forces in Europe. This was primarily a NATO mission since Gen. John B. Montgomery fought to have SAC freed of this commitment as far back as 1949.[5]

Although the JCS assigned SAC a certain number of targets, SAC planners found the list insufficient and produced their own annex to JCS war plans, which had over 1,700 designated ground zeros. Furthermore, the Navy officer noted, SAC plans emphasized the near-simultaneous destruction of each target on the list. Unclassified projections placed the number of nuclear weapons in the U.S. arsenal at one thousand during fiscal year 1954. By fiscal year 1956 the nuclear stockpile would nearly double, providing more than enough weapons to cover SAC's expanded list. The single, massive blow SAC planned provided another benefit: the near-simultaneous penetration of Soviet airspace by all of SAC's bombers. SAC predicted that the overwhelming number of bombers hitting the entire perimeter of Soviet airspace at the same time would severely degrade Soviet air defenses; they simply would not be able to handle all the bombers in the air. SAC's bombers would then enter Soviet airspace, strike their targets, and leave as rapidly as possible.[6] General LeMay explained SAC's rationale for expanding the JCS war plan: "Our job in SAC was not to promulgate a national policy or an international one. Our job was to produce. And we produced," he explained. "We put America in that situation of incipient power which she occupied at the time."[7]

While SAC had meticulously worked out the intricacies of its war plan, problems remained. At the time, one of the major coordination setbacks with SAC's EWP was scheduling planes through the various nuclear storage facilities in order to load the nuclear weapons. General Chris Adams began his career in the Air Force in 1952 and served in SAC for thirteen years as a B-36 and B-52 pilot. He recalled how his B-36 crew would execute its war plan if, in his words, "the balloon had really gone up." "We would deploy from our home base at Biggs Air Force Base, Texas, to Kirtland Air Force Base, New Mexico," Adams explained, "where the munitions crews at the Manzano nuclear storage facility would load on the prescribed weapons for the mission. From there, we would fly to a designated forward staging base, refuel, rest if possible, and await further orders to launch a strike."[8] Estimates put the complete round trip to the Soviet Union and back at roughly twenty hours. Such a plan, based on nuclear weapons separate from their delivery vehicles, assumed a certain level of warning about a possible attack. The coming missile age altered these assumptions as well as the custody arrangement of nuclear weapons.

As General Old finished his briefing, Captain Moore made two overall observations regarding SAC's plans. With 600 to 750 bombers and weapons approaching Russia from many directions to overload the air defenses, Moore wrote, his "final impression was that virtually all of Russia would be nothing but a smoking, radiating ruin at the end of two hours." Moore also came away with the sense that SAC was, in effect, a sort of "elite corps" dominated by a forceful and dedicated commander. LeMay, in Moore's eyes, had complete confidence in SAC's ability to crush Russia quickly by massive atomic bombing attacks. The SAC commander seemed to give no consideration to the moral aspect of his plan; nor did he discuss or appear concerned with the long-range effects of such attacks. Nevertheless, Moore observed, SAC was confident that when the bell rang, it would get the weapons needed to cover the expanded target list, no matter what the JCS allocations were at the moment.[9]

Moore's exposure to SAC culture revealed more than the planning assumptions that went into pre-1957 war plans. As an outsider, Moore observed the elite mentality with which SAC operated. Most members within the organization during this period viewed SAC as a step above the rest of the Air Force. "Better organized, better disciplined," "a very special outfit," and "the only way to adequately describe SAC is to say: SAC should run the world"—these were just some of the phrases former SAC members used to describe their organization in 2006.[10] SAC members even differentiated their bomber command and commands that flew other types of airplanes. In reference to the Military Air Transport Service, which flew cargo and passengers, one SAC member stated, "They were trying to figure out if they were a commercial airline or a military organization."[11] Don Shea expressed a similar view about the lack of discipline in Tactical Air Command (TAC). Shea's commander referred to the organization as simply a "raggedy ass militia." Whereas SAC planned every mission in minute detail, the perception existed that fighter pilots simply showed up at their jets to "kick the tires [perform a preflight]—light the fires [start engines]—first one to the hold line is lead—brief on guard [a radio channel reserved only for emergencies]."[12] SAC, in its members' eyes, had more professionalism, discipline, and purpose than its sister organizations or even its sister services. General Old recalled an instance during his time in SAC that highlighted the perception that only the best should join the organization. At an Omaha party during LeMay's tenure, a local judge approached the commander and said, "Well, General LeMay, I did you a favor today. I had this young man up there, and when I got ready to have his case I told him that if he would join the Air Force I wouldn't put him in jail." LeMay replied, "Goddamn, you say you did me a favor? That's the most stupid goddamn thing I ever head in my life. Do you really think that is the kind of people we want in the Air Force?"[13]

SAC's Bunker

Although SAC prided itself on showing power and displaying its prestige, Soviet advances in long-range bombers and the prospect of a surprise attack by guided missiles forced some operations underground. In January 1957 SAC moved its operations into a new command center on Offutt Air Force Base, Nebraska. Rather than simply being named a "headquarters" building, SAC called its new super structure a "control center" to indicate that all of SAC's operations would be centrally controlled from one location. Costing more

than $9 million, the three-story underground portion of the head-
quarters building became its central feature. In designing the new
building, SAC's official history explained the thought that went into
moving its main control center underground: "Since this headquarters would control, in a world-wide basis, the strategic forces' nuclear
retaliation campaign, its security was an important factor in the
Nation's defense posture."[14] SAC's center boasted the largest bomb
shelter in the nation at the time, capable of withstanding all but a
direct nuclear hit.[15] Supplies of dry food along with a separate power
supply to keep the facility running in case of attack ensured members'
underground survival. Probably more impressive were the two-story-
high maps highlighted by rows of spotlights and the 2,500 telephones
designed to give SAC commanders up-to-the-minute information
on the status of its forces.[16]

An elite force guarded the nerve center. Air police monitored
closed-circuit televisions and verified the credentials of all people seeking access. The unique uniforms of these air police showed how SAC
set itself apart from the rest of the Air Force. They wore distinctive
berets and an ascot embossed with the organizational insignia. Perhaps
more noticeable were the pearl-handled revolvers they carried. The
purpose was to create in the air police the same type of esprit felt
by SAC's aircrews.[17] The air police became primarily a security force,
responsible for securing the nerve center, instead of a police force,
which served in a traditional law enforcement role. Given the growth
of SAC air bases and the increase in perimeters to protect, 70 percent
of SAC's policemen concentrated on security versus law enforcement.
Rather than trying to cover every inch of base perimeters, SAC pulled
its forces closer to the airplane. Just like the aircrews, SAC continued
to challenge its security forces. People volunteered for the sabotage
teams despite the dangers involved. One moonlit night at Carswell Air
Force Base, Texas, a sabotage team leader tried to get on the base by
swimming across Lake Worth, which bordered the base. As he neared
the shore, a shot rang out and a ricocheting rifle bullet flew too close
to the would-be saboteur. The team leader changed his mind about
his attempt and reportedly made the trip back across the lake in near-
record time.[18]

In addition to security, the ability to execute worldwide command and control became a feature of SAC's new nerve center. Communicating with all the forces in real time required a sophisticated communications suite inside the complex. First, the control center maintained an elaborate teletype system that enabled it to send and receive instant messages or reconnaissance photos worldwide from its forward operating bases in the United Kingdom, Japan, Guam, and North Africa.[19] The new command structure reflected a different operating mentality. Previously, SAC argued, commanders thought they had to control the action of their forces from a Quonset hut close to the front. Technology—both the airplane and sideband radio—now meant that SAC could fight the war from a hole in the ground in the center of the United States.[20]

A closer examination of the command center reveals how other artifacts testified to the worldwide nature of the organization's operations. Eight different clocks—each set to a different time zone—hung within view of the "cab," the two-story structure resembling a football press box from which the SAC commander and his staff would centrally control the forces. Across from the cab hung maps and display boards that showed the disposition of SAC's forces, the current weather, and the projected routes should the EWP be executed. Inside the control cab, a red phone sat within arm's reach of the SAC commander. By entering five digits, the commander could set off alarm bells and flashing lights in each of the more than forty different SAC control rooms in the United States. When the command assumed "alert status" by late 1957, General Power could have SAC's entire alert fleet airborne within three to fifteen minutes of his order. Due to the expansiveness of the facility and the need for real-time information, LeMay and Power had closed-circuit televisions installed so the command staff could receive weather and intelligence briefings from the floor.[21] In the cab, the staff monitored boards of information as "cat-footed specialists slide any of a hundred huge information-bearing panels." As one reporter put it: "They move in and out of view as though a titanic poker player were shuffling a cosmic deck of cards."[22]

Another feature of the SAC control center, the EWP computer, captured the detailed planning and order that characterized SAC behavior. Planning the near-simultaneous penetration of Soviet airspace by over seven hundred bombers in addition to synchronizing and coordinating the delivery of almost two thousand nuclear weapons required computer-processing power. General Everett Holstrom, a SAC planner at the time, described the computer. "This was a big one," Holstrom remembered. "It took up rooms. . . . Big wheels turning and all that stuff." Indicative of the developing military, industrial, and academic complex the United States used to fight the Cold War, SAC initially contracted with the University of Chicago to put its entire war plan on the computer.[23] Eventually, people within the organization learned how to perform the task faster because the command needed to produce operations orders when conditions changed. The computer electronically stored information pertaining to SAC forces. Upon activation of the EWP, the big computer would record the progress of the strike force by means of punch cards. Using this process, SAC commanders received immediate updates on the status of the strike force and could adjust its operations accordingly.[24] Working with war plans and the computer required dedicated men willing to put in long hours. Holstrom recalled that it was dark when he arrived on duty and it was usually dark when he left; he rarely saw the light of day, leading him to add, "We felt like a bunch of moles down in the underground portion of SAC HQ."[25]

SAC wanted to keep its forces abreast of their role in the war plan and how their actions directly affected operations. Therefore, the organization began the "First Team Program" to reward its select crews. Don Shea remembered when his "select" crew earned the privilege to visit SAC's control center. Crews would receive a detailed briefing on the center's operations. What left the biggest impression on Shea, however, was how everything his crew did fed directly into the SAC headquarters, including the location of his aircraft in flight.[26]

A New SAC Leader: Thomas Power

More changes occurred in SAC during 1957 than just the move into the new control center. In the spring of 1957, the Air Force announced that President Eisenhower had appointed Nathan Twining to become chairman of the Joint Chiefs, the first Air Force officer to hold that position. Thomas White, the current vice chief of staff of the

Air Force, would move up to assume General Twining's former position. White had a reputation for being an extremely intelligent officer but did not have the operational experience of some of the Air Force's other four-star generals. To fill the vacant vice chief position, the Air Force turned to LeMay.[27] LeMay brought operational experience to the Air Force leadership team and an affinity for impressing members of Congress with his knowledge of bomber operations. The first vacancy at SAC in nine years generated considerable speculation as to LeMay's replacement, since many aspiring Air Force leaders wanted what many considered the premier combat job in the Air Force.

LeMay wanted to leave the command in the hands of someone he could trust and who thought like he did. Therefore, he played an active role in selecting his successor. General Francis Griswold served as SAC's deputy commander after Thomas Power left that position and continued in the same position under LeMay's replacement. The person LeMay chose to replace him seemed to have at least two qualifications the outgoing commander valued: he was a "SAC type" individual, and he enjoyed flying. Griswold described what a "SAC type" meant: "The SAC type of person was someone who was dedicated and had the feeling that this was the command that would keep peace in the world. They were not facetious about it, or smart about it, or anything else. They were just dedicated people that felt that SAC had the capability and the power."[28] In addition to being a SAC type, LeMay's replacement had to have flying credentials. When an interviewer asked Griswold what LeMay looked for in commanders, besides an ability to meet SAC's demanding requirements, Griswold simply replied, "The most important thing they had to do was fly airplanes. People lose sight of that. What is the whole Air Force for? Flying airplanes."

James Edmundson knew firsthand that LeMay wanted his generals to be flying leaders. "He brought in a lot of young generals in SAC," Edmundson said. "I was one of them. There were the guys that he promoted ahead of their contemporaries and he said he wanted them to be known as flying generals and he used to keep track of those that were flying in the tactical equipment." While Edmundson served as deputy director of operations at SAC headquarters in 1957, LeMay asked the staff to rate the best group and wing commanders in SAC. To prove his point that flyers made better commanders, LeMay then compared the staff ranking to the number of flying hours each leader in SAC accumulated. The correlation between the two lists was almost exact; SAC's best commanders were those who flew. "He wanted his generals to fly," Edmundson stated. "And he wanted his kids that had to put their ass on the line to know that their bosses were aviators."[29]

To replace him, LeMay recommended a "SAC guy" and a flyer: Thomas Power. Since his departure from SAC in 1954, Power had commanded the Air Research and Development Command. Under Power's tenure, the command oversaw the procurement of new bombers and, more importantly, the development of ballistic missiles. LeMay, however, found it difficult to get Power named as his replacement. According to LeMay's aide, David Jones, Secretary of the Air Force Donald Quarles fought LeMay over the recommendation.[30] Early speculation centered on Gen. Emmett "Rosie" O'Donnell, who had served in two wars, including leading SAC's initial participation in the Korean War.[31] Power, however, was LeMay's choice. Quarles left his position as secretary of the Air Force to become the deputy secretary of defense, which allowed LeMay to convince incoming secretary of the Air Force James Douglas to push for Power's appointment.[32] Not missed by the press was the fact that Power, unlike O'Donnell, had not gone to West Point. Upon his announcement, the papers reported that "like his predecessor, [Power] is not a West Point graduate."[33] Power had gone to prep school, but he was not a college graduate. Nevertheless, on July 1, 1957, Thomas S. Power assumed command of SAC.

SAC Culture under General Power

Power did little to alter SAC culture. He had served as LeMay's deputy and had played a critical role in implementing the policies that turned SAC around in the late 1940s and early 1950s. The two men, however, had different leadership styles. Power lived up to his name and led SAC in a manner conducive to the iron fist that symbolized the organization. Griswold, SAC deputy under both men, summarized the distinction. "I would say that General LeMay's appeal was personal and General Power's appeal was to duty," Griswold recalled. "For General LeMay you wanted to do it. For General Power you felt you should do it." Power's exposure to research and development gave him the ability to look deeper into the way things operated. Whereas LeMay looked at the whole operation, Griswold remembered, Power became a nitpicker, almost a micromanager.[34] This leadership trait elevated the level of fear in SAC. LeMay claimed that he never "fired" anyone; he just transferred them to new assignments.[35] On the other hand, General Power took a different approach. General Horace Wade, who served under Power as well, explained, "LeMay was a kind hearted man . . . always has been. He got a lot of credit for being mean as a result of General Power. General LeMay didn't go around firing people. General Power did." Power continued LeMay's practice of having wing commanders brief the SAC commander on flying accidents. Under LeMay, the wing commander typically left with a recommendation. With Power, however, nine times out of ten the wing commander got fired. Wade also did not appreciate the way Power treated his staff: "He delighted getting a group in his office for a briefing and then making an ass out of the briefing officer. He thought it was the way to make good leaders."[36] General Old, a numbered air force commander under both men, found in Power traits similar to those seen by Wade and Griswold. "I don't think he was . . . he was not tough," Old recalled. "He was mean."[37] Meanwhile, changes in the circumstances and assumptions of the Cold War only compounded the anxiety Power's leadership brought to SAC.

SAC Goes on Alert

Immediately after assuming command, Power began to work on altering SAC's EWP. Holstrom worked on the plan and recalled how Power's assumptions differed from LeMay's. Whereas LeMay had assumed advanced warning on the employment of SAC's force, Power had the war plans division working on a new EWP, which assumed only fifteen minutes' notice. Perhaps through his work overseeing missile development, Power understood that at most there would be twenty minutes' notice once the United States detected the launch of a Soviet missile. Although SAC planners could develop a plan that would assume only fifteen minutes' notice, the plan had several problems that would take time to iron out.[38] First, alert required a new nuclear weapons custodial relationship between civilian and military agencies. Second, there was no facility next to the runway to house aircrew so they could get to their aircraft quickly enough. Initial plans had the crews housed at barracks as close as possible to the runway. The "alert" life would become a hallmark of SAC culture; it would add visible and invisible elements to the organization's culture.

Although implemented under Power, the planning for alert had begun under LeMay. Alert grew out of SAC's plans to deploy its forces from the United States. Despite having all forces back in the United States under SAC control, planners recognized the need to develop a "quick strike" operations plan. SAC anticipated that the Soviet Union would, by 1960 to 1964, have considerable strength in its intercontinental bomber fleet and possess missiles in quantity. Therefore, SAC began to study and seek approval for ground alert as early as 1955. Realizing that SAC forces could be caught completely off guard, the command proposed the idea that 100 percent of its forces should be on alert. For a command that considered itself at war, 100 percent alert was the next logical step. Resource costs—especially money and manpower—proved prohibitive. Therefore, SAC decided to propose placing one-third of its force on alert status, ready to launch within fifteen minutes of notification. One-third of SAC's forces still amounted to a large force of bombers and tankers. SAC planned on having thirty-nine bomber wings and fifty-two air-refueling squadrons by 1960. Therefore, the total alert force would number 585 bombers and 364 tankers for a total of 949 aircraft.[39]

Placing aircraft on alert required a new nuclear weapons custodial relationship coupled with new infrastructure to support the operating concept. Maintaining aircraft on alert, ready to launch on their war mission with only fifteen minutes' notice, meant SAC planes could no longer fly from their bases to Atomic Energy Commission storage sites for weapons loading. The nuclear weapons had to be readily available to SAC forces. As early as May 4, 1956, the JCS created a new AEC–Department of Defense memorandum of understanding that automatically transferred custody of "finished" weapons to the military. This presidential action made sure that weapons were "available to meet the commanders' needs without being restricted by custodial requirements."[40] The increased intensity of the Cold War enabled SAC to gain control over the one asset that had eluded its grasp since the original conception of the EWP: the nuclear weapons themselves.

SAC tested several concepts of its alert plan but, in a move uncharacteristic of its culture, implemented a program before the command had the training and infrastructure in place. On October 1, 1957, General Power placed several bases in the United States and overseas on alert. Writing to his crewmembers, the new commander explained the importance of alert operations: "As long as the Soviets know that, no matter what means they employ to stop it, a sizeable percentage of SAC's strike force will be in the air for counterattack within a few minutes after they have initiated aggression, they will think twice before undertaking such aggression."[41] His actions came only three days prior to the Soviet Union's launch of Sputnik, which ratcheted up Cold War tensions and created anxiety within the American populace. One month later, to calm fears, General Power informed the public that SAC aircrews were sitting alert at the end of U.S. runways. Although Power announced that he would maintain "as much as one-third of our strike forces on continuous alert," the actual numbers failed to reach that goal for several years.[42] The organization put 11 percent of its forces on alert in 1957 and gradually increased that amount (to 12 percent in 1958 and to 20 percent in 1959) until it attained the goal of 33 percent in 1960.[43]

SAC took years to reach its goal because it implemented the program before the organization could firmly establish the infrastructure and procedures required for alert. Although implemented in fiscal year 1958, the military budget for that year contained few resources to build alert facilities at SAC bases. Initially, SAC crews lived in barracks and quarters close to the runway, but in fiscal year 1959 the Air Force gained the money to build another artifact of SAC culture: the alert facility. In Power's eyes, crews with a first-priority mission deserved first-priority treatment. Facilities at sixty-three bases were to be comfortable and have adequate living space to provide not only sleeping quarters but also places for crews to enjoy television, games, and special alert cooking.[44] Located close to the runway, aircrews would be able to reach their planes at a moment's notice.

Allowing crews to live within minutes of their aircraft was one way to ensure SAC could meet its goal of getting the alert force airborne within fifteen minutes. In addition, SAC developed a unique ramp design and special tactics to ensure survival of the alert fleet in case of an attack. Instead of parking planes conventionally at ninety-degree angles, wing commanders built alert aircraft parking spots at forty-five-degree angles. The configuration—known as the herringbone—provided quicker exit from the alert stub to the taxiway, reduced taxi distance, provided more stubs for a given section of pavement, and reduced problems associated with taxiing heavy aircraft.[45] Although officially termed the herringbone, SAC members referred to the newest cultural artifact as simply the "Christmas tree" because when seen from the air, it resembled the holiday symbol.

The final aspect to launching SAC's alert force quickly was another tactic, or cultural routine, exclusive to the organization: the minimum interval takeoff (MITO). During MITO launches, bombers and tankers would take off with a fifteen-second spacing between aircraft. On runways where aircraft could be staggered on either side of the runway, SAC reduced the takeoff interval to seven and a half seconds. Like everything else, crews had to practice MITOs on a regular basis. Takeoffs by themselves were considered a critical phase of flight that only became more dangerous and harrowing with the implementation of MITOs. The weights of the aircraft loaded with fuel and nuclear weapons meant the need for additional thrust to get the lumbering bombers and tankers off the runway. B-47s could use jet-assisted takeoffs in which essentially up to thirty-two rockets were strapped around the bomber in a "horse collar" to give the B-47 additional thrust during takeoff. Eventually, all tankers and bombers used "water injection" during their takeoffs for additional thrust. Filtered water would be injected into the intake airstream of the jet's engines, increasing the density of the intake air and resulting in a corresponding increase in engine performance. The drawback to this method was the trail of black smoke water injection produced. In addition to the likelihood of flying through the preceding aircraft's wake turbulence because of the reduced separation, visibility could be momentarily reduced to zero when flying through the trailing black smoke. The recollection of one B-47 pilot was not the successes but the accidents he heard of or witnessed at the 509th and 100th Bomb Wings.[46] Although SAC had the lowest accident rate in the Air Force, most pilots recalled the MITO as the most hazardous and gripping moment in their SAC flying career.

Crews found that alert did not provide them a break from the realism of SAC training. SAC initially gave their members alert tours of two to three days. Although housed in nice alert facilities, crews could expect at least once during their tour to be forced to respond to a practice alert. If crews were visiting places outside the alert facility on base, they would park in places reserved for alert vehicles. For example, at the base theater, crews sat in the back of the theater close to the exit, and an alert light above the screen would flash upon initiation of an alert response. Upon notification of an alert, crews rushed to their vehicles—the first person there became the driver—and together they rushed to their aircraft. While the crews were en route, the aircraft's ground crew had already arrived to begin pulling intake covers off the engines and manning the fire extinguisher in case crews were required to start engines.[47] Once at the aircraft, crews had to determine the type of response. No one knew if the alert was real or an exercise until they established contact with the command center. SAC devised three levels of response to test their crews. During an ALPHA response, crews proceeded to the aircraft, checked in with the wing control center, and reported ready to start engines. A BRAVO alert required crews to start engines and report when ready to taxi. The third option—a COCO alert—had crews perform all the previous steps and in addition taxi to the runway, apply full power for a simulated takeoff, and then terminate the exercise when the aircraft reached fifty knots.[48] The job of the alert crew was to make sure they understood the type of response commanded by the message. No one wanted to be the only aircraft rolling down the runway while the rest of the alert force remained in their parking stubs. Fear by leadership, one SAC member said, started at the top and propagated down to the crew level. The reward for doing a good job—getting the alert right—was to not be punished.[49]

SAC challenged crews with alert responses in the United States and at forward bases overseas. Headquarters in Omaha ended ninety-day rotations to forward operating bases but continued to rotate crews overseas to the United Kingdom, North Africa, and Guam. SAC tasked B-47s with the mission since the medium bombers did not have the range of the B-52s, which were replacing the aging B-36 fleet. "Reflex" was the term SAC used to describe the forward alert tasking. Instead of ninety days, B-47 bomber crews pulled a three-week tour, spending two weeks on alert with a one-week break in between. Combined with alert tours in the United States, bomber crewmembers could expect to spend six weeks out of twelve away from their families.[50] General William Martin, who commanded the first B-52/KC-135 wing, said that eventually, "Alert status was a way of life. The crews accepted it." Besides providing the comforts of home in alert facilities, Martin recalled, SAC provided ways for wives and families to visit their spouses on alert in the United States, usually at picnic areas close to the facility.[51]

Life on alert took on a culture of its own. For example, the competition pervading SAC culture found new forms. Crews would pony up money to form pools based on the expected alert response during their tour. As one crewmember explained it, "The teams get up pools; kick in a buck or so apiece just to make the alert more interesting. The guys that report in first they're ready to roll get the pool."[52] Gambling became the most popular form of diversion on alert. While some members found "action" at the alert facility pool tables or the "back-alley"-type crap games, SAC became famous for its poker games. Stories circulated about airmen losing great sums of money or even the family car while on alert.[53] Wives began complaining about the games, and commanders felt they were beginning to erode the distinction between officers and enlisted airmen. According to Sigmund Alexander, his commander began cracking down on gambling during alert.[54] In addition to SAC leadership, members blamed the John F. Kennedy administration for the reductions in gambling. Defense Secretary Robert McNamara's "whiz kids" reduced the amount of per diem paid to B-47 crews pulling alert on "Reflex" operations, which meant less disposable income for gambling activities.[55]

Alert elicited different responses from those who served time in the alert facility. By 1959, when Edward Jedrziewski began pulling alert, tours in the United States were typically a week long. Jedrziewski identified what he considered to be the different categories of individuals who pulled alert. He labeled his first group "those who like it," which in his estimation had the fewest members but saw alert as a way to get away from the wife and kids for some peace and quiet. "It is possible that this type," Jedrziewski added, "had a strong, self-sufficient wife, maybe the kind that wore the pants in the family." On the opposite end of the spectrum, the B-47 crewmember found "the worrier." This person believed his wife and kids could not get along without him, a situation in which the husband was dominant and ended up spending a lot of time on the phone running the household from afar, not unlike the way SAC directed its members' lives. Jedrziewski's third category was the "horny complainer" who grumbled vocally about the imposed week of celibacy. Upon leaving alert, this person would say, "When I get home from alert, the second thing I am going to do is put my suitcase down." The fourth category, in Jedrziewski's estimation, was the professional crewmember who spent the entire alert tour reading technical orders and quoting some obscure fact he learned about SAC procedures. Finally, Jedrziewski identified the hobbyist, a person who spent the alert tour engaged in hobbies such as model building or gunstock carving. Jedrziewski remembered a fellow crewmember who spent an entire tour aiming the pistol he shot competitively. While only one person's viewpoint, these descriptions demonstrate the varied responses SAC members had when forced to live away from their families. Some used the opportunity to focus more on their jobs, perhaps in the hope of becoming a select crewmember. Others found it an escape. One fact remained: there was no escaping their crewmates. Everything in SAC revolved around the crew. Bombers had crews, tankers had crews, and soon the newest member of SAC's arsenal would have a crew as well.

Alert Expands to New Concepts and Artifacts

The introduction of the ballistic missile triggered a whole new "alert era" in SAC history. The increasing emphasis on alert to preserve a retaliatory force in case of a sudden missile attack by the Soviet Union altered routines and created new artifacts strictly unique to SAC and its culture. As the organization reached its objective of one-third of aircraft on alert, it began testing the new idea of airborne alert. The Eisenhower administration felt the expectations of a surprise strategic attack were unfounded, but General Power testified before Congress that with three hundred missiles, the Soviet Union could eliminate

America's entire nuclear arsenal, bombers, and missiles. In his testimony to Congress, Power stated, "I feel strongly that we must get on with this airborne alert. . . . we must impress Mr. Khrushchev that we have it, and that he cannot strike this country with impunity."[56]

The Eisenhower administration rejected attempts by Congress and Power to seek additional funding for airborne alert, calling Power a "parochial general."[57] But from 1959 to 1961, SAC did receive funding to test the concept. Flying six thousand sorties in those two years, Power argued, demonstrated the feasibility of the concept.[58] Those who flew the missions labeled them "Chrome Dome" because the myth was that flying with a helmet on for twenty-four hours could make crewmembers bald. Those who flew airborne alert considered it essential to national defense. "I don't mind ground alert because I know it's necessary . . . but I like air alert so much better. . . . Instead of sitting around and waiting for something to happen, I do what I know and like best—flying." Another crewmember added, "If General Power could invite that guy Khrushchev to fly a [airborne training mission] . . . the experience would keep him peaceful for a while."

Perhaps more revealing about SAC culture was a crewmember's statement about airborne alert in relation to other services: "Think of the money we could save because we could do away with the Army, the Navy and the rest of the Air Force."[59] Airborne alert provided some SAC crewmembers with the feeling that they were actually engaged in war. They flew toward the Soviet Union, armed with nuclear weapons, and throughout their mission retained the ability to strike that nation on a moment's notice. More importantly, SAC's people saw their mission as "the" way to deter the Soviet Union. The assumptions of SAC's founders had become the espoused beliefs of its members.

Alert produced another striking artifact of SAC culture: the airborne command post. According to Holstrom, General Power grew concerned that SAC had too much centralization in the organization's alert communications system. The "red phone" system—although enclosed in a bunker—was still too vulnerable. One good nuclear strike, Power feared, could knock out SAC's communications and leave the alert force without a commander. In addition to dispersing antennas and transmitters to remote areas, SAC tested and fielded a converted KC-135 (termed "Looking Glass") with a general officer aboard supplied with an extensive communications suite capable of launching and controlling the alert force.[60] Although LeMay had designated deputy commanders (known as SAC X-Ray, Zebra, Victor, Yoke, and Oboe) in other theaters, General Power wanted a deputy commander airborne twenty-four hours a day who could direct SAC's alert force in case of a surprise attack. SAC began testing "Looking Glass" in July 1960. After six months of testing, the airborne command post began actual operations on February 3, 1961.[61] General Wade explained the purpose of the airborne commander:"He has all the war plans . . . he is up there . . . he has radio contact. He has authority when the National Command Authority is no longer there to push the button."[62] "Looking Glass" offered another insight into the evolution of SAC artifacts. This plane was a derivative of a tanker design. Previously, SAC used bomber platforms when creating new platforms—tankers and recon planes—for a specific mission. Because of the versatility of the airframe, tankers served as the derivative platform for creating platforms for a specific mission. The RC-135, an electronic reconnaissance plane, would replace the EB/RB-47. By the end of the 1960s, tankers would outnumber bombers in the organization.[63]

In the 1960s the SAC commander gained the authority to launch the entire alert force as further insurance that America could preserve its retaliatory capability. Fear was one of the factors that led to the implementation of positive control. During a war game, explained Horace Wade, SAC had to deal with a specific scenario. If the ballistic missile early warning system indicated a launch and the president could not be reached or intelligence could not confirm a positive launch of Soviet missiles, how could SAC preserve the alert force given the time constraint of twenty minutes to make a decision?[64] Therefore, the president entrusted the SAC commander with the ability to launch the alert force under "positive control." If launched, crews would proceed along their preplanned mission until reaching a go/no-go point. Crews would only continue their mission and attack the Soviet Union if they confirmed the right code word from the president. In its earliest form, crews would receive a code word that they would compare with a code word enclosed in an envelope aboard the aircraft. If the crews received no code word or the code words did not match, they remained at their control point or returned to base, depending on their preplanned instructions. Aboard the aircraft, it took three crewmembers to open a safe and verify receipt of a valid go code. Much like airborne alert and the airborne command post, SAC tested the concept for months before implementation.

Alert Pay Reconsidered

When General Power and SAC initially pursued alert, one of the ground rules the SAC commander established was that "no reduction in flying or ground safety standards would be permitted."[65] SAC already had its own special promotion system, but the assumption of alert, in General Power's eyes, further differentiated his command from the rest of the Air Force and from the other military services. As early as December 30, 1957, General Power sought special compensation for the alert force, asking the Air Staff to approve alert pay, which would give alert members an additional $10 a day. The Air Staff opposed his request for several reasons: other commands (such as Air Defense Command) were also pulling alert; SAC had less personnel turmoil than other commands and did not need the bonus; and the morale of the SAC force was already high without the extra incentive. Addressing Congress in 1959, Power raised the issue again: "I would like to have alert pay for these crews. It is psychological rather than a matter of getting rich."[66] In the end, it was LeMay, sensing the opposition in Washington to giving SAC any more special benefits, who informed Power that alert pay was a lost cause. "I am convinced that even if [alert pay] were to be revived under a new name," LeMay wrote in April 1960, "it would only receive similar reaction at that level. For this reason, no action will be taken on your request at this time."[67]

Power sought special pay because alert had placed an extreme burden on his aircrews. Although SAC reached its goal of one-third of its bombers on alert in 1960, the Kennedy administration raised the level to 50 percent in 1961.[68] The level of crew manning—approximately 1.6 crews for every bomber—meant that airmen were working in excess of seventy hours a week. By now, crews were pulling one-week alerts and given three and a half days of combat crew rest and recuperation following alert duty, during which they were not scheduled to fly or perform other official duties. This usually left about two and a half weeks in a month for the crews to fly their mandatory three sorties. Given the rigorous schedule, Power did all he could to reduce the aircrew workload by having crews perform ground training on alert. Nevertheless, SAC accepted the fact that its members were putting in long hours and stated that no crewmember could average more than seventy-four hours a week in any four-month period. The typical workweek, including alert, averaged seventy to seventy-two hours.[69] Although under LeMay's tenure the command had provided various clubs for airmen to use in their off-duty time, crewmembers simply stated they did not have the time to enjoy them because of the demands on their time.[70] By the time 50 percent of the force assumed alert, 90 percent of combat-ready crewmembers were married with children, which made off-duty time a precious commodity.[71]

The Language and Look of SAC:
Losing Fighters, Gaining Bombers

Jargon, the specialized language used by those in the same organization, represents a form of organizational culture. It not only identifies members of the organization but also sets them apart from nonmembers.[72] The loss of SAC's fighters in 1957 served as an example of a subculture becoming "SACumsized," a term repeated often by members of the organization with some cynicism to describe what happened when a person completed indoctrination into the SAC mentality.[73] In 1957 SAC had its strategic fighter wings either reassigned to TAC or deactivated. The phaseout of the B-36 and the continued acceptance of all-jet B-52s reduced the need for fighter escorts.[74] Furthermore, the fighters had been "SACumsized." As early as 1952, SAC explored the development of a tactical atomic bomb and the ability to deliver it with fighter aircraft. General LeMay did not mind equipping fighters with nuclear weapons as long as it preserved command relationships already established and kept the force from being controlled by theater commanders.[75] SAC may have given up its fighters, but by the time they left, they were nuclear carriers steeped in SAC culture and would still come under SAC's control in case the organization executed its EWP. Although SAC lost most of its fighter support—the organization still had interceptor squadrons overseas—it gained a new bomber in 1960, the B-58 Hustler.

As in any organization, symbols—the physical icons or objects that represent the organization—have meaning.[76] SAC was a bomber organization. It first embraced the strategic bomber (B-17, B-24, and B-29/50), then the intercontinental strategic bomber (B-36), and finally, the all-jet intercontinental strategic bomber (B-52). The latest bomber to enter SAC's fleet, the B-58 Hustler, represented a significant departure from LeMay's emphasis on intercontinental range. Bombers conducted independent operations, and intercontinental bombers symbolized that freedom. On August 1, 1960, Power accepted SAC's latest medium-range bomber capable of flying twice the speed of sound.[77] While commander of the Air Research and Development Command, Power oversaw the development and production of the B-58. The delta wing design of the B-58 and its speed gave SAC a fast, sleek appearance. Even the name, "Hustler," represented the capability of the aircraft to go fast. According to LeMay's former aide, Gen. Paul Carlton, who commanded a B-58 wing, "LeMay originally opposed procurement of the B-58 because he perceived it to be range limited and not of real value to him in terms of strategic operations."[78] For LeMay, strategic missions required intercontinental bombers but not fast, darting, fighter-looking planes.[79] The limited range of the B-58 would possibly mean keeping overseas bases. LeMay wanted all of SAC's forces under his control—not in some other theater. Power, however, had different ideas. The development by the Soviets of the SA-2 surface-to-air missile had forced all of SAC's bombers to begin low-level training. Under Power's EWP, B-58s would penetrate enemy airspace at low altitude and supersonic speeds to deliver their atomic weapons.[80]

The B-58 may have given SAC a new sleek look, but it proved to be impractical for SAC's operations. First, it consumed too much fuel at a time when tankers were a limited commodity. When going over Goose Bay, Canada, or Iceland, the B-58 usually required two tankers for each aircraft to off-load the fuel required to reach Soviet airspace. Second, the targets assigned to the B-58 were not very deep inside the Soviet Union. Deterrence, in SAC's estimation, meant the ability to penetrate deep inside the Soviet Union. The B-58 simply did not live up to the task. Finally, the "Hustler" cost too much to maintain. Carlton remembered the B-58 exceeding B-52 maintenance costs by two or threefold.[81] General Holstrom also struggled with his command of a B-58 wing. When a B-58 from the 43rd Bomb Wing (from Carswell Air Force Base, Texas) crashed at the Paris air show, General Power—true to his reputation—fired the wing commander immediately. Despite Holstrom's plans for a trip to Mexico with his wife, Power ordered him to take over the wing. Upon arriving, Holstrom discovered significant problems in the maintaining of his B-58s. One of Holstrom's SAC mentors told the new wing commander that the problem was that his maintenance officer was a TAC-trained guy, not yet "SACumsized." He advised Holstrom: "You've got to go down there and fire all those fighter guys. That's the first thing you've got to do." Holstrom also discovered that his wing simply worked too many hours to try to get the B-58 up to SAC standards. On Sundays, Holstrom got into his staff car and drove down the flightline. If he found anyone working, he would run them off.[82] Despite the extra maintenance hours and costs, the B-58 continually lagged other bombers by an average of ten points in terms of the percentage of the fleet that could execute its war mission at any time.[83] The B-58, as an organizational symbol, simply did not have the look, the feel, or the capability to be a true SAC bomber.

Control Begins to Slip:
Promotions, Education, and the U-2

Alert gave SAC greater control over its dominant force structure of tankers and bombers. In 1957, however, there were indications that the control SAC maintained over its various subcultures of reconnaissance and fighter aircraft had started to wane. First, its fighters either were reassigned to TAC or the units were disbanded. Furthermore, SAC found itself continually justifying its spot promotion program. Every time Power gave a spot promotion, another command had to give up one of its slots in that rank because of congressional limitations on the number of officers in each rank. General Martin remembered the continual battles fought to maintain this program: "Where spot promotion had served its purpose early on, it was now becoming a problem in the Air Force. SAC fought the problem with the Air Staff. . . . we went to Washington and took our best talents to try to convince the Air Staff."[84] Another indication of the loss of SAC control came from an unsuspecting source, LeMay himself. His time in Washington opened his eyes to the importance of military education in the development of senior officers. Seeing the importance of having SAC experience on the Air Staff, LeMay decreed that nobody would be taken off the senior service school list without permission.[85] While LeMay had previously fought to keep people in SAC, the former commander realized the importance these schools played in developing future generals. General Russ Dougherty remembered vividly when General Old informed him and David Jones about their acceptance to senior service school. When Jones turned to his friend and asked, "Did we just get fired?" Dougherty replied, "You're damn right we did."[86]

SAC's control over its own personnel policies and fighters was not the only thing slipping; SAC had to give up some of its control over certain aspects of its flying operations. Initial reconnaissance platforms were derived essentially from bomber designs (RB–36 or RB–47). For bombers, SAC selected the crews, planned the missions, maintained the planes, and monitored the planes in flight. Despite its reconnaissance fleet, the command still lacked the ability to see deep inside the Soviet Union to determine the state of the Russian missile program and to find targets for the ballistic missiles that would soon enter operational service. Desperate for intelligence, SAC released balloons equipped with cameras in Norway, England, and Turkey, and retrieved them off the coast of Japan and Alaska using cargo planes equipped with hooks.[87] In 1957 SAC began flying a plane designed specifically for reconnaissance, the U–2. Designed in a highly secret program and funded and managed by the Central Intelligence Agency (CIA), the U–2 became part of SAC's inventory. From the start, General LeMay questioned the relationship. "[The] CIA was able to get money to develop the U–2 . . . but they had no capability of operating the airplane and no knowhow to do it. We had to do this for them," LeMay recalled. "But then they controlled how these things were going to be used. I questioned the concept from the start and fought it right from the start but lost the battle."[88] SAC maintained the system and recommended pilots for the program. Due to the political implications of flying over enemy territory in a spy plane, pilots resigned their commissions and became civilian pilots for the CIA. Furthermore, the CIA dictated the rules for employment and designed the operational mission. In terms of symbols and organizational culture, the U-2 was the first nonbomber derivative reconnaissance plane in SAC's inventory. With that distinction came a loss of SAC's power over every phase of its operations. It was a compromise SAC was willing to make to keep some aspect of command over reconnaissance operations. SAC would soon place an organizational symbol on alert that forced SAC to compromise its core beliefs: the ICBM.

Missiles and SAC: Ambivalent Acceptance

The history of the Air Force and missiles could be described as ambivalent at best. A brief overview of the Air Force and ICBMs shows the difficult issues an organization headed by pilots wrestled with over these "unmanned strategic bombers." Following World War II, LeMay led in recognizing the importance of missiles. Writing to General Spaatz in September 1946, LeMay stated: "The long-range future of the AAF lies in the field of guided missiles. Machines have greater endurance, will stand more severe ambient conditions, will perform more functions accurately, will dive into targets without hesitation. The AAF must go to guided missiles for the initial heavy casualty phase of future wars."[89]

Rather than cooperating with the Navy on missile development, LeMay got the Army Air Forces to define its own rocket and satellite concepts.[90] Despite the initial enthusiasm for developing ballistic missiles, the idea was essentially shelved from 1947 to 1951 because of several factors: scarce funds were put toward bigger bombers and jet aircraft development; the assumption was made of American superiority in aviation; "blue-sky" air officers were preferred for manned bombers; and there was scientific pessimism about overcoming technical problems. Hitting the target from a manned aircraft with a time of fall of sixty seconds proved difficult enough. It was hard to convince pilots that a missile was going to hit its target half a world away while the earth continued to rotate throughout the missile's thirty-minute time of flight. Priorities during the initial stages of the Cold War centered on production of nuclear bombs and the B-36.[91] Although the Air Force downplayed missiles within the organization, it urged missile development at the expense of other services. Some argued that the Air Force resistance to the ICBM became a cultural resistance to unmanned vehicles; only when threats arose from the enemy or a sister service did the Air Force become interested in developing ICBMs.[92]

During the Eisenhower administration, the development of ICBMs became the president's number-one priority. By presidential decree on September 8, 1955, Eisenhower announced that the ICBM would become America's chief focus in terms of its military arsenal.[93] SAC commander LeMay expressed his thoughts on the ICBM: "I consider an ICBM with capability of instantaneous launch and with acceptable reliability, accuracy, and yield to be the ultimate weapon in the strategic inventory."[94] The problem, as LeMay and other SAC generals saw it, was that the ICBM had not demonstrated either reliability or accuracy. Initially, ICBMs were seen as an aid to penetrating bombers and having little capability to actually destroy entire target complexes. The launch of Sputnik provided emergency impetus to the Air Force program for the deployment of ICBMs.[95]

In the months following, Chief of Staff Thomas White announced plans to take the Air Force's missile development program operational. The Air Force would transfer control of Cooke Air Force Base, California, to SAC, and SAC would assume operational responsibility for intermediate range missiles and ICBMs. Although given command of missiles in 1957, it would be two years before SAC would accept the first Atlas missile at Vandenberg Air Force Base, California, because of technical problems, not resistance to missiles themselves. Production delays, propellant contamination, and other maintenance problems forced SAC to accept missiles piecemeal.[96]

SAC commander Power was optimistic about the integration of missiles into SAC and, in an article published in *Air Force Magazine*, explained how he envisioned the integration of SAC and missiles: "SAC must always have, first, an adequate quantity of weapon systems that reflect the latest advances in technology, and, second, a global and centrally controlled organization flexible enough to be readily adaptable to any new weapon system or technique, no matter how revolutionary." Power explained that SAC "will be exceedingly helpful in the integration of missiles which is now in process." He pointed out, however, that "the manned bomber is still the only operational weapon system that can be employed successfully against strategic targets, regardless of their location, size, and character. Even the first operational strategic missiles will still be inferior to the bomber with respect to accuracy, payload, and reliability."[97] Despite Power's optimism, missiles—pilotless strategic bombers—represented a subculture with a different operating mentality than that of the pilots who ran SAC. One editorial mused that missiles, which had their own internal guidance and operating system, could put pilots on the breadline.[98]

Bombers versus Missiles:
Operational and Cultural Comparisons

Bomber pilots dominated SAC culture and would share few commonalities with those who would employ missiles. The integration of missiles into SAC would actually prove more difficult than Power suggested, since the operating characteristics of those who flew bombers and those who "launched" missiles were totally different. The different cultural routines associated with each system created operational and cultural distinctions. Bomber pilots flew long-duration missions in cramped cockpits over enemy territory. These pilots refueled in flight to reach their targets, and they flew over enemy air defenses, risking their lives, to drop bombs on targets. Furthermore, pilots attended survival school, in case they were shot down behind enemy lines, and learned to stay alive on their own until rescued. Missileers did none of those things. They readied their missiles for launch within a matter of minutes and with the push of a button sent the weapon on its way. Once launched, missileers had no control over their weapons system. More importantly, pilots from Power's and LeMay's generation went through pilot training at a time when they had to prove they had the inherent skills required to fly. What were the inherent skills needed to "pilot" a missile? One graduate of missile training explained what it took to become a missileer. Missiles, in his estimation, required more knowledge and technical expertise, which is why everyone in the missile force—that he knew—had a college degree.[99] Pilots used their hands and eyes; missileers were thinkers.

Even the operating characteristics of the two systems—missiles and bombers—stood in contrast. Airplanes at their inception were seen as restoring chivalry to warfare, and that aura of romance lasted even into the era of mass nuclear destruction. Launching a missile would not be a battle; "It would be a colossally murderous engineering operation."[100] One SAC planner stated simply, "There is no way to build guts into a computer."[101] There was no chivalry, no battle, no duel in the air as missiles passed one another en route to their targets. Bombers and their pilots were air breathers; they need oxygen to complete their mission. Unlike bombers, missiles did not need oxygen when they flew, they did not need to be refueled to reach their target, and they did not have to return to base when their mission was complete.[102] Power claimed the speed and range of ballistic missiles were their greatest attributes. These characteristics made them suitable for an organization committed to strategic operations. Given SAC's mission to "conduct strategic air operations on a global basis so that, in the event of sudden aggression, SAC could immediately mount simultaneous nuclear attacks designed to destroy the vital elements of the aggressor's warmaking capability to the extent that he would no longer have the will nor the ability to wage war," Power said that missiles were essential to the global, immediate, and simultaneous aspects of SAC's mission.[103] Although missiles fit into the strategic mission, the organization made sure a pilot oversaw the integration of the very things that threatened to put pilots out of a job.

When the first group of airmen graduated missile training, Maj. Gen. Alfred Kalberer, 15 AF deputy commander, told them, "Today marks the initial step in the integration of missiles and missile airmen into Strategic Air Command."[104] Thomas Power assigned Gen. David Wade, his chief of staff, to oversee SAC's missile program. Newspaper accounts reported that Wade was a "long-time bomber man."[105] As SAC brought in missileers, a pilot, not a missileer, would show them the way things are done in the organization. Establishing "rules of the game," implicit, unwritten rules for getting along in the organization, is an element of organizational culture.[106] General Power wanted the best people to guide missiles to alert status. "We broke a lot of hearts," Gen. Horace Wade recalled. "People who came in the Air Force to fly airplanes and all of a sudden they are now out supervising the people that are going to be sitting in the missile silos and capsules underground." SAC considered giving its rated officers assigned to missile units "accrued" credit that would safeguard their flying status.[107]

Like their bomber counterparts, missileers learned the importance of working around the clock. The need to produce a credible missile force became so important that classes were held around the clock in six-hour segments. Charlie Simpson remembered his excitement at having the early class: "I was in the morning class—0600–1200; the 0000–0600 class had to be a real joy."[108] Missileers, as a group, discovered that combat-ready status in SAC meant a significant amount of training and was not something easily earned. Grant Secrist's combat certification consisted of one hour of emergency procedures testing, four hours for a written examination, several tests regarding positive control procedures, and fourteen to eighteen hours of performance evaluation in the launch complex. His recollection was that close to 50 percent of combat crews failed to pass the evaluation. Like aircrew members, missileers would have standardization and evaluation crews and be subjected to constant ORIs.[109]

Throughout 1958 SAC activated strategic missile wings that existed without really having any missiles assigned. Crews may have been ready, but the missiles were not. On September 1, 1959, General Power accepted the first Atlas missile, a liquid-fueled rocket capable of reaching targets five thousand miles away. Atlas missiles were powered by combining 11,500 gallons of rocket propellant and 18,600 gallons of an oxidizer (liquid oxygen). SAC leadership thought Vandenberg would become a missile training base, but Power said, "No, we are going to put them on alert. We are going to put warheads on them and put them on alert. If anything happens, we are going to fly those missiles."[110] The growing fear of a missile gap made it essential to demonstrate a U.S. missile launch capability. Following a test launch of the Atlas missile, General Power officially put three missiles on alert. This ran counter to the "SAC way," which was to focus on one squadron—get it to combat-ready status—and then move on to the next. In order to maintain a quick-strike capability, the Atlas missile had to be fueled prior to launch since liquid oxygen could not be stored on the missiles. Within eleven minutes, crews could fill the rocket's tanks. Loading liquid oxygen was extremely hazardous; one spark could trigger an explosion.[111] Although Power put a few missiles on alert for diplomatic and political reasons, the advanced technology created doubt in SAC leadership about the missile's reliability and its accuracy.

After a year of operation, Power considered the reliability of the entire missile program to be zero. In the last sixteen test launches from Vandenberg, only three missiles had actually reached the target. The majority of missiles aborted, failed on liftoff, or fell short of the target.[112] The problems with the missile program did not escape David Jones, then serving in the manned systems branch in the Pentagon. Jones reviewed the operational reports from Vandenberg and put a briefing together for LeMay that showed how problems could have prevented every operational launch. Following the presentation to LeMay, Jones flew out—under LeMay's orders—to brief the SAC commander. Jones, accompanied by his friend Russ Dougherty, went in to brief Power in a large conference room at SAC headquarters. As was Power's style, he tried to destroy the credibility of the briefer before Jones even spoke. "Now before the briefing, I would like to establish the credentials of the briefer. Colonel Jones, how many times have you been out to a missile site?" Jones continued with his briefing, refusing to be intimidated. After the brief, Power approached Jones and said, "Now, I hope you didn't take that personally." More importantly, Power traveled to Washington, D.C., three days later to demand $180 million to improve the reliability of the missiles.[113]

When LeMay and Power took over SAC in 1948, the chief challenge was training and procedures. SAC faced a new and different problem with missiles. It was not the crews causing zero reliability, but the technology itself. When several SAC leaders, including Horace Wade, went out to observe a missile test launch, "We watched it burn up on the pad. It ignited—never lifted off—burned up right there on the pad." SAC prided itself on on-time takeoffs and hitting the target as scheduled. Missiles were not making scheduled "takeoffs"; they were blowing up on the ramp. When a bomber missed its target, there was someone to hold accountable. Who did commanders hold accountable when a missile missed its target? This period caused a lot of angst in SAC's leadership. General Wade describe this period as "hard days for SAC. . . . [It] divided the force between the bomber force and the missile force and not knowing any more about missiles than we knew and placing as much reliance on it as evidently we were going to place in the future on a weapons system we couldn't fly—we couldn't test—we didn't know what the reliability was. . . .

[Missiles] just didn't make a lot of sense to a lot of people in SAC."[114] Missiles had the potential to greatly expand SAC's offensive capability, with their ability to reach the target in thirty minutes. SAC's leader, however, noted that missiles still lacked the "accuracy and reliability of the tried-and-proven manned bomber."[115]

Missiles slowly became a part of SAC's operations, but the manned bomber remained the dominant weapons system. Missiles lacked the characteristics, in SAC's eyes, that made the manned bomber the optimum SAC weapon. Bombers were flexible and unpredictable; they could be recalled in flight, and unlike missiles, the enemy could not predict their flight path. Finally, SAC's commander believed that "there will always be need for man over enemy territory because no missile computer can match the reason power of the human mind. It is that uncanny capacity which is needed to deal with unpredictable situations and to make decisions on the spot."[116]

As SAC missileers began to sit alert, the distinction between bomber and missile routines and rituals became more obvious. Bombers pulled alert just like missile crews, but bomber crews still had to fly three sorties a month when off alert. Missile crews did not "fly" anything when off alert. A study found that missile crews spent 5 percent of their time on required tasks when not on alert. This stood in stark contrast to the 76 percent of the time bomber crews spent on nonalert duty requirements.[117] When bomber crews sat alert, they were required to practice alert exercises that challenged their ability to respond to their jets, start engines, and be ready to take off within minutes. Missile crews practiced "refueling exercises." Another disparity between the two groups was how SAC evaluated their ability to execute its war plan. Bomber crews were subject to "no-notice" inspections. In the initial days of missile integration, Power felt that missile crews were not sufficiently familiar with these new weapons; therefore, SAC subjected missile crews to "shakedowns," where crews had to complete two successful loadings of missiles with their liquid fuel combination.[118]

Missiles eventually increased in reliability, accuracy, and ability to respond rapidly. The Titan, which came into the inventory after the Atlas, could be placed in missile silos for its refueling procedure. The next-generation missile, the Minuteman (1962), had solid-fuel propellant, which eliminated the need for the dangerous and time-consuming fueling procedures. In 1961, as more missiles went on alert, SAC renamed strategic missile wings after well-known bombardment units from World War II. According to Power, "This meets several objectives: helps maintain traditions which are limited in the Air Force as compared to other service, builds esprit de corps by identifying personnel with a battle-proven organization, and shows continuity in mission even though the methods of achieving this mission have changed."[119] Culturally, missiles were now part of an organization steeped in flying. Although missileers only turned a key to launch their bombs, they became a part of the strategic bombing tradition that was Strategic Air Command.

In 1961 SAC created another cultural routine indicative of the organization—the Single Integrated Operations Plan (SIOP). By 1960 the Navy had developed the ability to launch missiles from its submarines. Despite this capability, SAC wanted control over all planning for offensive operations against the Soviet Union. General Power argued that this was the only "way we make sure that the offensive forces will operate within a common war plan and use each weapon as a complement instead of in competition."[120] On August 16, 1960, Secretary of Defense Thomas Gates announced the creation of the Joint Strategic Target Planning Staff directed by the SAC commander. Rear Admiral Edward Parker would serve as deputy of the staff because Navy ballistic missile submarines were becoming part of the strategic force under the SIOP. SIOP 62 was the first war plan that integrated all nuclear offensive capabilities, including submarine-launched ballistic missiles and tactical fighters carrying nuclear bombs stationed in Europe.[121] One year later, Cold War tensions would force SAC to begin implementation of its plan.

Conclusion

From 1957 to 1962, SAC grew and evolved in response to the Cold War. The threat of nuclear bombardment by intercontinental ballistic missiles added an element of fear to SAC: fear of a surprise attack that could wipe out the U.S. ability to respond to any aggression. Alert duty became a new ritual for SAC's crewmembers and eventually its missile force. With alert came other cultural rituals: alert responses, MITOs, "reflex" operations, and positive control launches. At the same time, SAC culture took on new symbols that showed the organization was entering the missile age: the alert facility, the Christmas tree (alert parking ramp), the airborne command post, and the missile itself. An organization that prided itself on showing its distinctiveness now found itself driven underground by the threat of nuclear bombardment. By the end of the decade, SAC had gained a new bomber, the B-58, and a new reconnaissance plane, the U-2. The B-58 brought a sleek, faster image, but gave the organization that demanded reliability more problems than the plane was worth. Between the B-58 and the missile, the organization learned that faster was not always better.

Reliability, readiness, responsiveness: these were the elements SAC looked for in its alert force. Missiles were struggling to show they had any of these characteristics. Bomber pilots refueled in the air and flew over the target to deliver their nuclear payloads. Missiles were launched by their "operators" from a control center with the push of a button. Since missileers represented a new subculture, the organization assigned a pilot to lead their integration. SAC pilots also served on missile crews to show the newest members the "SAC way." This new group would be "SACumsized." Because of its operating characteristics and proven track record, manned bombers would always remain a fixture of SAC culture for two reasons. First, manned bombers were bullets that could literally be stopped in flight due to positive control. Missiles—once fired—could not be recalled. Second, deterrence required the projection of power. As Power put it, "Bombers on airborne alert or on special missions represent a clearly visible expression of national intent and demonstrate this country's determination and capability to protect its interests and those of his allies." Missiles in underground silos do not impress the citizens of distant countries, Power felt, "but the huge bombers patrolling the skies above or nearby can provide unmistakable warning to our foes."[122] SAC would have an opportunity to test Power's thesis in October 1962.

Epilogue and Conclusion

Deterrence of aggression is composed of three basic elements—forces in being, public understanding of this force, and national determination to use the force if necessary. These are three elements that make our force credible to our friends and to our enemies. If any of them is missing, credibility suffers proportionately.

—CURTIS LeMAY

Epilogue: The Week SAC Went to War

On October 12, 1962, SAC commander Thomas Power, returning from an overseas inspection of his bases, met with the secretary of the Air Force, Eugene Zuckert, and Curtis LeMay, who had become the Air Force chief of staff on July 1, 1961. The meeting was not about the status of forces overseas but an island right off the coast of the United States, Cuba. During the meeting, Zuckert and LeMay directed Power to implement Brass Knob, an operations plan for U-2 flights over Cuba, as soon as possible. The next day, 2 AF sent the execution message for SAC's R-47K (a B-47 derivative) to begin weather reconnaissance flights around the island. Two days after the implementation of Brass Knob, Maj. Richard S. Heyser took off from Edwards Air Force Base, California, at midnight so that by daybreak on the East Coast, his U-2 was in a position to fly the first high-altitude sortie over the island. Upon landing at McCoy Air Force Base, Florida, intelligence analysts examined the photos taken by the spy plane. Heyser's photos, in addition to photos from two more U-2 flights the following day, confirmed the presence of Soviet nuclear missiles in Cuba.[1]

In accordance with the current DEFCON and under JCS direction, SAC began carrying out certain aspects of its dispersal plan on October 19, 1962. Nonalert aircraft at Homestead, MacDill, and McCoy Air Force Bases in Florida were loaded with the nuclear weapons in ferry configuration (unarmed) and flown to military and civilian airfields away from Cuba. The following day, October 20, Power directed that missile units would immediately place on alert all missiles currently being accepted from the contractor. The missiles would bypass the operational testing phase they usually went through before assuming alert.[2]

First Lieutenant William Stocker, a missile maintenance officer at Mountain Home Air Force Base, Idaho, got a call from his supervisor to report to the command post for a secret message. Stocker's supervisor was in the middle of a dinner party and asked Stocker if he would read the message. The young lieutenant grew excited at the prospect of reading a classified message. Upon arriving at the command post, Stocker recognized a serious tension in the air. His suspicions were confirmed when he read the message that said, "Put sorties C-02 and A-01 on Alert ASAP . . . War time safety rules apply." The person working command post duty that night verified the accuracy of the message and informed Stocker that the wing's three B-47 squadrons were being loaded with nuclear weapons. Upon receipt of the message, the missile squadron implemented a recall and started procedures to get the missiles ready. "It was scary," Stocker remembered.[3]

As a sign of the intensity of the operation before them, SAC cancelled all scheduled operational readiness inspections. SAC was not going to test a unit's war plans since some of its organizations were already executing portions of them. All leave except emergency leave was cancelled as well. Another indication of the seriousness of the situation was that SAC ordered all missiles be brought to a readiness configuration and authorized field units to bypass normal procedures and regulations to accomplish the task. Each missile had two crews assigned to maintain a constant alert status. For John Nailen, a missile crewmember at Walker Air Force Base, New Mexico, the most memorable experience was the fact that his unit took missiles directly from contractors to alert status in a matter of days.[4] By October 22, SAC had dispersed seven B-52 and twenty-six B-47 nonalert bombers from Florida. Security around all SAC bases increased to the highest levels, but SAC suspended all sabotage operations, indicating the gravity of the moment.[5]

On October 22, President Kennedy addressed the nation about the missiles in Cuba, saying, "We will not prematurely or unnecessarily risk the costs of worldwide nuclear war in which even the fruits of victory would be ashes in our mouth—but neither will we shrink from that risk at any time it must be faced."[6] Charlie Simpson, a missile maintenance officer at Mountain Home Air Force Base, remembered when the nation went to DEFCON 3 that day. "Almost all our bombers and tankers left," Simpson recalled. "We missileers were left alone and on alert."[7] That same day Power implemented the "one-eighth airborne alert" plan and over the next twenty-four hours would continually launch enough B-52s to keep sixty-six airborne. SAC's own KC-135 tankers kept the air armada aloft. For tanker pilot Tom Cantarano, it felt like he was refueling a B-52 every five minutes to keep the nuclear-armed planes in the air.[8] By the end of the following day, all the required bombers, 183 B-47s, had arrived at their dispersal locations. Not every phase of the operation went flawlessly; one B-47 crew remembered they did not have the required government credit card on the aircraft to purchase fuel at their civilian dispersal airfield. Therefore, the aircraft commander had to use his own credit card to fuel the jet to place it on nuclear alert.[9]

When the United States imposed a quarantine around Cuba, the DEFCON level was raised to 2—one level below war. Charlie Simpson remembered the words Power spoke that day across the SAC alert system: "This is General Power speaking. I am addressing you for the purpose of reemphasizing the seriousness of the situation the nation faces. We are in an advanced state of readiness to meet any emergencies, and I feel that we are well prepared. I expect each of you to maintain strict security and use calm judgment during this tense period." The SAC commander went on to say, "Our plans are well prepared and are being executed smoothly. Review your plans for further action to insure [sic] that there will be no mistakes or confusion. I expect you to cut out all nonessentials and put yourself in a maximum readiness condition. If you are not sure what you should do in any situation, and if time permits, get in touch with us here." Simpson thought, "We are very close to nuclear war." For the next four days, not knowing how long the crisis would last, missile crews sat ready to load liquid oxygen on their missiles and launch within fifteen minutes.[10] SAC would have 1,436 bombers ready to launch and 183 ICBMs ready to fly within fifteen minutes; 90 percent of the Western world's firepower, more than two thousand nuclear weapons containing seven thousand megatons of explosive power, were under Power's control.[11] SAC had achieved centralized control of a majority of the nation's strategic air operations.

The tension continued to mount. When a B-47 crashed on October 27 and a U-2 was shot down the same day over Cuba, Simpson remembered thinking that "war seemed unavoidable."[12] The next day there was a break in the standoff as the United States and the Soviet Union reached a diplomatic understanding. SAC, however, continued to operate in its war mode until November 21, when SAC forces reverted to DEFCON 4, which meant that 50 percent of SAC's bombers were sitting alert instead of the entire force.[13] While the rest of the Air Force reverted to DEFCON 5, SAC, due to its alert posture, continued at DEFCON 4. This was the normal SAC status, one level closer to war than the rest of the Air Force or the other military services. Throughout the crisis, SAC's airborne alert aircraft flew 2,088 missions, logged 47,000 flying hours, traveled 20 million miles, and conducted 4,076 air refuelings without a single accident.[14] SAC personnel had demonstrated what close to fifteen years of a "we are at war" mentality and culture had produced.

Addressing the American Ordnance Association on December 5, 1962, LeMay reflected on the Cuban Missile Crisis: "Our umbrella of strategic power represented 'deterrence in action' and was, in the final analysis, what made President Kennedy confident that his decision to quarantine Cuba would not leave us with the 'ashes in our mouth.' It seems to me . . . Cuba proved that, short of guaranteed disarmament, there is no substitute for superior strength at the strategic level." More telling was what LeMay said were his lessons from the crisis: "The first lesson is the need for swift action. When and if forces are called to act, they must be able to do so instantly. We must stay prepared to handle emergencies half way around the world with speed and decision. Another lesson is that military airpower must be designed and operated by people who have spent their lives operating airplanes and who are dedicated professionals."[15] LeMay's last lesson was more of a real-ization that the Kennedy administration was not going to make the investment in strategic airpower and in SAC that had occurred for the last fifteen years.

Two statistics from the 1960s revealed that SAC was about to lose its primacy in the military establishment. First, SAC had 282,723 people in the organization in 1962, the highest number ever in its history. Within six years, the organization would lose 120,000 people. Additionally, in 1962 SAC would accept the last of its B-52s and B-58s. This was the first year since 1946 that SAC did not have a bomber in production.[16] The Kennedy administration, with Robert McNamara as secretary of defense, had cancelled the program for the B-70, LeMay's dream design for a supersonic intercontinental bomber. National security was moving away from strategic airpower. For Paul Carlton, LeMay's former aide, the Cuban Missile Crisis demonstrated SAC's overwhelming supremacy. In the summer of 1962 Carlton was finishing his year at the National War College and knew, even before the Cuban Missile Crisis, that a new direction in military strategy was coming. He remembered his instructors being told as he left the school, "You have got to start a class in contingency warfare, guerrilla forces, [and] anti-guerrilla forces." Carlton said he knew right away what that new direction would mean for SAC: "That meant the end of the strategic day and all the money going to SAC. You are going to have a guerrilla campaign. We have got to build up the Army; we have got to build up the tactical air forces of the Air Force." The tran-sition away from SAC, Carlton felt, came from his recollection of what President Kennedy said: "There has got to be a better way than to contain communism with a direct confrontation nuclear bombwise." For Carlton, "Maxwell Taylor [Military Representative to the Presi-dent (1961) and Chairman of the Joint Chiefs of Staff (1962)] came through with his *Uncertain Trumpet* and guerrilla warfare is the way to go. . . . Instead of fighting in Cuba, we fought in Vietnam."[17]

The new policy was flexible response. The concept, according to political scientist Lawrence Freedman, was "based upon a flexible and balanced range of appropriate response, conventional and nuclear, to all levels of aggression or threats of aggression. These responses, subject to appropriate political control, are designed, first to deter aggression and thus preserve peace."[18] Massive retaliation was no longer the U.S. response, which meant that the investment in SAC would never be as great. On April 21, 1964, SAC had as many missiles sitting alert as it did bombers. From that day forward, the number of missiles on alert would continue to increase as the number of bombers decreased. Power retired from the Air Force in 1964 after seven years as SAC commander. LeMay had commanded SAC for nine years; no other SAC leader would come close to the longevity of either one.[19] In 1965, LeMay retired and, almost ironically, spot promotions in SAC ended the same year. SAC's prestige would wane over the coming decades as fighter pilots flying missions in Vietnam gained more combat experience and better positioned themselves for leadership than SAC pilots sitting nuclear alert. SAC bombers would conduct bombing missions in Vietnam, but SAC continued to pull alert throughout the conflict. As if in a reversal of fortune, SAC pilots would become qualified as fighter pilots to serve tours in Vietnam to help meet the need for more pilots.

In 1982 Charles Gabriel became the chief of staff of the Air Force; he was the first general with no bomber experience in his background to lead the organization. In 1991 President George H. W. Bush, signaling an end to the Cold War, took all SAC planes off alert. Within a year, SAC as a separate organization ceased to exist. The missiles became part of the newly formed United States Strategic Command, and SAC's bombers joined Tactical Air Command. SAC had existed for close to five decades, during which the organization developed its unique and distinctive culture—the SAC mentality.

SAC's organizational culture began with the assumptions of Air Force leaders who believed that strategic airpower should be organized under one military commander, not subordinate to a theater commander. This provided the initial values and doctrine for the organization. The shared historical experiences of those who fought in World War II added the tactics and cultural rituals that became part of SAC culture. As SAC organized, trained, and, in the minds of its people, fought the Cold War, other organizational routines, rituals, symbols, and language evolved. Because of his long tenure with the organization, Curtis LeMay became synonymous with SAC. Perhaps no better story captures the impact of LeMay and SAC than one told by someone who served and led the organization himself.

Gen. Russell Dougherty served in SAC and commanded it from 1974 to 1977. When Dougherty took command of SAC, he recalled LeMay's words to him when Dougherty was in the organization: "Everything we must do must be real, consequential, and meaningful, and it must be recognizable as such by the Soviet Union. No bluff, no smoke and mirrors, just raw and recognizable capability to exact unacceptable punishment, and with the unquestioned ability of our force to employ effectively under all circumstances."[20] For Dougherty, the Cold War was a different type of war: "The *kick the tires and light the fires, damn the torpedoes, and follow me* élan of the World War II period gave way over the Cold War years to more sober and thoughtful acts of major commanders whose arsenals allowed no mistakes, because mistakes, once made, could cause a global catastrophe."[21] When Dougherty assumed command of SAC, LeMay attended the ceremony and warned the new SAC commander that "his nuclear responsibilities to this nation were such that I could not afford to fail, that I could never do anything wrong myself, nor condone mistakes on the part of others, that affected the mission of my command." LeMay ended his advice with this comment: "Don't you be remembered in history for a single mistake." SAC culture emphasized standardized procedures, perfection in detail, and most of all physical presence, because this was the type of war the nation was fighting. "Every single procedure and requirement for employing those weapons," Dougherty recalled, "had to be seen to be believable, robust, and reliable."[22] For laying that foundation in SAC, Dougherty said he would argue that "there were no truly heroic military commanders of the Cold War period. Only Gen. Curtis LeMay comes up on my screen as a Cold War commander of truly unusual stature.... He championed military actions that made military deterrence work over the Cold War years.... I think he was exactly right when he cautioned me, as I assumed command of SAC: 'Russ, make sure that you are not remembered in history.'"[23]

Many do remember SAC and LeMay, especially those who were members of the organization. So strong was the culture that members continue to meet periodically to recall their experiences and tell stories of what SAC life was like. Other military organizations have reunions, but the interesting aspect of SAC reunions is the memory

of those who gather. At a reunion for the association of the B-47—a
plane that never dropped a bomb in the Cold War yet sat alert from its
inception—a member rose to give a historical briefing on some aspect
of his experience in the B-47. Before he spoke, he simply shouted,
"We kicked their butt," and was greeted by the cheers of the audience.[24] Even the missileers, the stepchild subculture of SAC, have positive memories. Printed across the complimentary briefcase handed
out at the Association of Air Force Missileers reunion is the association's motto, "Victors in the Cold War."[25] For many, SAC culture
embodied the central purpose of a military organization: victory in
peace through strength.

Notes

Introduction

1. Dino A. Brugioni, *Eyeball to Eyeball: The Inside Story of the Cuban Missile Crisis,* ed. Robert F. McCort, 1st ed. (New York: Random House, 1991), 364.
2. Office of SAC History, *Chronology of SAC Participation in the Cuban Crisis* (Offutt Air Force Base, Neb.: Strategic Air Command, 1972), 7.
3. Scott Douglas Sagan, *The Limits of Safety: Organizations, Accidents, and Nuclear Weapons* (Princeton, N.J.: Princeton University Press, 1993), 62.
4. Ibid., 62–63.
5. Curtis E. LeMay, "Deterrence in Action," *Ordnance* (March–April 1963): 527.
6. R. Michael Worden, *Rise of the Fighter Generals: The Problem of Air Force Leadership, 1945–1982* (Maxwell Air Force Base, Ala.: Air University Press, 1998), 103–4.
7. The United States and the Soviet Union never directly confronted each other. Instead, these two superpowers opposed each other through "proxy" nations in Asia (Korea, Vietnam, Afghanistan) and South America (El Salvador, Nicaragua, Guatemala).
8. For an explanation of how tactical fighter leadership replaced bomber leadership in the Air Force, see Worden, *Rise of the Fighter Generals.*
9. Howard Aldrich and Martin Ruef, *Organizations Evolving*, 2nd ed. (Thousand Oaks, Calif.: Sage Publications, 2006), 6–7.

10. Ibid., 16–20.
11. Harrison Miller Trice and Janice M. Beyer, *The Cultures of Work Organizations* (Englewood Cliffs, N.J.: Prentice Hall, 1993), 2–11.
12. Ibid., 2.
13. Joanne Martin, *Cultures in Organizations: Three Perspectives* (New York: Oxford University Press, 1992), 55–59.
14. Edgar H. Schein, *Organizational Culture and Leadership*, 3rd ed. (San Francisco: Jossey-Bass, 2004), 25–30; Joanne Martin, *Organizational Culture: Mapping the Terrain* (Thousand Oaks, Calif.: Sage Publications, 2002), 65.
15. Trice and Beyer, *The Cultures of Work Organizations*, 77.
16. Ibid., 79–80.
17. Martin, *Organizational Culture*, 3–4.
18. Ibid., 94–99.
19. Schein, *Organizational Culture and Leadership*, 2.
20. Ibid., 17.
21. Ibid., 11.
22. Kurt Lang, *Military Institutions and the Sociology of War* (Beverly Hills, Calif.: Sage Publications, 1972), 10.
23. Ibid., 58.
24. Samuel P. Huntington, *The Soldier and the State: The Theory and Politics of Civil-Military Relations* (Cambridge, Mass.: Belknap Press of Harvard University Press, 1957).
25. Morris Janowitz, *The Professional Soldier: A Social and Political Portrait* (New York: Free Press, 1960), 38.
26. Morris Janowitz and Roger William Little, *Sociology and the Military Establishment*, 3rd ed. (Beverly Hills, Calif.: Sage Publications, 1974), 34.
27. Janowitz, *The Professional Soldier*, viii.
28. Ibid., 4.
29. Janowitz and Little, *Sociology and the Military Establishment*, 98–100.
30. Janowitz, *The Professional Soldier*, xiii.
31. Ibid., xiii–xiv.
32. Sagan, *The Limits of Safety*, 14–27.
33. Allan D. English, *Understanding Military Culture: A Canadian Perspective* (Montreal: McGill-Queen's University Press, 2004), 5.

34. Isabel V. Hull, *Absolute Destruction: Military Culture and the Practices of War in Imperial Germany* (Ithaca, N.Y.: Cornell University Press, 2005), 329.

35. English, *Understanding Military Culture,* 10.

36. Hull, *Absolute Destruction,* 333.

37. Carl H. Builder, *The Masks of War: American Military Styles in Strategy and Analysis* (Baltimore: Johns Hopkins University Press, 1989), 3–5.

38. Ibid., 19.

39. Ibid., 21.

40. George R. Mastroianni, "Occupations, Cultures, and Leadership in the Army and Air Force," *Parameters* (Winter 2005–06): 82–83.

41. Ibid., 80.

42. Builder, *The Masks of War,* 26.

43. Mastroianni, "Occupations, Cultures, and Leadership in the Army and Air Force," 78–79.

44. Builder, *The Masks of War,* 27.

45. Borowski made the argument that SAC was a "hollow threat" in its initial years (1946–50); see Harry R. Borowski, *A Hollow Threat: Strategic Air Power and Containment before Korea* (Westport, Conn.: Greenwood Press, 1982).

Chapter 1. "A Different Breed of Cat"

Epigraph. William Mitchell, *Winged Defense: The Development and Possibilities of Modern Air Power—Economic and Military* (New York: G. P. Putnam's Sons, 1925), 19.

1. Schein, *Organizational Culture and Leadership,* 278–89.

2. Steven L. McShane and Mary Ann Von Glinow, *Organizational Behavior,* 3rd. ed. (New York: McGraw-Hill, 2005), 478.

3. For a discussion of the early days of flying and the Wright brothers' attempt to sell planes to the Air Force, see Alfred F. Hurley and William C. Heimdahl, "The Roots of U.S. Military Aviation," in *Winged Shield, Winged Sword: A History of the United States Air Force,* vol. I, ed. Bernard Nalty (Washington, D.C.: Air Force History and Museums Program, 1997).

4. I. B. Holley, *Ideas and Weapons* (Washington, D.C.: Air Force History and Museums Program, 1997), 26–28.

5. James P. Tate, *The Army and Its Air Corps: Army Policy toward Aviation, 1919–1941* (Maxwell Air Force Base, Ala.: Air University Press, 1998), 1. For a complete work of Spaatz's life, see David R. Mets, *Master of Airpower: General Carl A. Spaatz* (New York: Presidio Press, 1997). An official biography of Air Force general officers (past or present) is available at http://www.af.mil.bois. Biographical information on Air Force generals contained in this work came from published works, oral interviews, or the above listed web site.

6. Joseph J. Corn, *The Winged Gospel: America's Romance with Aviation, 1900–1950* (New York: Oxford University Press, 1983), 8.

7. See Henry H. Arnold, *Global Mission* (New York: Harper & Brothers, 1949).

8. Hurly and Heimdahl, "The Roots of U.S. Military Aviation," in Nalty, *Winged Shield, Winged Sword*, 26–27.

9. Tate, *The Army and Its Air Corps,* 22.

10. James J. Cooke, *Billy Mitchell* (Boulder, Colo.: Lynne Rienner, 2002), 50–53.

11. Tate, *The Army and Its Air Corps,* 22.

12. Ibid.

13. Gen. Hunter Harris, USAF, interview by Hugh N. Ahmann, November 1974 and March 1979, Air Force Historical Research Agency (AFHRA) K239.0512–811.

14. Gen. Horace M. Wade, USAF, interview by Hugh N. Ahmann, October 1978, AFHRA K239.0512–1105.

15. Lt. Gen. Earl W. Barnes, USAF, interview by Hugh N. Ahmann, January 1975, AFHRA K239.0512–828.

16. Harris interview.

17. Curtis E. LeMay and MacKinlay Kantor, *Mission with LeMay: My Story* (Garden City, N.Y.: Doubleday, 1965), 21–23.

18. Ibid., 42–44.

19. Wade interview.

20. Barnes interview.

21. LeMay and Kantor, *Mission with LeMay,* 58–59.

22. Gen. Jacob E. Smart, USAF, interview by Arthur W. McCants and James C. Hansdorff, November 1978, AFHRA K239.0512–1108.

23. Harris interview.

24. Ibid.

25. Maj. Gen. John B. Montgomery, USAF, interview by Mark C. Cleary, May 1984, AFHRA K239.0512–1586.

26. The school began as the Air Service Field Officers School (1920), became the Air Service Tactical School (1922), and evolved into the Air Corps Tactical School (1926) with the establishment of the Air Corps.

27. William C. Sherman, *Air Warfare* (Maxwell Air Force Base, Ala.: Air University Press, 1926; reprint, 2002), 11–12.

28. William "Billy" Mitchell made the medieval knight comparison in his 1925 work *Winged Defense*. Sherman had drafted his work in the early 1920s, before Mitchell, but he was not as vocal an advocate as Mitchell for the advantages in airpower.

29. A majority of pilots were officers; however, some enlisted personnel earned their wings as well. The story of enlisted pilots is told in Lee Arbon, *They Also Flew: The Enlisted Pilot Legacy, 1912–1942* (Washington, D.C.: Smithsonian Institution Press, 1998).

30. Corn, *The Winged Gospel,* 11.

31. Gen. Haywood S. Hansell, USAF, interview by Edgar F. Puryear, February 1979, AFHRA K239.0512–1433.

32. Lt. Gen. James V. Edmundson, USAF, interview with Edgar F. Puryear, July 1978, AFHRA K239.0512–1411.

33. Gen. Russell E. Dougherty, USAF, interview with Edgar F. Puryear, March 1979, AFHRA K239.0512–1407.

34. Corn, *The Winged Gospel,* 12.

35. Alfred Thayer Mahan, *The Influence of Sea Power Upon History, 1660–1805* (New York: Dover Publications, 1894; reprint, 1987), 50–58.

36. Richard H. Kohn and Joseph H. Harahan, eds., *Strategic Air Warfare: An Interview with Generals Curtis E. LeMay, Leon W. Johnson, David A. Burchinal, and Jack J. Catton* (Washington, D.C.: U.S. Government Printing Office, 1988), 21.

37. Corn, *The Winged Gospel,* 10.

38. DeWitt S. Copp, *A Few Great Captains: The Men and Events That Shaped the Development of U.S. Air Power* (McLean, Va.: EPM Publications, 1989), 6, 82–85.

39. Gen. Emmett "Rosie" O'Donnell, USAF, interview by Edgar F. Puryear, December 1967, AFHRA K239.052–1476.

40. Wade interview.

41. Montgomery interview.

42. Gen. Curtis LeMay, USAF, interview by Edgar F. Puryear, November 1976, AFHRA K239.0512–1450.

43. LeMay and Kantor, *Mission with LeMay,* 113–16.

44. LeMay earned his reputation as a navigator on several high-profile missions demonstrating the B-17's ability to find ships at sea. He served as the lead navigator in finding the Navy's *Utah* off the Pacific Coast and the Italian liner *Rex* off the Atlantic Coast; see Copp, *A Few Great Captains,* 394–98, 419–23.

45. LeMay interview by Puryear.

46. Holley, *Ideas and Weapons,* 14.

47. For a complete discussion of airpower in World War I, see Lee B. Kennett, *The First Air War, 1914–1918* (New York: Free Press, 1999).

48. G. Sensever and L. Baillif, *Le Combat Aerien* (Paris, 1914), as quoted in ibid., 63.

49. Mark A. Clodfelter, "Molding Airpower Convictions: Development and Legacy of William Mitchell's Strategic Thought," in *The Paths of Heaven: The Evolution of Air Power Theory,* ed. Phillip S. Meilinger (Maxwell Air Force Base, Ala.: Air University Press, 2001), 83.

50. Robert F. Futrell, *Ideas, Concepts, Doctrine: 1907–1960,* 4th ed. (Washington, D.C.: U.S. Government Printing Office, 2002), 21–23.

51. Cooke, *Billy Mitchell,* 88–95; Futrell, *Ideas, Concepts, Doctrine,* 27.

52. Hurley and Heimdahl, "The Roots of U.S. Military Aviation," 27.

53. Phillip S. Meilinger, "Giulio Douhet and the Origins of Airpower Theory," in Meilinger, *The Paths of Heaven,* 4–7.

54. Giulio Douhet, *The Command of the Air,* trans. Dino Ferrari (Washington, D.C.: Air Force History and Museums Program, reprint, 1998), 7–10. *Command of the Air* first appeared in Italian in 1921; English translations began to appear in 1930.

55. Ibid., 3–15.

56. Ibid., 51.

57. Ibid., 24–25.

58. Ibid., 19.

59. Ibid., 32.

60. During World War I, Mitchell wore a nonregulation uniform and sped through France in a Mercedes, the fastest car in the country; see Tate, *The Army and Its Air Corps,* 4. For his views on air command, see Mitchell, *Winged Defense,* 113–14.

61. Carl H. Builder, *The Icarus Syndrome: The Role of Air Power Theory in the Evolution and Fate of the U.S. Air Force* (New Brunswick, N.J.: Transaction Publishers, 1994), 31.

62. Futrell, *Ideas, Concepts, Doctrine,* 30–36.

63. Mitchell, *Winged Defense,* 4.

64. Ibid., 67–76.

65. William Mitchell, *Skyways: A Book on Modern Aeronautics* (Philadelphia: J. B. Lippincott Co., 1930), 253.

66. Johnny R. Jones, *William "Billy" Mitchell's Air Power* (Maxwell Air Force Base, Ala.: Airpower Research Institute, 1997), 6–9, 60.

67. Clodfelter, "Molding Airpower Convictions," 95–97.

68. Futrell, *Ideas, Concepts, Doctrine,* 46.

69. "Col Mitchell's Statements on Government Aviation," *Aviation,* no. 11 (September 14, 1925), 318.

70. Cooke, *Billy Mitchell,* 178–84.

71. Ibid., 187–217.

72. Following World War II, when the Air Force became an independent service, the Air Force established the Air University at its current home at Maxwell Air Force Base, Alabama.

73. Peter R. Faber, "Interwar U.S. Army Aviation and the Air Corps Tactical School: Incubators of American Airpower," in Meilinger, *The Paths of Heaven,* 211–13.

74. Sherman, *Air Warfare,* 97, 178–79.

75. Robert T. Finney, *History of the Air Corps Tactical School, 1920–1940* (Maxwell Air Force Base, Ala.: Air University Press, 1992), 55–73.

76. Barnes interview.

77. Kohn and Harahan, *Strategic Air Warfare,* 29.

78. Lt. Gen. George W. Mundy, USAF, interview by Mark C. Cleary, September 1984, AFHRA K239.0512–1610.

79. Tami Davis Biddle, *Rhetoric and Reality in Air Warfare: The Evolution of British and American Ideas About Strategic Bombing, 1914–1945* (Princeton, N.J.: Princeton University Press, 2002), 206–7.

80. Ibid., 206–8.

81. Hansell interview.

82. Biddle, *Rhetoric and Reality,* 160–75. Biddle's book offers the best research to date on the differences between the English and American approaches to strategic bombing in World War II.

83. Corn, *The Winged Gospel,* 11.

Chapter 2. Shared Experiences

Epigraph. Gen. Curtis LeMay, USAF, interview by Max Rosenberg, January 1965, AFHRA K239.0512–714.

1. Trice and Beyer argue that "organizations . . . tend to produce and preserve shared responses and shared experiences of uncertainty and chaos"; see Trice and Beyer, *The Cultures of Work Organizations,* 4.

2. Kohn and Harahan, *Strategic Air Warfare,* 26.

3. LeMay and Kantor, *Mission with LeMay,* 216–26; Kohn and Harahan, *Strategic Air Warfare,* 27.

4. Kohn and Harahan, *Strategic Air Warfare,* 35.

5. Lt. Gen. Carlos M. Talbott, USAF, interview by Hugh N. Ahmann, June 1985, AFHRA K239.0512–1652.

6. Kenneth Ray Chidster, "Bomber Down: A True Story of Kenneth Ray Chidster" (unpublished, 2004), 23–25.

7. Wade interview.

8. Ralph H. Nutter, *With the Possum and the Eagle: A Memoir of a Navigator's War over Germany and Japan* (Denton: University of North Texas Press, 2005), 29–30.

9. Gen. Curtis LeMay, USAF, interview by Bill Peck, March 1965, AFHRA K239.0512–785.

10. Wade interview.

11. LeMay and Kantor, *Mission with LeMay,* 237–39; Kohn and Harahan, *Strategic Air Warfare,* 33.

12. Coffey, *Iron Eagle,* 35.

13. Nutter, *With the Possum and the Eagle,* 34–36.

14. LeMay interview by Rosenberg.

15. *Lead Crew Manual, 3rd Bombardment Division, Combat Crew Handbook, 3rd Bomb Division,* and *Combat Crew Manual, XX Bomber Command* were all published during World War II and outlined standardized procedures for each crew position. Curtis E. LeMay Papers, Box B4, Library of Congress (hereafter LOC), Washington, D.C.

16. Maj. Gen. Curtis E. LeMay, *Combat Crew Handbook, 3rd Bomb Division,* LeMay Papers, LOC.

17. Montgomery interview.

18. LeMay interview by Peck.

19. Lt. Gen. William K. Martin, USAF, interview by David L. Olson, February 1988, AFHRA K239.0512–1791.

20. LeMay eventually became commander of the 3rd Bomb Division. For more of LeMay's accolades in Europe, see Charles Wilfred Bosanko, "The Architecture of Armageddon: A History of Curtis Lemay's Influence on the Strategic Air Command and Nuclear Warfare" (Fullerton: California State University, master of arts thesis, 2000), 14–20.

21. For a discussion of the evolution of Field Manual 100–20, see Futrell, *Ideas, Concepts, Doctrine,* 135–38.

22. War Department, Field Manual 100–20, *Command and Employment of Air Power,* July 21, 1943, http://www.ibiblio.org/hyperwar/USA/ref/FM/FM100-20/index.html.

23. Futrell, *Ideas, Concepts, Doctrine,* 138.

24. Kohn and Harahan, *Strategic Air Warfare,* 46–47.

25. Hansell interview.

26. Aldrich and Ruef, *Organizations Evolving,* 114.

27. For a history of the Twentieth Air Force's operations against Japan and Arnold's justification, see Kenneth P. Werrell, *Blankets of Fire: U.S. Bombers over Japan During World War II* (Washington, D.C.: Smithsonian Institution Press, 1996), 90–91.

28. LeMay and Kantor, *Mission with LeMay,* 324–25.

29. Thomas M. Coffey, *Iron Eagle: The Turbulent Life of General Curtis LeMay* (New York: Crown Publishers, 1986), 22–23.

30. Nutter, *With the Possum and the Eagle,* 41–49. Nutter's insights into LeMay come from someone who was part of the organization and learned of the LeMay myth from secondhand sources.

31. See Schein, *Organizational Culture and Leadership,* 2. Schein argued that if an organization is successful, the leaders will repeat their assumptions and values. LeMay's success in Europe provided him a template for addressing his mission in the Pacific, which then laid the foundation for the type of values and assumptions he brought to SAC when he assumed command.

32. Gen. Paul K. Carlton, USAF, interview by Scottie S. Thompson, August 1979, AFHRA K239.0512–1138.

33. Kohn and Harahan, *Strategic Air Warfare,* 59–60.

34. Ibid., 61.

35. Werrell, *Blankets of Fire,* 145–46.

36. Gen. Jack J. Catton, USAF, interview by James C. Hasdorff, July 1977, AFHRA K239.0512–952.

37. Werrell, *Blankets of Fire,* 117.

38. Edmundson interview. Edmundson told this story secondhand based on his conversations with Gen. Walter "Cam" Sweeney.

39. Montgomery interview.

40. Gen. Curtis LeMay, USAF, interview by Robert Futrell et al., June 1972, AFHRA K239.0512–592.

41. Kohn and Harahan, *Strategic Air Warfare,* 58.

42. Catton interview.

43. Kohn and Harahan, *Strategic Air Warfare,* 62. Emphasis in original.

44. Martin interview. General Martin remembered flying only as an observer with some of LeMay's crews because he insisted upon crew integrity.

45. Hansell interview.

46. LeMay interview by Rosenberg.

47. Montgomery interview.

48. "General H. H. Arnold, Commander Twentieth Air Force, to Major General Curtis E. LeMay, Commander XXI Bomber Command, 21 March 1945," in Gen. Thomas Power, USAF, Papers, AFHRA, CH-79–01, text-fiche, frame 487.

49. Montgomery interview.

50. Thomas E. Griffith, *MacArthur's Airman: General George C. Kenney and the War in the Southwest Pacific* (Lawrence: University Press of Kansas, 1998), 227; Werrell, *Blankets of Fire,* 328.

51. Hansell interview.

52. LeMay interview by Rosenberg.

53. Arnold, *Global Mission,* 598.

54. Trice and Beyer, *The Cultures of Work Organizations,* 6.

Chapter 3. Beginnings

Epigraph. Testimony before Congress in 1949; see William R. Conklin, "Spaatz Calls B-36 and Bomb 'Greatest Forces for Peace,'" *New York Times,* August 23, 1949.

1. These steps are part of the evolutionary approach to organizations; see Aldrich and Ruef, *Organizations Evolving,* 16–27.

2. Biddle, *Rhetoric and Reality,* 9.

3. *The United States Strategic Bombing Surveys: Summary Report* (1945; repr., Maxwell Air Force Base, Ala.: Air University Press, 1987), 13.

4. Ibid., 37.

5. Ibid., 107.

6. Futrell, *Ideas, Concepts, Doctrine,* 207.

7. Army Air Forces Headquarters, AAF Regulation No. 20–20, "Organization: Strategic Air Command," October 10, 1946, 1.

8. The AAF became the Air Force when President Harry Truman signed the National Security Act of 1947 on July 26, 1947. See Herman S. Wolk, "The Quest for Independence," in Nalty, *Winged Shield, Winged Sword,* 395.

9. Ronald H. Cole et al., *The History of Unified Command, 1946–1993* (Washington, D.C.: Joint History Office, 1995), 11–21. A specified command is a command established by the president and usually consists of a single service. In this case, SAC had an organize, train, and equip mission as well as a warfighting mission.

10. Department of the Air Force, "Topical Digest of Testimony Before the House Armed Services Committee During Hearings on the B-36 and Related Matters: Section II," October 1949, AFHRA Roll 33780, Frame 891, text-fiche.

11. Carl Spaatz, "Testimony before U.S. Senate Military Affair Committee," November 7, 1945, Spaatz Papers, LOC.

12. Carl Spaatz, "Air Power and American Independence: The Heavy Bomber," July 4, 1947, Spaatz Papers, LOC.

13. Maj. Gen. Elwood "Pete" Quesada, USAF, "Address by Pete Quesada," June 23, 1947, Elwood Quesada Papers, LOC.

14. Carl Spaatz, "Presentation to Senate Armed Forces Committee," January 27, 1948, Spaatz Papers, LOC.

15. Carl Spaatz, "Airpower and the Future," October 11, 1945, Spaatz Papers, LOC.

16. Carl Spaatz, "Spaatz Board Report," October 23, 1945, Spaatz Papers, LOC.

17. Ibid.

18. Ibid.

19. Futrell, *Ideas, Concepts, Doctrine,* 231.

20. Air Staff, *Strategic Implications of the Atomic Bomb,* quoted in Lawrence Freedman, *The Evolution of Nuclear Strategy* (New York: St. Martin's Press, 1981), 54.

21. Kenneth Gantz, "The Atomic Present," *Air Force Magazine,* March–April 1946, quoted in Futrell, *Ideas, Concepts, Doctrine,* 215.

22. Joint Chiefs of Staff, "Statement of Effect of Atomic Weapons on National Security and Military Organization," April 1, 1946, Record Group (RG) 341, Entry 335, National Archives and Records Administration (NARA).

23. Ibid.

24. Catton interview.

25. Carlton interview by Thompson.

26. Society of the Strategic Air Command, *America's Shield: The Story of the Strategic Air Command and Its People* (Paducah, Ky.: Turner Publishing Co., 1997), 16.

27. Walton S. Moody, *Building a Strategic Air Force* (Washington, D.C.: Air Force History and Museums Program, 1996), 175.

28. Marcelle Size Knaack, *Encyclopedia of U.S. Air Force Aircraft and Missile Systems,* vol. 2: *Post–World War II Bombers* (Washington, D.C.: U.S. Government Printing Office, 1988), 3–15; Futrell, *Ideas, Concepts, Doctrine,* 231–32.

29. USAF Weapons and Aircraft Board Reports, "Approved Heavy and Medium Bombardment Development," August 19, 1947, AFHRA, Roll 33780, Frame 574, IRIS Number 1030448, text-fiche.

30. Jeffrey Pfeffer and Gerald R. Salancik, *The External Control of Organizations: A Resource Dependence Perspective* (New York: Harper & Row, 1978).

31. SAC's resources depended heavily on the nature of the Cold War. The organization was not created in response to the Cold War; however, it disbanded as a result of the end of the Cold War. President George H. W. Bush took bombers off alert in the fall of 1991; within a year, the Air Force disbanded SAC and created new organizations in its place.

32. Melvyn P. Leffler, *A Preponderance of Power: National Security, the Truman Administration, and the Cold War* (Stanford, Calif.: Stanford University Press, 1992). Leffler showed how relations in the Cold War revolved around the concept of power and that the United States decided to pursue a national security strategy that embraced a preponderance of power to deter Soviet aggression.

33. Warner R. Schilling, "The Politics of National Defense: Fiscal 1950," in *Strategy, Politics, and Defense Budgets,* ed. William Fox (New York: Columbia University Press, 1962), 1–266. Schilling's in-depth analysis of the construction of the fiscal year 1950 defense budget revealed the many factors that led the Truman administration to rely on strategic airpower as the way to deter possible Soviet aggression. See Steven Rearden's chapter on the fiscal year 1950 budget in Steven L. Rearden, *History of the Office of the Secretary of Defense,* vol. I: *The Formative Years 1947–1950* (Washington, D.C.: Office of the Secretary of Defense Historical Office, 1984), 335–60.

34. Ibid., 13–14.

35. Ibid., 313–15.

36. David Alan Rosenberg, "American Atomic Strategy and the Hydrogen Bomb," *Journal of American History* 66, no. 1 (1979): 68.

37. Recorded by David Lilienthal as quoted in David G. McCullough, *Truman* (New York: Simon & Schuster, 1992), 650.

38. Carl A. Spaatz, "The Air-Power Odds against Us," *Reader's Digest,* June 1951, 11–12.

39. Forrestal diary as quoted in Moody, *Building a Strategic Air Force,* 159.

40. Phillip S. Meilinger, *Hoyt S. Vandenberg: The Life of a General* (Bloomington: Indiana University Press, 1989), 131.

41. The Navy would not give up its fight for a part of the strategic mission. With the development of missile technology, the Navy pursued the submarine-launched Polaris missile and became part of the U.S. strategic triad.

42. The United States did not become a garrison state—in which the government directs all forms of economics and industry for the purposes of generating military power—for several reasons. Those reasons are outlined in Aaron L. Friedberg, *In the Shadow of the Garrison State: America's Anti-Statism and Its Cold War Strategy* (Princeton, N.J.: Princeton University Press, 2000).

43. Steven T. Ross, *American War Plans, 1945–1950: Strategies for Defeating the Soviet Union* (Portland, Ore.: Frank Cass, 1996), 15–28, 54.

44. For a further discussion of Kenney's achievements in the Pacific, see Griffith, *MacArthur's Airman.*

45. Ibid., 227–28.

46. Gen. George C. Kenney, USAF, interview by James C. Hasdorff, August 1974, AFHRA K239.0512–806.

47. Gen. Carl Spaatz, commanding general, Army Air Forces, memorandum to Gen. George Kenney, commanding general, Strategic Air Command, May 1, 1946, Harry Borowski Papers, United States Air Force Academy.

48. Borowski, *A Hollow Threat,* 141.

49. Kohn and Harahan, *Strategic Air Warfare,* 74.

50. Statistics provided by SAC's official history for 1946 as quoted in Borowski, *A Hollow Threat,* 45.

51. Ibid., 135.

52. Kohn and Harahan, *Strategic Air Warfare,* 74.

53. Ibid., 75.

54. Brig. Gen. Everett W. Holstrom, USAF, interview by James C. Hasdorff, April 1988, AFHRA K239.0512–1793.

55. Bomb scores were measured in circular error probable, which is the radius of a circle in which one-half of a plane's bombs fall. In grading crews and bomb squadrons, lower bomb scores mean a greater chance of hitting the target. Therefore, lower scores were better. Combat readiness was measured by the percentage

of assigned personnel considered ready for combat duty. Hence, higher rates were considered better.

56. Holstrom interview.

57. "Gen. Kenney Pleads for No. 1 Air Force," *New York Times*, May 17, 1949; "Kenney Minimizes Our Bomber Strength," *New York Times*, May 18, 1949.

58. Gen. Carl Spaatz, commanding general, Army Air Forces, to Gen. George C. Kenney, commanding general, Strategic Air Command, May 30, 1947, Borowski Papers.

59. W. Stuart Symington, assistant secretary of war for air, to Gen. George C. Kenney, commanding general, Strategic Air Command, May 30, 1947, Borowski Papers.

60. Moody, *Building a Strategic Air Force*, 180.

61. Borowski, *A Hollow Threat*, 148–49.

62. Moody, *Building a Strategic Air Force*, 221.

63. Montgomery interview.

64. Gen. Lauris Norstad, USAF, interview by Edgar F. Puryear, August 1977, AFHRA K239.0512–1473.

65. Office of SAC History, *The Development of Strategic Air Command* (Offutt Air Force Base, Neb.: Strategic Air Command, 1972), 13.

66. Meilinger, *Hoyt S. Vandenberg*, 105.

67. Charles Lindberg, "Report to General Vandenberg," September 14, 1948, Emmett O'Donnell Papers, United States Air Force Academy.

68. Ibid.

69. Meilinger, *Hoyt S. Vandenberg*, 106–7.

Chapter 4. "We Are at War Now"

Epigraph. LeMay and Kantor, *Mission with LeMay*, 436.

1. Schein, *Organizational Culture and Leadership*, 2–37. Schein argued that values can eventually become artifacts. Artifacts can take physical form.

2. Gen. Curtis LeMay, USAF, interview by John Bohn, March 1971, AFHRA K239.0512–736.

3. "Bombers at the Ready," *Newsweek*, April 18, 1949, 25.

4. LeMay interview by Bohn.

5. Gen. Hoyt S. Vandenberg, chief of staff, United States Air Force, memorandum to commanding general, Strategic Air Command,

subject: Relocation of Headquarters, Strategic Air Command, December 11, 1947, Hoyt Vandenberg Papers, LOC.

6. Gen. George Kenney, commander, Strategic Air Command, memorandum to chief of staff, United States Air Force, subject: Recommendation on Movement of Strategic Air Command Headquarters, SAC 686, December 17, 1947, Vandenberg Papers, LOC.

7. Moody, *Building a Strategic Air Force,* 82.

8. Gen. Hoyt S. Vandenberg, chief of staff, United States Air Force, memorandum to secretary of the Air Force, Stuart Symington, subject: Relocation of Headquarters, Strategic Air Command, May 12, 1948, Vandenberg Papers, LOC.

9. Gen. Hoyt S. Vandenberg, chief of staff, United States Air Force, memorandum to commanding general, Strategic Air Command, subject: Relocation of Headquarters, Strategic Air Command, June 8, 1948, Vandenberg Papers, LOC.

10. Daniel L. Haulman, "Air Force Bases, 1947–1960," in *Locating Air Force Base Sites: History's Legacy,* ed. Frederick J. Shaw (Washington, D.C.: Air Force History and Museums Program, 2004), 57; "Strategic Air Force to Shift to Nebraska," *New York Times,* May 22, 1948.

11. Montgomery interview.

12. Tactical Air Command's first commanding general, Elwood Quesada, made Langley Field, Virginia, the headquarters for the command because he wanted it close to the Army Ground Forces Command at Fort Monroe, Virginia. See Thomas Alexander Hughes, *Overlord: General Pete Quesada and the Triumph of Tactical Air Power in World War II* (New York: Free Press, 1995), 311–12.

13. LeMay interview by Bohn.

14. Norman Polmar, *Strategic Air Command: People, Aircraft, and Missiles* (Annapolis, Md.: Nautical and Aviation Publishing Company of America, 1979), 13.

15. Kohn and Harahan, *Strategic Air Warfare,* 78–79.

16. LeMay interview by Bohn.

17. Catton interview.

18. LeMay and Kantor, *Mission with LeMay,* 431.

19. LeMay interview by Bohn.

20. Werrell, *Blankets of Fire,* 161–62.

21. Emmett Curry, "The Story of SAC." The date and publication of this article are unknown—although the year was probably 1949, since it describes the new SAC leadership. Archie Old Papers, AFHRA K168.7141–14.

22. LeMay and Kantor, *Mission with LeMay,* 430.

23. Curtis LeMay, "Talk by General LeMay before Omaha Chamber of Commerce," November 16, 1946, LeMay Papers, LOC.

24. Curtis LeMay, "Notes for Discussion with General Vandenberg," November 4, 1948, LeMay Papers, LOC.

25. Catton interview.

26. Moody, *Building a Strategic Air Force,* 190–201, 30–31; Ross, *American War Plans, 1945–1950,* 90–98.

27. Office of SAC History, "Presentation Phase One (Transcript): Exercise Dualism (6–8 December 1948)" (Offutt Air Force Base, Neb.: Strategic Air Command, 1948), 206.

28. Gen. Curtis E. LeMay, USAF, interview by Robert Kipp and John Bohn, November 1972, AFHRA K239.0512–1774.

29. Office of SAC History, "Presentation Phase One (Transcript)," 206–7.

30. Ibid., 224.

31. From the transcript of the Dualism conference as quoted in Moody, *Building a Strategic Air Force,* 231.

32. Lt. Gen. Curtis LeMay, commander, Strategic Air Command, memorandum to Lt. Gen. Lauris Norstad, deputy chief of staff, operations, December 15, 1948, AFHRA K416.201–3.

33. Maj. Gen. S. E. Anderson, director, plans and operations, memorandum to Lt. Gen. Curtis LeMay, commander, Strategic Air Command, January 14, 1949, AFHRA K416.201–3.

34. LeMay and Kantor, *Mission with LeMay,* 436.

35. Curtis LeMay, "Commanding General's Diary," LeMay Papers, LOC. According to his diary, LeMay visited Forbes Air Force Base, Kansas, on December 10, Kearney Air Force Base, Nebraska, on December 13, Carswell Air Force Base, Texas, on December 16, Biggs Air Force Base, Texas, and Davis-Monthan Air Force Base, Arizona, on December 17, and Castle Air Force Base, California, on December 29, 1948. All references to the trip from here are based on LeMay's diary.

36. Ibid.

37. LeMay received resistance from local unions that were afraid SAC cooks were taking up union jobs in the local hotels. LeMay assured them that the cooks would remain in the service once their training was complete. See LeMay and Kantor, *Mission with LeMay,* 438.

38. Curtis LeMay, "Commanding General's Diary," LeMay Papers, LOC.

39. LeMay and Kantor, *Mission with LeMay,* 436.

40. LeMay interview by Bohn.

41. Ibid.

42. Kohn and Harahan, *Strategic Air Warfare,* 79.

43. LeMay and Kantor, *Mission with LeMay,* 432.

44. Kohn and Harahan, *Strategic Air Warfare,* 79.

45. LeMay and Kantor, *Mission with LeMay,* 432–33.

46. In 1947, before LeMay took command, SAC implemented the Hobson plan. Under this reorganization, "wing headquarters bearing the same numerical designation as the bombardment and fighter groups were organized and placed in a supervisory capacity over all combat and support elements on a base. Prior to this reorganization, the base or installation commander, who was often a non-flying administrator, was the immediate superior of the combat group commander." Polmar, *Strategic Air Command,* 12.

47. Curtis LeMay, "Commander's Diary," LeMay Papers, LOC. LeMay visited Carswell Air Force Base, Texas, on December 16, 1948.

48. Kohn and Harahan, *Strategic Air Warfare,* 80.

49. LeMay interview by Bohn.

50. Kohn and Harahan, *Strategic Air Warfare,* 84.

51. Robert K. Weinkle, "The Progression of the Standardization/Evaluation Program in Strategic Air Command" (Maxwell Air Force Base, Ala.: Air University, 1965), 19.

52. Ibid., 7.

53. LeMay and Kantor, *Mission with LeMay,* 256–57.

54. Office of SAC History, *Lead Crew School and Combat Crew Standardization School,* History Study no. 8 (Offutt Air Force Base, Neb.: Strategic Air Command, 1951), 1–10.

55. Weinkle, "The Progression of the Standardization/Evaluation Program in Strategic Air Command," 10–11.

56. "Man in the First Plane," *Time,* September 4, 1950, 17.

57. Office of SAC History, *History of Strategic Air Command, 1949* (Offutt Air Force Base, Neb.: Strategic Air Command, 1950), 141.

58. LeMay and Kantor, *Mission with LeMay,* 439–40.

59. "U.S. Grounds B-29s as Another Crash Kills 5 in Florida," *New York Times,* November 19, 1949, 1.

60. Montgomery interview.

61. LeMay and Kantor, *Mission with LeMay,* 439.

62. Office of SAC History, *Development of Strategic Air Command,* 26.

63. LeMay and Kantor, *Mission with LeMay,* 436.

64. SAC Historical Branch, "Radar Bomb Scoring Activities in Strategic Air Command: Origins and Growth through 1952" (Offutt Air Force Base, Neb.: Strategic Air Command, 1952), 10.

65. Office of SAC History, "Presentation Phase One (Transcript)," 206.

66. Martin interview.

67. Ibid.

68. Society of the Strategic Air Command, *America's Shield,* 16.

69. SAC Historical Branch, *Development of Evasion and Escape and Air Evacuation Program,* Historical Study no. 14 (Offutt Air Force Base, Neb.: Strategic Air Command, 1951), 7–8.

70. Ibid., 23.

71. "Commanding General's Diary," May 5–7, 1950, LeMay Papers, LOC.

72. SAC Historical Branch, *Development of Evasion and Escape and Air Evacuation Program,* 59–62.

73. Schein, *Organizational Culture and Leadership,* 26. Schein argues that organizational culture begins with assumptions, unconscious beliefs, and perceptions. These assumptions become espoused values in organizational strategies or philosophies. Eventually, organizational culture takes physical form in an organization's structures of process. Schein does note the process can work in reverse.

74. Harold Martin, "Are Our Big Bombers Ready?," *Saturday Evening Post,* December 30, 1950, 65.

75. Carlton interview by Thompson.

76. Walter H. Waggoner, "First in History," *New York Times,* March 3, 1949, 1.

77. Polmar, *Strategic Air Command,* 18–19.

78. Harris interview.

79. Society of the Strategic Air Command, *America's Shield,* 21.

80. LeMay and Kantor, *Mission with LeMay,* 437.

81. Ibid., 443.

82. Harris interview.

83. "Man in the First Plane," 16.

84. "Bombers at the Ready," 24.

85. "Commanding General's Diary," June 11–12, 1950, LeMay Papers, LOC.

86. LeMay and Kantor, *Mission with LeMay,* 446.

87. Curtis LeMay, "Commander's Conference Agenda," January 13, 1949, LeMay Papers, LOC.

88. Wade interview.

89. Edmundson interview.

90. Martin, "Are Our Big Bombers Ready?," 65.

91. Quoted in Office of SAC History, *The Strategic Air Command Spot Promotion Program: Its Rise and Fall,* Historical Study no. 167 (Offutt Air Force Base, Neb.: Strategic Air Command, 1978), 3.

92. Martin interview.

93. Office of SAC History, *Development of Strategic Air Command,* 16.

94. Gen. George Kenney, commander, Air University, to Gen. Hoyt Vandenberg, chief of staff, United States Air Force, "Observations on Commander's Conference," April 29, 1950, AFHRA 168.15–10.

95. SAC Inspector General report as quoted in Office of SAC History, *Development of Strategic Air Command Security Program,* Historical Study no. 17 (Offutt Air Force Base, Neb.: Strategic Air Command, 1951), 2.

96. Ibid., 4.

97. LeMay and Kantor, *Mission with LeMay,* 479.

98. Montgomery interview.

99. "Bombers at the Ready," 25.

100. See Schein, *Organizational Culture and Leadership,* 25–27.

101. "Commanders Conference (transcript)," April 25–27, 1950, Ramey Air Force Base, Puerto Rico, AFHRA 168.15–10.

Chapter 5. Taking Charge

Epigraph. LeMay and Kantor, *Mission with LeMay,* 482.

1. Rearden, *History of the Office of the Secretary of Defense,* vol. I: *The Formative Years 1947–1950,* 315–17.

2. For more on the Revolt of the Admirals and the B-36 decision, see Jeffrey G. Barlow, *Revolt of the Admirals: The Fight for Naval Aviation, 1945–1950* (Washington, D.C.: Brassey's, 1998), and Paul Y. Hammond, "Super Carriers and B-36 Bombers: Appropriations, Strategy, and Politics," in *American Civil Military Relations,* ed. Harold Stein (Birmingham: University of Alabama Press, 1963).

3. Polmar, *Strategic Air Command,* 13–20.

4. George M. Watson, *The Office of Secretary of the Air Force, 1947–1965* (Washington, D.C.: U.S. Government Printing Office, 1993), 104.

5. Wade interview.

6. See chapter 6 for more information on actual reconnaissance profiles.

7. Office of SAC History, *The Development of Strategic Air Command,* 13.

8. "Strategic Air Command Altered," *New York Times,* March 8, 1950; "Strategic Air Command," *Army and Navy Journal* 87, no. 28 (March 11, 1950): 732.

9. LeMay and Kantor, *Mission with LeMay,* 368–70.

10. "Commanding General's Diary," March 28, 1950, LeMay Papers, LOC.

11. Perhaps the most comprehensive one-volume work that chronicled the air war in Korea is Robert F. Futrell, *The United States Air Force in Korea, 1950–1953,* rev. ed. (Washington, D.C.: Office of Air Force History, 1983). Many aspects of the strategic air campaign in Korea are also covered in Conrad C. Crane, *American Airpower Strategy in Korea, 1950–1953* (Lawrence: University Press of Kansas, 2000).

12. "Commanding General's Diary," June 27, 1950, LeMay Papers, LOC.

13. SAC Historical Branch, *The Deployment of Strategic Air Command Units to the Far East* (Offutt Air Force Base, Neb.: Strategic Air Command, 1950), 15.

14. Edmundson interview.

15. Kohn and Harahan, *Strategic Air Warfare,* 87.

16. Hoyt Vandenberg, General, United States Air Force, to George Stratemeyer, General, FEAF, "Redline to Stratemeyer from Vandenberg," July 3, 1950, LeMay Papers, LOC.

17. Edmundson interview.

18. Quoted in SAC Historical Branch, *The Deployment of SAC Units to the Far East,* 7.

19. Gen. David C. Jones, USAF, interview by Melvin Deaile, January 2006.

20. Montgomery interview.

21. Wade interview.

22. Conrad C. Crane, "Raiding the Beggar's Pantry: The Search for Airpower Strategy in the Korean War," *Journal of Military History* 63, no. 4 (October 1999): 889.

23. LeMay and Kantor, *Mission with LeMay,* 88.

24. Carlton interview by Thompson. Carlton was LeMay's aide during the Korean War and noted that LeMay did not want to use precious atomic weapons against Korea when they were required for SAC war plans against the Soviet Union.

25. Futrell, *U.S. Air Forces in Korea,* 186.

26. Ibid., 187.

27. "Rosie" O'Donnell, CG/FEAF Bomber Command, to George Stratemeyer, CG/FEAF, July 19, 1950, LeMay Papers, LOC.

28. Crane, "Raiding the Beggar's Pantry," 890.

29. "Rosie" O'Donnell, CG/FEAF Bomber Command, to Curtis LeMay, CG/SAC, July 21, 1950, LeMay Papers, LOC.

30. Ibid.

31. Extract of letter from O'Donnell to LeMay published in Crane, "Raiding the Beggar's Pantry," 890.

32. Futrell, *U.S. Air Forces in Korea,* 188–98.

33. Ibid., 198–207.

34. Edmundson interview. Edmundson recalled Jones' ability as an aircraft commander and stated he was given a spot promotion. Jones, however, said he never benefited from spot promotions; see Gen. David C. Jones, USAF, interview by Maurice Maryanow and Richard Kohn, August 1985–March 1986, AFHRA K239.0512–1664.

35. Colonel Robert H. Hinckley, Director Military Personnel Actions, to Wing Commander J. R. Beggs, Director of USAF Personnel Planning, "FEAF Report on Spot Promotions," RG 341, Entry 130, Deputy Chief of Staff, Personnel, NARA.

36. At the beginning of the decade, SAC had roughly 962 airplanes and 19 bases in the zone of the interior. By the end of the decade, SAC controlled 2,992 aircraft (300 percent increase) housed on 46 bases (250 percent increase). In comparison, Air Defense Command had twenty-one bases, and Tactical Air Command controlled thirty-one bases. See Haulman, "Air Force Bases, 1947–1960," in Shaw, *Locating Air Force Base Sites*, 62–74.

37. SAC Historical Branch, *Strategic Air Command History,* vol. 1: *January–June 1951* (Offutt Air Force Base, Neb.: Strategic Air Command, 1951), 2.

38. "Discussion Recorded During the Air Force and Wing Commanders Conference," December 6–8, 1950, LeMay Papers, LOC.

39. Polmar, *Strategic Air Command*, 25.

40. Harris interview.

41. SAC Historical Branch, *Strategic Air Command Expansion Program*, Historical Study no. 19 (Offutt Air Force Base, Neb.: Strategic Air Command, 1951), 24.

42. Wade interview.

43. Ibid.

44. Lt. Gen. Archie J. Old, USAF, interviewed by Hugh N. Ahmann, November 1982, AFHRA K239.0512–1357.

45. Archie Old, 7 AD Commander, to Curtis LeMay, SAC/CG, April 26, 1951, LeMay Papers, LOC.

46. Old interview. This is the story as related by Old. The other interesting fact is that Old believed the assignment ignited McConnell's career.

47. Curtis LeMay, Lt. General, CG/SAC, memorandum to Archie Old, Major General, 5 AD/CG, July 27, 1951, Archie Old Papers, AFHRA K168.1741.

48. SAC Historical Branch, *Strategic Air Command Expansion Program*, 38.

49. Old interview.

50. Curtis LeMay, CG/SAC, to John P. McConnell, CG/7 AD, "Appointment of Deputy Commanding General, SAC (ZEBRA)," January 3, 1952, LeMay Papers, LOC.

51. Futrell, *Ideas, Concepts, Doctrine,* 434. In 1954, SAC established 3rd Air Division (AD) to control all SAC units in the Far East. 3 AD had a command relationship similar to 7 AD (UK) and 5 AD (Morocco); see Polmar, *Strategic Air Command,* 35.

52. *The Public Papers of Harry S. Truman,* March 14, 1946, as quoted in Peter Feaver, *Guarding the Guardians: Civilian Control of Nuclear Weapons in the United States* (Ithaca, N.Y.: Cornell University Press, 1992), 99.

53. Ibid., 107–13.

54. McCullough, *Truman,* 649–50.

55. Moody, *Building a Strategic Air Force,* 334.

56. Assertive control is a term used by Peter Feaver to describe the Atomic Energy Commission, the civilian agency responsible for custody and handling of nuclear weapons. Feaver used the term delegative control to explain the situation when electronic locks on nuclear weapons replaced physical control of nuclear weapons. See Feaver, *Guarding the Guardians,* 7–12.

57. "Commanding General's Diary," July 1, 1950 (page 2), LeMay Papers, LOC.

58. Moody, *Building a Strategic Air Force,* 425.

59. William S. Borgiasz, *The Strategic Air Command: Evolution and Consolidation of Nuclear Forces, 1945–1955* (Westport, Conn.: Praeger, 1996), 20–21.

60. Feaver, *Guarding the Guardians,* 146.

61. Alwyn T. Lloyd, *A Cold War Legacy: A Tribute to Strategic Air Command, 1946–1992* (Missoula, Mont.: Pictorial Histories Publishing, 2000), 163; Polmar, *Strategic Air Command,* 29.

62. These were random phrases not attributable to any one person but heard at three different SAC reunions held during 2006: SAC Association Reunion, May 24–27, 2006, Tucson, Arizona; B-52 Association Reunion, August 3–5, 2006, Minot, North Dakota; and B-47 Association Reunion, September 21–23, 2006, Wichita, Kansas.

63. These recollections are not attributable to any one person but were general comments offered during the B-47 Association Reunion.

64. Old interview.

65. General comments offered during the B-47 Association Reunion.

66. Hunter Harris and John Montgomery both recalled LeMay's hand in redesigning the B-52; see Harris interview and Montgomery interview.

67. LeMay and Kantor, *Mission with LeMay,* 467.

68. "Barracks Brief Notes for General LeMay," Commanding General's Diary, no date given but in the fall of 1950, SAC devised a plan to replace a burned-out barracks on Offutt Air Force Base with the new SAC design. LeMay Papers, LOC.

69. LeMay and Kantor, *Mission with LeMay,* 467.

70. Holstrom interview.

71. Lt. Gen. John B. McPherson, USAF, interview by Hugh N. Ahmann, December 1985 and February 1991, AFHRA K239.0512–2014.

72. Commanding General's Diary, January 8, 1951, LeMay Papers, LOC.

73. LeMay and Kantor, *Mission with LeMay,* 450.

74. Carlton interview by Thompson.

75. LeMay and Kantor, *Mission with LeMay,* 451.

76. Carlton interview by Thompson.

77. This is one of the main arguments Edgar Schein makes in his work on organizational culture; see Schein, *Organizational Culture and Leadership,* 1–23.

78. Explanation of the magazine's origin found on the title page of the first issue of *Combat Crew* 1, no. 1 (November 1950). The earliest editions of *Combat Crew* can only be found at the Air University Library, Maxwell Air Force Base, Alabama.

79. Carlton interview by Thompson.

80. W. F. Schaub, Chief, Military Division, Bureau of the Budget, to H. Lee White, Assistant Secretary of the Air Force, August 7, 1953, LeMay Papers, LOC.

81. Curtis LeMay, CG/SAC, to Nathan Twining, CSAF, July 20, 1953, LeMay Papers, LOC.

82. Curtis LeMay, CG/SAC, to Nathan Twining, CSAF, August 26, 1953, LeMay Papers, LOC.

83. "Twining to Keep Post: Decision to Shift Jobs with LeMay Cancelled by Air Force," *New York Times,* October 29, 1952.

84. Edgar Schein argues that tenure and longevity contribute to the development of organizational culture. If a leader is successful, his

values can define an organization's culture for generations; see Schein, *Organizational Culture and Leadership,* 1–20.

Chapter 6. SAC Life

Epigraph. James Edmundson, "Six Churning and Four Burning," *Klaxon,* 1995, 1.

1. For more on the "New Look," see Futrell, *Ideas, Concepts, Doctrine,* 424–27; Friedberg, *In the Shadow of the Garrison State,* 130–33.
2. Freedman, *The Evolution of Nuclear Strategy,* 89.
3. SAC had nearly 266,788 people in the organization by the close of the 1950s; the maximum number of people was 282,723, which SAC reached in 1962. See Polmar, *Strategic Air Command,* 61–79.
4. Martin, *Organizational Culture,* 65.
5. Wade interview.
6. LeMay and Kantor, *Mission with LeMay,* 479.
7. Office of SAC History, *Development of Strategic Air Command Security Program,* 8–9.
8. LeMay and Kantor, *Mission with LeMay,* 479.
9. Lt. Col. Tom Cantarano, USAF (Ret.), interview by Melvin Deaile, April 2006.
10. Carlton interview.
11. Moody, *Building a Strategic Air Force,* 402–3.
12. One way to discover organizational culture is to interview those members of the organization. Although not statistically significant, a discernable majority of those attending SAC's various reunions or respondents to surveys answered that they did believe SAC was at war.
13. Trice and Beyer, *The Cultures of Work Organizations,* 105.
14. Carlton interview.
15. Story offered with Richard Purdam's consent at the B-47 Association Reunion.
16. LeMay and Kantor, *Mission with LeMay,* 480.
17. Story offered with George Gott's consent at the B-47 Association Reunion.
18. Trice and Beyer, *The Cultures of Work Organizations,* 107.
19. Edwin C. Ross, "Flying the B-47," in *Boeing B-47 Stratojet: True Stories of the Cold War,* ed. Mark Notola (Atglen, Pa.: Schiffer Military History, 2002), 44–45.

20. Sigmund Alexander, *B-47: Centurion of the Cold War* (San Antonio, Tex.: C. C. C. P. Publishing, 2002), 203–4.

21. Checklist information and procedures are listed in *Flight Handbook: B-47B and B-47E, Tech Order (T.O.) 1B-47E-1* (St. Louis, Mo.: Universal Printing Company, June 30, 1955, rev. September 30, 1955), 99. Tech orders provided courtesy of Frank Sweet's family—Mr. Sweet flew SAC B-47s.

22. Alexander, *B-47: Centurion of the Cold War*, 205.

23. Ross, "Flying the B-47," 47.

24. James Wells offered his memory through a survey collected when he attended a SAC reunion in 2006.

25. Ross, "Flying the B-47," 51.

26. Alexander, *B-47: Centurion of the Cold War*, 205.

27. Polmar, *Strategic Air Command*, 50.

28. Lloyd, *A Cold War Legacy,* 125.

29. Jones interview.

30. "Unarmed Atom Bomb Hits Carolina Home, Hurting 6," *New York Times,* March 12, 1958. The newspaper report indicated a "mechanical malfunction of the plane's bomb lock." SAC members at the B-47 Association Reunion revealed what they remembered as the "real" cause of the incident.

31. Most missions flown with nuclear weapons were either missions testing nuclear weapons or those ferrying nuclear weapons. In 1957 SAC began flying nuclear airborne alert (see chapter 7), which meant flying with armed nuclear weapons on a regular basis. Training bombs were used to practice the IFI maneuver.

32. Alexander, *B-47: Centurion of the Cold War*, 206.

33. "It's a Girl," a story published under the "Reflections" section of the Seventh Bomb Wing, B-36 Association website, http://www.7bwb-36assn.org/reflect.html, accessed August 8, 2006.

34. Anecdote relayed by a former SAC crewmember who wanted to remain anonymous but felt the story highlighted the importance SAC placed on bomb scores. Relayed at the B-47 Association Reunion.

35. Col. Donald Shea, USAF, interview by Melvin Deaile, March 2007.

36. Andrew Labosky, interview by Melvin Deaile, September 2006.

37. Edmundson, "Six Churning and Four Burning," 8.

38. Curtis LeMay, CG/SAC, to Hoyt Vandenberg, CSAF, "Strategic Air Command Physical Conditioning Program," June 16, 1952, Power Papers, AFHRA, CH-79–01, text-fiche, frame 269.

39. "Rooms with Bath; Air Force Policy," *New York Times,* March 3, 1952.

40. "Survival Training" a story published under the "Reflections" section of the Seventh Bomb Wing (7 BW), B-36 Association web site, http://www.7bwb-36assn.org/reflect.html. The interesting aspect of the story's post is the fact that most remembered how others bypassed the SAC system.

41. Edmundson, "Six Churning and Four Burning," 9.

42. Ken Blank, "Recon Crews Snoop from 40,000 Feet," *Air Force Magazine* 35, issue 6 (June 1952): 31–33, 56.

43. Harold Austin, "A Cold War Overflight of the USSR," B-47 Association web page, http://www.b-47.com/stories/austin/austin.html.

44. Thomas Swanton, comments provided on a SAC survey at the B-47 Association Reunion.

45. Wade interview.

46. LeMay interview by Kipp and Bond.

47. Office of SAC History, *The Strategic Air Command Spot Promotion Program*, 9.

48. Alexander, *B-47: Centurion of the Cold War*, 204.

49. Labosky interview.

50. Shea interview.

51. Ed Fields, "Recollections of the 19th Air Refueling Squadron, Homestead AFB, FL (May 1956–July 1958)," unpublished, 2.

52. Typical problems associated with the crew leave system expressed by members of the B-47 Association Reunion.

53. Fields, "Recollections of the 19th Air Refueling Squadron," 2.

54. Office of SAC History, *The Strategic Air Command Spot Promotion Program*, 8–14.

55. Ibid., 11.

56. Shea interview.

57. LeMay and Kantor, *Mission with LeMay,* 470.

58. LeMay interview by Kipp and Bond.

59. Ibid.

60. Comments on housing provided by Donald Shea, USAF, phone interview by Melvin Deaile, March 2007.

61. "What About Air Force Housing?," *Air Force Magazine* 34, no. 10 (October 1951): 32–34, 79–80.

62. Martin interview.

63. In 1959, the United States put on an exhibit in Moscow attended by Vice President Richard Nixon and Soviet premier Nikita Khrushchev. The United States used the exhibit as a form of propaganda to show the way modern Americans lived in their modern kitchens. When Vice President Nixon pointed out all the comforts of the American kitchen, Khrushchev simply replied, "All our houses have this kind of equipment." See Walter L. Hixson, *Parting the Curtain: Propaganda, Culture, and the Cold War, 1945–1961,* 1st ed. (New York: St. Martin's Press, 1997), 179.

64. "What About Air Force Housing?," 32–34, 79–80.

65. Montgomery interview.

66. *The Enlisted Experience: A Conversation with Chief Master Sergeants of the Air Force,* ed. Janet R. Bednarek (Washington, D.C.: U.S. Government Printing Office, 1995), 49.

67. "Air Force Wife Explains Problems of Dislocation," *New York Times,* May 29, 1956.

68. "Strategic Air Command I: An Analysis of Program for Building Force for Keeping the World's Peace," *New York Times,* October 27, 1955.

69. Ruth Lindquist, "Marriage and Family Life of Officers and Airmen in Strategic Air Command" (Chapel Hill, N.C.: Institute for Research in Social Science, 1952), i. This study provided considerable insight into the lives of SAC wives. While wives did attend the SAC Association reunions, few of the wives wanted to share their memories. Lindquist's study provides an in-depth analysis of SAC life on the home front during the early 1950s.

70. Ibid., ii.

71. Ibid., 12.

72. Ibid., 19–20.

73. Ibid.

74. "Strategic Air Command," *New York Times,* October 28, 1955.

75. "The Problem of Army Morale," *New York Times,* December 5, 1954.

76. Wade interview.

77. "How Wives Are Organized to Serve in Our Strategic Air Command," *U.S. Lady* 1, no. 6 (May 1956): 9, 42–43.

78. Comments from unidentified wives and husbands at SAC reunions held during the summer of 2006.

79. Shea interview. Shea recalled his commander addressing the airmen about giving to the SAC aid fund.

80. Curtis LeMay, General, USAF, CG/SCA, to Laurence S. Kuter, Lt. General, Deputy Chief of Staff, Personnel, February 26, 1952, LeMay Papers, LOC.

81. Laurence S. Kuter, Lt. General, Deputy Chief of Staff, Personnel, to Curtis LeMay, General, USAF, CG/SAC, May 19, 1952, LeMay Papers, LOC.

82. R. M. Montgomery, Colonel, USAF, Deputy Chief of Staff, SAC, to Curtis LeMay, General, USAF, CG/SAC, June 2, 1952, LeMay Papers, LOC.

83. R. O. Cork, Brigadier General, USAF, Comptroller, SAC, "Memorandum for Record: Turner Sports Car Races," June 16, 1953, LeMay Papers, LOC.

84. "Omaha Auto Race Taken by M'Afee," *New York Times,* July 5, 1954.

85. "Extract of Telephone Conversation, 6 May 1954, Between General Twining and General LeMay," LeMay Papers, LOC.

86. Walter Sweeney, Major General, USAF, CG/15 AF, to Curtis LeMay, General, USAF, CG/SAC, November 9, 1954, LeMay Papers, LOC.

87. Jones interview by Deaile.

88. Carlton interview.

89. "Air Dispersal Planned: Strategic Command Bombers Will Shift to 11 Bases," *New York Times,* August 8, 1956.

90. Above the gate at Minot Air Force Base, North Dakota, a SAC base created due to dispersal, a sign read "Only the Best Go North." Fighter pilots would use the same saying in the 1960s to describe those pilots flying missions in North Vietnam.

91. Curtis E. LeMay, "Aerospace Power Is Indivisible," *Air Force Magazine* 44 (November 1961): 67.

92. Lawrence H. Suid, *Guts & Glory: The Making of the American Military Image in Film,* rev. ed. (Lexington: University Press of Kentucky, 2002), 221.

93. Starr Smith, *Jimmy Stewart: Bomber Pilot* (St. Paul, Minn.: Zenith Press, 2005), 263.

94. Jimmy Stewart, "Strategic Air Command," *Air Force Magazine* 38 (April 1955): 40–43.

95. Ibid.

96. Anthony Mann, *Strategic Air Command* (Hollywood, Calif: Paramount Pictures, 1955).

97. Ibid.

98. Ibid.

99. Ibid.

100. Ibid.

101. Ibid.

102. The picture of LeMay using Mitchell's sword to cut the cake appeared in Lloyd, *A Cold War Legacy,* 229.

103. Polmar, *Strategic Air Command*, 44.

104. Hanson W. Baldwin, "Strategic Air Command II," *New York Times,* October 28, 1955.

105. Chris Adams, *Inside the Cold War: A Cold Warrior's Reflections* (Maxwell Air Force Base, Ala.: Air University Press, 1999), 6.

Chapter 7. Living in the Missile Age

Epigraph. General Power wrote the introduction to the summer 1958 issue of *Skyline* magazine. The entire issue was devoted to various aspects of SAC; see Power's quote in *Skyline* 16, no. 2 (Summer 1958).

1. Story as told by Polmar, *Strategic Air Command,* 60.

2. Wade interview.

3. Declassified RAND study, "RAND Memorandum 1075, Possible Offensive Capability Against the U.S.," quoted in Calvin W. Fite, "Reduction of Vulnerability to Atomic Attack of SAC Air Base System" (Maxwell Air Force Base, Ala.: Air War College, 1955), 7.

4. David Alan Rosenberg, "Smoking Radiating Ruin at the End of Two Hours: Documents on American Plans for Nuclear War

with the Soviet Union, 1954–55," *International Security* 6, no. 3 (1981): 8–9.

5. Montgomery interview.

6. Rosenberg, "Smoking Radiating Ruin at the End of Two Hours," 1–10.

7. LeMay and Kantor, *Mission with LeMay,* 482.

8. Adams, *Inside the Cold War,* 8.

9. Rosenberg, "Smoking Radiating Ruin at the End of Two Hours," 28.

10. Phrases randomly selected from responses to the question "Was SAC different from other Air Force commands during the time you served?" on surveys distributed to former SAC members at various reunions throughout the summer of 2006.

11. Statement made by a B-52 reunion member at the B-52 Association Reunion.

12. Shea interview.

13. Old interview.

14. Office of SAC History, *History of Strategic Air Command: 1 January 1957–30 June 1957,* Historical Study no. 68 (Offutt Air Force Base, Neb.: Strategic Air Command, 1957), 6.

15. Cheyenne Mountain, which houses the North American Air Defense Command, opened in 1962.

16. "Nuclear Shelter Unveiled by SAC," *New York Times,* October 27, 1956.

17. A. R. Sorrells, "Omaha," *Skyline* 16, no. 2 (1958): 5–6.

18. David Wade, "SAC Security: How SAC Tackles Its Security Problems," *Air Force Magazine* 39, no. 4 (April 1956): 60–62.

19. Rosenberg, "Smoking Radiating Ruin at the End of Two Hours," 22.

20. Sorrells, "Omaha," 6.

21. Ibid.

22. Sidney Hyman, "The Men Who Fly with the Bomb," *New York Times,* September 17, 1961.

23. Holstrom interview.

24. Hyman, "The Men Who Fly with the Bomb."

25. Holstrom interview.

26. Shea interview.

27. Jack Raymond, "LeMay New Air Vice Chief; Army Moves Up Lemnitzer," *New York Times,* April 5, 1957.

28. Griswold interview.

29. Edmundson interview.

30. During Secretary Quarles' term, the secretary of the Air Force and the Air Staff had a tenuous relationship. On several occasions, Quarles openly disputed the testimony of his generals, especially before former secretary of the Air Force Senator Stuart Symington's committee. The disputes centered on the estimate of Russian capabilities and funding for the Air Force. Quarles, in the Air Force's eyes, held the Eisenhower administration line on budget spending rather than promoting increases in Air Force spending. See Watson, *The Office of Secretary of the Air Force, 1947–1965,* 158–75.

31. "AF Speculates on LeMay's Successor," *The Military Register,* April 13, 1957.

32. Jones interview by Deaile.

33. Jack Raymond, "Gen. Power Head Key Air Command," *New York Times,* May 21, 1957.

34. Griswold interview.

35. This fact was repeated by his aides: Carlton interview by Thompson, Jones interview by Deaile.

36. Wade interview.

37. Old interview.

38. Holstrom interview.

39. Office of SAC History, "The SAC Alert Program: 1956–1959" (Offutt Air Force Base, Neb.: Strategic Air Command, 1992), 4–6.

40. Arleigh Burke, Admiral, Chief of Naval Operations, to Charles E. Wilson, Secretary of Defense, "Revision to AEC-DOD Memorandum of Understanding for the Transfer of Atomic Weapons (4 May 1956)," JCSM-223–59, June 15, 1959, Nathan Twining Papers, LOC.

41. Office of SAC History, *Strategic Air Command and the Alert Program: A Brief History* (Offutt Air Force Base, Neb.: Strategic Air Command, 1988), 1.

42. "Strategic Air Chief Puts Third of Force on Alert," *New York Times,* November 9, 1957.

43. Office of SAC History, *Strategic Air Command and the Alert Program: A Brief History*, 3.

44. Office of SAC History, "The SAC Alert Program: 1956–1959," 32–34.

45. Ibid., 28–29.

46. Alexander, *B-47: Centurion of the Cold War*, 205.

47. A. R. Sorrells, "Alert," *Skyline* 16, no. 2 (1958): 13.

48. Office of SAC History, "The SAC Alert Program: 1956–1959," 16.

49. Edward W. Jedrziewski, "Alert," in *Boeing B-47 Stratojet: True Stories of the Cold War in the Air,* ed. Robert M. Robbins (Atglen, Pa.: Schiffer Military History, 2002), 76.

50. Alexander, *B-47: Centurion of the Cold War*, 204.

51. Martin interview.

52. Sorrells, "Alert," 13.

53. SAC members at the B-47 Association Reunion offered these anecdotes and remembrances, but no one offered specific names.

54. Col. Sigmund Alexander, USAF, interview by Melvin Deaile, February 2007.

55. What is interesting about this member's recollections is how the Kennedy administration eventually earned a reputation among a lot of SAC members for the decline in prestige of SAC; Jedrziewski, "Alert," 74.

56. The *New York Times* reported Power's testimony; see Jack Raymond, "Power Again Bids U.S. Put Bombers on Flying Alert," *New York Times,* February 3, 1960. Power's testimony is quoted in Polmar, *Strategic Air Command*, 63.

57. "Some B-52s in Air Around the Clock," *New York Times,* November 19, 1961. Scholarship on Eisenhower's administration suggests that by the president's second term, he had moved away from massive retaliation, seeing the futility in thermonuclear war. See Campbell Craig, *Destroying the Village: Eisenhower and Thermonuclear War* (New York: Columbia University Press, 1998).

58. "Some B-52s in Air Around the Clock."

59. Comments taken from a SAC history of alert; see Office of SAC History, *Strategic Air Command and the Alert Program: A Brief History,* 6.

60. Holstrom interview.

61. Polmar, *Strategic Air Command*, 75.

62. Wade interview.

63. Polmar, *Strategic Air Command*, 112.

64. Ibid.

65. Office of SAC History, "The SAC Alert Program: 1956–1959," 15.

66. Ibid., 40–41.

67. Letter from LeMay to Power quoted in Robert K. Reece, "Strategic Air Command 74 Hour Duty Week: An Analysis," Air War College, 1966, 8.

68. Polmar, *Strategic Air Command*, 73.

69. Carroll H. Goyne, "The Strategic Air Command Aircrew Duty Week: An Analysis," Air War College, 1965, 21.

70. Although a representative sample, a number of respondents to the SAC survey of 2006 stated that they did not have time to use the various "hobby shops" on SAC bases.

71. Hyman, "The Men Who Fly with the Bomb."

72. Trice and Beyer, *The Cultures of Work Organizations*, 90.

73. The term "SACumsized" could not be traced to a specific date or event. Members, however, throughout the 2006 reunions commonly used the term when describing what happened to them as they became exposed to SAC's organizational culture.

74. Polmar, *Strategic Air Command*, 51–52.

75. "Commanding Generals Diary," January 7–9, 1952, January 12, 1952, LeMay Papers, LOC.

76. Gerald W. Driskill and Angela Laird Brenton, *Organizational Culture in Action* (Thousand Oaks, Calif.: Sage Publications, 2005), 43.

77. Polmar, *Strategic Air Command*, 67.

78. Gen. Paul Carlton, USAF, interview by Cargill Hall, September 1980, AFHRA K239.0512–1277.

79. General LeMay, as SAC commander, vice chief of staff, and even as chief of staff of the Air Force, sought the development of the B-70 Valkyrie, a long-range supersonic bomber; the Dyna-Soar, a chemically powered high-altitude long-range bomber; and even entertained the idea of a nuclear-powered bomber.

80. Carlton interview by Hall.

81. Ibid.

82. Holstrom interview.

83. Carlton interview by Hall.

84. Martin interview.

85. Catton interview.

86. Gen. Russell Dougherty, USAF, interview by Melvin Deaile, January 2006. Interestingly, despite their apprehensions about senior service school, Jones became chairman of the Joint Chiefs (1978–82), and Dougherty rose to command SAC from 1974 to 1977.

87. Wade interview.

88. LeMay interview by Bohn and Kipp.

89. Major General Curtis LeMay to General Carl Spaatz, September 20, 1946, in Edmund Beard, *Developing the ICBM: A Study in Bureaucratic Politics* (New York: Columbia University Press, 1976), 39.

90. Martin J. Collins, *Cold War Laboratory: Rand, the Air Force, and the American State, 1945–1950* (Washington, D.C.: Smithsonian Institution Press, 2002), 74.

91. Beard, *Developing the ICBM,* 82.

92. Ibid., 100–5, 219–25.

93. Ibid., 195; Office of SAC History, "SAC Missile Chronology, 1939–1988" (Offutt Air Force Base, Neb.: Strategic Air Command, 1990), 10.

94. Jacob Neufeld, *Ballistic Missiles in the United States Air Force, 1945–1960* (Washington, D.C.: Office of Air Force History, 1990), 142–43.

95. For a discussion on Sputnik, U.S. space policy, and Eisenhower's politics, see Walter McDougall, . . . *The Heavens and the Earth: A Political History of the Space Age* (Baltimore, Md.: Johns Hopkins University Press, 1985).

96. Neufeld, *Ballistic Missiles,* 208.

97. Thomas S. Power, "Ballistic Missiles and the SAC Mission," *Air Force Magazine* 41, no. 76 (April 1958): 76.

98. Arthur Widder, "ICBM: Prelude to Pushbutton Pilots," *The National Guardsman,* no. 10 (May 1956): 5.

99. Comment made by a former SAC missileer, Association of Air Force Missileers Reunion, September 27–30, 2006, Cheyenne, Wyoming.

100. Walter Mills, "Ultimate Weapons—Ultimate Questions," *New York Times,* April 14, 1957.

101. Quoted by General Power in a book on defense policy he published after retirement; see Power, *Design for Survival,* 169.

102. Widder, "ICBM: Prelude to Pushbutton Pilots," 6.

103. Thomas S. Power, "SAC and the Ballistic Missile," *Air University Quarterly* 9, no. 4 (Winter 1957–58): 4–5.

104. "First Group of Missile Airmen Ends Training on Coast," *New York Times,* December 18, 1957.

105. "SAC to Control Strategic Missiles," *Air Force Times,* December 7, 1957. Cooke Air Force Base was renamed Vandenberg Air Force Base in 1958 after the Air Force's second chief of staff.

106. Schein, *Organizational Culture and Leadership,* 13.

107. "Missile Duty Could Be Costly," *Army Navy Air Force Journal,* December 19, 1959.

108. Charlie Simpson, "Getting Started in the Titan I," *Association of Air Force Missileers Newsletter* 9, no. 4 (December 2001), 6.

109. Grant E. Secrist, "Combat Crew Duty with the 308th Strategic Missile Wing: Personal Perspective on the Early Years," January 24, 2006, unpublished paper.

110. Wade interview.

111. Neufeld, *Ballistic Missiles,* 202–4.

112. Ibid., 216.

113. Jones interview by Maryanow and Kohn.

114. Wade interview.

115. Thomas S. Power, "SAC: Peace Is Our Profession," *Air Force Times,* April 11, 1959, 1.

116. Power, *Design for Survival,* 168.

117. Goyne, "The Strategic Air Command Aircrew Duty Week: An Analysis," 15.

118. Neufeld, *Ballistic Missiles,* 204.

119. General Power, CG/SAC, to General Thomas White, CSAF, January 17, 1961, Thomas White Papers, LOC.

120. "Air Force Seeks Centralized SAC Control of All U.S.-Allied Strategic Weapons," *Army Navy Air Force Journal,* March 8, 1958.

121. For the development of the first SIOP and its strategy, see David Alan Rosenberg, "The Origins of Overkill: Nuclear Weapons and American Strategy, 1945–1960," *International Security* 7, no. 4 (Spring 1983).

122. Power, *Design for Survival,* 170–71.

Epilogue and Conclusion

Epigraph: LeMay, "Aerospace Power Is Indivisible," 67.

1. Office of SAC History, *Chronology of SAC Participation in the Cuban Crisis,* 2–3.
2. Ibid., 4–5.
3. Anecdote offered by Col. William F. Stocker, USAF (Ret.), on a SAC survey collected at the Air Force Association of Missileers Convention, September 27–30, 2006.
4. Anecdote offered by Maj. John Nailen, USAF (Ret.), on a SAC survey collected at the Air Force Association of Missileers Convention.
5. Office of SAC History, *Chronology of SAC Participation in the Cuban Crisis,* 5.
6. John F. Kennedy, "Radio-TV Address of the President to the Nation: 22 October 1962," in *The Cuban Missile Crisis: A National Security Archive Documents Reader,* ed. Laurence Chang and Peter Kornbluh (New York: The New Press, 1998), 162.
7. Charlie Simpson, "Missileers and the Cuban Missile Crisis," *Association of Air Force Missileers Newsletter* 10, no. 4 (September 2002): 5.
8. Cantarano interview.
9. Anecdote told by unattributed B-47 crewmember at the B-47 Association Reunion.
10. Simpson, "Missileers and the Cuban Missile Crisis," 6.
11. Sagan, *The Limits of Safety,* 65; Richard Rhodes, *Dark Sun: The Making of the Hydrogen Bomb* (New York: Simon & Schuster, 1995), 575.
12. Simpson, "Missileers and the Cuban Missile Crisis," 6.
13. Office of SAC History, *Chronology of SAC Participation in the Cuban Crisis,* 33.
14. Sagan, *The Limits of Safety,* 67–68.
15. Curtis E. LeMay, "SAC's Power Is Lesson of Cuba (Speech Excerpts)," *Army Navy Air Force Journal and Register,* December 15, 1962, 19–23.
16. Polmar, *Strategic Air Command,* 79–109.
17. Carlton interview.
18. Freedman, *The Evolution of Nuclear Strategy,* 285.
19. Lloyd, *A Cold War Legacy,* 666–76.

20. LeMay as quoted in Russell E. Dougherty, "Leadership During the Cold War: A Four-Star General's Perspective," in *Warriors and Scholars: A Modern War Reader,* ed. Peter R. Lane and Ronald E. Marcello (Denton: University of North Texas Press, 2005), 117.

21. Ibid., 119.

22. Ibid., 118–19.

23. Ibid., 124.

24. Observed at the B-47 Association Reunion.

25. Observed at the Association of Air Force Missileers Reunion.

Bibliography

Archives
Air Force Historical Research Agency (AFHRA)
Archie J. Old Papers, AFHRA K168.7141–14.
Department of the Air Force, "Topical Digest of Testimony Before the House Armed Services Committee During Hearings on the B-36 and Related Matters: Section II," October 1949, AFHRA Roll 33780, Frame 891, text-fiche.
Thomas Power Papers, CH-79–01, text-fiche.

U.S. Air Force Oral History Program
Barnes, Earl W., Lt. Gen., USAF, interview by Hugh N. Ahmann, January 1975.
Carlton, Paul, Gen., USAF, interview by Scott Thompson, August 1979.
_____. Interview by Cargill Hall, September 1980.
Catton, Jack C., Gen., USAF, interview by James C. Hasdorff, July 1977.
Dougherty, Russell E., Gen., USAF, interview by Edgar F. Puryear, March 1979.
Edmundson, James V., Lt. Gen., USAF, interview by Edgar F. Puryear, July 1978.
Griswold, Francis, Lt. Gen., USAF, interview by Robert Kipp, April 1970.
Hansell, Haywood S., Gen., USAF, interview by Edgar F. Puryear, February 1979.
Harris, Hunter, Gen., USAF, interview by Hugh N. Ahmann, November 1974, March 1979.
Holstrom, Everett W., Brig. Gen., USAF, interview by James C. Hasdorff, April 1988.

Jones, David C., Gen., USAF, interview by Maurice Maryanow and Richard Kohn, August 1985–March 1986.

Kenney, George C., Gen., USAF, interview by James C. Hasdorff, August 1974.

Kuter, Laurence S., Gen., USAF, interview by Edgar F. Puryear, November 1996.

LeMay, Curtis, Gen., USAF, interview by Max Rosenberg, January 1965.

_____. Interview by Robert Futrell et al., June 1972.

_____. Interview by Bill Peck, March 1965.

_____. Interview by Edgar F. Puryear, November 1976.

_____. Interview by John Bohn, March 1971.

_____. Interview by John Bohn and Robert Kipp, November 1972.

Martin, William K., Lt. Gen., USAF, interview by David L. Olson, February 1988.

McPherson, John B., Lt. Gen., USAF, interview by Hugh N. Ahmann, December 1985, February 1991.

Montgomery, John B., Maj. Gen., USAF, interview by Mark C. Cleary, May 1984.

Mundy, George W., Lt. Gen., USAF, interview by Mark C. Cleary, September 1984.

Norstad, Lauris, Gen., USAF, interview by Edgar F. Puryear, August 1977.

Old, Archie J., Lt. Gen., USAF, interview by Hugh N. Ahmann, November 1982.

O'Donnell, Emmett "Rosie," Gen., USAF, interview by Edgar F. Puryear, December 1967.

Ryan, John D., Gen., USAF, interview by Edgar F. Puryear, August 1981.

Smart, Jacob E., Gen., USAF, interview by Arthur W. McCants and James C. Hansdorff, November 1978.

Talbott, Carlos M., Lt. Gen., USAF, interview by Hugh N. Ahmann, June 1985.

Wade, Horace M., Gen., USAF, interview by Hugh N. Ahmann, October 1978.

Library of Congress, Manuscript Division
Curtis LeMay Papers
Elwood "Pete" Quesada Papers

Carl Spaatz Papers
Nathan Twining Papers
Thomas White Papers
Hoyt Vandenberg Papers

National Archives and Records Administration
Record Group 341, Headquarters United States Air Force

Newspaper and Magazine Archives
Air Force Magazine
Air Force Times
Army and Navy Journal
Army, Navy, Air Force Journal and Register
Life
Newsweek
The New York Times Digital Archives
Klaxon Magazine

Former SAC Members
Sigmund Alexander
Tom Cantarano
Andrew Labosky
Don Shea

United States Air Force Academy Library
Harry Borowski Papers
Emmett "Rosie" O'Donnell Papers

Newspapers, Magazines, Monographs, and Reports
Adams, Chris. *Inside the Cold War: A Cold Warrior's Reflections.* Maxwell Air Force Base, Ala.: Air University Press, 1999.

Aldrich, Howard, and Martin Ruef. *Organizations Evolving.* 2nd ed. Thousand Oaks, Calif.: Sage Publications, 2006.

Alexander, Sigmund. *B-47: Centurion of the Cold War.* San Antonio, Tex.: C. C. C. P. Publishing, 2002.

Arbon, Lee. *They Also Flew: The Enlisted Pilot Legacy, 1912–1942.* Washington, D.C.: Smithsonian Institution Press, 1998.

Army Air Forces Headquarters. "AAF Regulation No. 20–20, Organization: Strategic Air Command." October 10, 1946.

Army Navy Air Force Journal. "Air Force Seeks Centralized SAC Control of All U.S.-Allied Strategic Weapons." March 8, 1958.

———. "Missile Duty Could Be Costly." December 19, 1959.

Arnold, Henry H. *Global Mission.* New York: Harper & Brothers, 1949.

Baldwin, Hanson W. "Strategic Air Command II." *New York Times.* October 28, 1955.

Barlow, Jeffrey G. *Revolt of the Admirals: The Fight for Naval Aviation, 1945–1950.* Washington, D.C.: Brassey's, 1998.

Beard, Edmund. *Developing the ICBM: A Study in Bureaucratic Politics.* New York: Columbia University Press, 1976.

Bednarek, Janet R., ed. *The Enlisted Experience: A Conversation with Chief Master Sergeants of the Air Force.* Washington, D.C.: U.S. Government Printing Office, 1995.

Biddle, Tami Davis. *Rhetoric and Reality in Air Warfare: The Evolution of British and American Ideas About Strategic Bombing, 1914–1945.* Princeton, N.J.: Princeton University Press, 2002.

Borgiasz, William S. *The Strategic Air Command: Evolution and Consolidation of Nuclear Forces, 1945–1955.* Westport, Conn.: Praeger, 1996.

Borowski, Harry R. *A Hollow Threat: Strategic Air Power and Containment before Korea.* Westport, Conn.: Greenwood Press, 1982.

Bosanko, Charles Wilfred. "The Architecture of Armageddon: A History of Curtis LeMay's Influence on the Strategic Air Command and Nuclear Warfare." California State University, Fullerton, 2000.

Brugioni, Dino A. *Eyeball to Eyeball: The Inside Story of the Cuban Missile Crisis.* Edited by Robert F. McCort. 1st ed. New York: Random House, 1991.

Builder, Carl H. *The Masks of War: American Military Styles in Strategy and Analysis.* Baltimore: Johns Hopkins University Press, 1989.

———. *The Icarus Syndrome: The Role of Air Power Theory in the Evolution and Fate of the U.S. Air Force.* New Brunswick, N.J.: Transaction Publishers, 1994.

Chidster, Kenneth Ray. "Bomber Down: A True Story of Kenneth Ray Chidster." Unpublished, 2004.

Clodfelter, Mark A. "Molding Airpower Convictions: Development and Legacy of William Mitchell's Strategic Thought." In *The Paths of Heaven: The Evolution of Air Power Theory.* Edited by Phillip S. Meilinger. Maxwell Air Force Base, Ala.: Air University Press, 2001.

Coffey, Thomas M. *Iron Eagle: The Turbulent Life of General Curtis LeMay.* New York: Crown Publishers, 1986.

Cole, Ronald H., et al. *The History of Unified Command, 1946–1993.* Washington, D.C.: Joint History Office, 1995.

Collins, Martin J. *Cold War Laboratory: Rand, the Air Force, and the American State, 1945–1950.* Washington, D.C.: Smithsonian Institution Press, 2002.

Conklin, William R. "Spaatz Calls B-36 and Bomb 'Greatest Forces for Peace.'" *New York Times.* August 23, 1949.

Cooke, James J. *Billy Mitchell.* Boulder, Colo: Lynne Rienner, 2002.

Copp, DeWitt S. *A Few Great Captains: The Men and Events That Shaped the Development of U.S. Air Power.* McLean, Va.: EPM Publications, 1989.

Corn, Joseph J. *The Winged Gospel: America's Romance with Aviation, 1900–1950.* New York: Oxford University Press, 1983.

Craig, Campbell. *Destroying the Village: Eisenhower and Thermonuclear War.* New York: Columbia University Press, 1998.

Crane, Conrad C. "Raiding the Beggar's Pantry: The Search for Airpower Strategy in the Korean War." *Journal of Military History* 63, no. 4 (October 1999): 885–920.

———. *American Airpower Strategy in Korea, 1950–1953.* Lawrence: University Press of Kansas, 2000.

Dougherty, Russell E. "Leadership During the Cold War: A Four-Star General's Perspective." In *Warriors and Scholars: A Modern War Reader.* Edited by Peter R. Lane and Ronald E. Marcello. Denton: University of North Texas Press, 2005.

Douhet, Giulio. *The Command of the Air.* Translated by Dino Ferrari. 1921. Reprint, Washington, D.C.: Air Force History and Museums Program, 1998.

Driskill, Gerald W., and Angela Laird Brenton. *Organizational Culture in Action.* Thousand Oaks, Calif.: Sage Publications, 2005.

Edmundson, James. "Six Churning and Four Burning." *Klaxon*, 1995.

English, Allan D. *Understanding Military Culture: A Canadian Perspective.* Montreal: McGill-Queen's University Press, 2004.

Faber, Peter R. "Interwar U.S. Army Aviation and the Air Corps Tactical School: Incubators of American Airpower." In *The Paths of Heaven: The Evolution of Airpower Theory.* Edited by Phillip S. Meilinger. Maxwell Air Force Base, Ala.: Air University Press, 2001.

Feaver, Peter. *Guarding the Guardians: Civilian Control of Nuclear Weapons in the United States.* Ithaca, N.Y.: Cornell University Press, 1992.

Fields, Ed. "Recollections of the 19th Air Refueling Squadron, Homestead Air Force Base, FL (May 1956–July 1958)." Unpublished.

Finney, Robert T. *History of the Air Corps Tactical School, 1920–1940.* Maxwell Air Force Base, Ala.: Air University Press, 1992.

Fite, Calvin W. "Reduction of Vulnerability to Atomic Attack of SAC Air Base System." Maxwell Air Force Base, Ala.: Air War College, 1955.

Freedman, Lawrence. *The Evolution of Nuclear Strategy.* New York: St. Martin's Press, 1981.

Friedberg, Aaron L. *In the Shadow of the Garrison State: America's Anti-Statism and Its Cold War Strategy.* Princeton, N.J.: Princeton University Press, 2000.

Futrell, Robert F. *The United States Air Force in Korea, 1950–1953.* Rev. ed. Washington, D.C.: Office of Air Force History, 1983.

———. *Ideas, Concepts, Doctrine: 1907–1960.* 4th ed. Washington, D.C.: U.S. Government Printing Office, 2002.

Goyne, Carroll H. "The Strategic Air Command Aircrew Duty Week: An Analysis." Maxwell Air Force Base, Ala.: Air War College, 1965.

Griffith, Thomas E. *MacArthur's Airman: General George C. Kenney and the War in the Southwest Pacific.* Lawrence: University Press of Kansas, 1998.

Hammond, Paul Y. "Super Carriers and B-36 Bombers: Appropriations, Strategy, and Politics." In *American Civil Military Relations.* Edited by Harold Stein. Birmingham: University of Alabama Press, 1963.

Haulman, Daniel L. "Air Force Bases, 1947–1960." In *Locating Air Force Base Sites: History's Legacy.* Edited by Frederick J. Shaw. Washington, D.C.: Air Force History and Museums Program, 2004.

Hixson, Walter L. *Parting the Curtain: Propaganda, Culture, and the Cold War, 1945–1961.* 1st ed. New York: St. Martin's Press, 1997.

Holley, I. B. *Ideas and Weapons.* Washington, D.C.: Air Force History and Museums Program, 1997.

Hughes, Thomas Alexander. *Overlord: General Pete Quesada and the Triumph of Tactical Air Power in World War II*. New York: Free Press, 1995.

Hull, Isabel V. *Absolute Destruction: Military Culture and the Practices of War in Imperial Germany*. Ithaca, N.Y.: Cornell University Press, 2005.

Huntington, Samuel P. *The Soldier and the State: The Theory and Politics of Civil-Military Relations*. Cambridge, Mass.: Belknap Press of Harvard University Press, 1957.

Hurley, Alfred F., and William C. Heimdahl. "The Roots of U.S. Military Aviation." In *Winged Shield, Winged Sword: A History of the United States Air Force*, vol. 1. Edited by Bernard Nalty. Washington, D.C.: Air Force History and Museums Program, 1997.

Hyman, Sidney. "The Men Who Fly with the Bomb." *New York Times*. September 17, 1961.

Janowitz, Morris. *The Professional Soldier: A Social and Political Portrait*. New York: Free Press, 1960.

Janowitz, Morris, and Roger William Little. *Sociology and the Military Establishment*. 3rd ed. Beverly Hills, Calif.: Sage Publications, 1974.

Jedrziewski, Edward W. "Alert." In *Boeing B-47 Stratojet: True Stories of the Cold War in the Air*. Edited by Robert M. Robbins. Atglen, Pa.: Schiffer Military History, 2002.

Jones, Johnny R. *William "Billy" Mitchell's Air Power*. Maxwell Air Force Base, Ala.: Airpower Research Institute, 1997.

Kennedy, John F. "Radio-TV Address of the President to the Nation: 22 October 1962." In *The Cuban Missile Crisis: A National Security Archive Documents Reader*. Edited by Laurence Chang and Peter Kornbluh. New York: The New Press, 1998.

Kennett, Lee B. *The First Air War, 1914–1918*. New York: Free Press, 1999.

Knaack, Marcelle Size. *Encyclopedia of U.S. Air Force Aircraft and Missile Systems*. Vol. 2: *Post–World War II Bombers*. Washington, D.C.: U.S. Government Printing Office, 1988.

Kohn, Richard H., and Joseph H. Harahan, eds. *Strategic Air Warfare: An Interview with Generals Curtis E. LeMay, Leon W. Johnson, David A. Burchinal, and Jack J. Catton*. Washington, D.C.: U.S. Government Printing Office, 1988.

Lang, Kurt. *Military Institutions and the Sociology of War.* Beverly Hills, Calif.: Sage Publications, 1972.

Leffler, Melvyn P. *A Preponderance of Power: National Security, the Truman Administration, and the Cold War.* Stanford, Calif.: Stanford University Press, 1992.

LeMay, Curtis E. "Aerospace Power Is Indivisible." *Air Force Magazine* 44 (November 1961).

————. "The Cuban Experience: Responses and Lessons." *Air Force Information Policy Letter Supplemental for Commanders,* no. 114 (December 1962).

————. "SAC's Power Is Lesson of Cuba (Speech Excerpts)." *Army Navy Air Force Journal and Register,* December 15, 1962.

————. "Deterrence in Action." *Ordnance* (March–April 1963): 526–28.

LeMay, Curtis E., and MacKinlay Kantor. *Mission with LeMay: My Story.* Garden City, N.Y.: Doubleday, 1965.

Lindquist, Ruth. "Marriage and Family Life of Officers and Airmen in Strategic Air Command." Chapel Hill, N.C.: Institute for Research in Social Science, 1952.

Lloyd, Alwyn T. *A Cold War Legacy: A Tribute to Strategic Air Command, 1946–1992.* Missoula, Mont.: Pictorial Histories Publishing, 2000.

Mahan, A. T. *The Influence of Sea Power Upon History, 1660–1805.* 1894. Reprint, New York: Dover Publications, 1987.

Mann, Anthony. *Strategic Air Command.* Hollywood, Calif.: Paramount Pictures, 1955.

Martin, Harold. "Are Our Big Bombers Ready?" *Saturday Evening Post,* December 30, 1950, 18–19, 65–67.

Martin, Joanne. *Cultures in Organizations: Three Perspectives.* New York: Oxford University Press, 1992.

————. *Organizational Culture: Mapping the Terrain, Foundations for Organizational Science.* Thousand Oaks, Calif.: Sage Publications, 2002.

Mastroianni, George R. "Occupations, Cultures, and Leadership in the Army and Air Force." *Parameters* (Winter 2005–06): 76–90.

McCullough, David G. *Truman.* New York: Simon & Schuster, 1992.

McDougall, Walter. . . . *The Heavens and the Earth: A Political History of the Space Age.* Baltimore, Md.: Johns Hopkins University Press, 1985.

McShane, Steven L., and Mary Ann Von Glinow. *Organizational Behavior*. 3rd ed. New York: McGraw-Hill, 2005.

Meilinger, Phillip S. *Hoyt S. Vandenberg: The Life of a General*. Bloomington: Indiana University Press, 1989.

———. "Giulio Douhet and the Origins of Airpower Theory." In *The Paths of Heaven: The Evolution of Air Power Theory*. Edited by Phillip S. Meilinger. Maxwell Air Force Base, Ala.: Air University Press, 2001.

Mets, David R. *Master of Airpower: General Carl A. Spaatz*. New York: Presidio Press, 1997.

Mills, Walter. "Ultimate Weapons—Ultimate Questions." *New York Times*. April 14, 1957.

Mitchell, William. *Winged Defense: The Development and Possibilities of Modern Air Power—Economic and Military*. New York, London: G. P. Putnam's Sons, 1925.

———. *Skyways: A Book on Modern Aeronautics*. Philadelphia: J. B. Lippincott Co., 1930.

Moody, Walton S. *Building a Strategic Air Force*. Washington, D.C.: Air Force History and Museums Program, 1996.

Neufeld, Jacob. *Ballistic Missiles in the United States Air Force, 1945–1960*. Washington, D.C.: Office of Air Force History, 1990.

New York Times. "Strategic Air Force to Shift to Nebraska." May 22, 1948.

———. "Gen Kenney Pleads for No. 1 Air Force." May 17, 1949.

———. "Kenney Minimizes Our Bomber Strength." May 18, 1949.

———. "U.S. Grounds B-29s as Another Crash Kills 5 in Florida." November 19, 1949.

———. "Strategic Air Command Altered." March 8, 1950.

———. "Rooms with Bath; Air Force Policy." March 3, 1952.

———. "Twining to Keep Post: Decision to Shift Jobs with LeMay Cancelled by Air Force." October 29, 1952.

———. "Omaha Auto Race Taken by M'Afee." July 5, 1954.

———. "The Problem of Army Morale." December 5, 1954.

———. "Strategic Air Command I: An Analysis of Program for Building Force for Keeping the World's Peace." October 27, 1955.

———. "Strategic Air Command." October 28, 1955.

———. "Air Force Wife Explains Problems of Dislocation." May 29, 1956.

————. "Air Dispersal Planned: Strategic Command Bombers Will Shift to 11 Bases." August 8, 1956.

————. "Nuclear Shelter Unveiled by SAC." October 27, 1956.

————. "Strategic Air Chief Puts Third of Force on Alert." November 9, 1957.

————. "First Group of Missile Airmen Ends Training on Coast." December 18, 1957.

————. "Unarmed Atom Bomb Hits Carolina Home, Hurting 6." March 12, 1958.

————. "Some B-52s in Air Around the Clock." November 19, 1961.

Newsweek. "Bombers at the Ready." April 18, 1949, 24–25.

Nutter, Ralph H. *With the Possum and the Eagle: A Memoir of a Navigator's War over Germany and Japan.* Denton: University of North Texas Press, 2005.

Office of SAC History. "Presentation Phase One (Transcript): Exercise Dualism (6–8 December 1948)." Offutt Air Force Base, Neb.: Strategic Air Command, 1948.

————. *History of Strategic Air Command, 1949.* Offutt Air Force Base, Neb.: Strategic Air Command, 1950.

————. *Development of Strategic Air Command Security Program.* Historical Study no. 17. Offutt Air Force Base, Neb.: Strategic Air Command, 1951.

————. *Lead Crew School and Combat Crew Standardization School.* Historical Study no. 8. Offutt Air Force Base, Neb.: Strategic Air Command, 1951.

————. *History of Strategic Air Command: 1 January 1957–30 June 1957.* Historical Study no. 68. Offutt Air Force Base, Neb.: Strategic Air Command, 1957.

————. *Chronology of SAC Participation in the Cuban Crisis.* Offutt Air Force Base, Neb.: Strategic Air Command, 1972.

————. *The Development of Strategic Air Command.* Offutt Air Force Base, Neb.: Strategic Air Command, 1972.

————. *The Strategic Air Command Spot Promotion Program: Its Rise and Fall.* Historical Study no. 167. Offutt Air Force Base, Neb.: Strategic Air Command, 1978.

————. *Strategic Air Command and the Alert Program: A Brief History.* Offutt Air Force Base, Neb.: Strategic Air Command, 1988.

————. "SAC Missile Chronology, 1939–1988." Offutt Air Force Base, Neb.: Strategic Air Command, 1990.

————. "The SAC Alert Program: 1956–1959." Offutt Air Force Base, Neb.: Strategic Air Command, 1992.

Pfeffer, Jeffrey, and Gerald R. Salancik. *The External Control of Organizations: A Resource Dependence Perspective.* New York: Harper & Row, 1978.

Polmar, Norman. *Strategic Air Command: People, Aircraft, and Missiles.* Annapolis, Md.: Nautical and Aviation Publishing Co. of America, 1979.

Power, Thomas S. "SAC and the Ballistic Missile." *Air University Quarterly* 9, no. 4 (Winter 1957–58).

————. "Ballistic Missiles and the SAC Mission." *Air Force Magazine* 41, no. 76 (April 1958).

————. "SAC: Peace Is Our Profession." *Air Force Times*, April 11, 1959.

————. *Design for Survival.* New York: Coward-McCann, 1964.

Raymond, Jack. "LeMay New Air Vice Chief; Army Moves Up Lemnitzer." *New York Times.* April 5, 1957.

————. "Gen. Power Head Key Air Command." *New York Times.* May 21, 1957.

————. "Power Again Bids U.S. Put Bombers on Flying Alert." *New York Times.* February 3, 1960.

Rearden, Steven L. *History of the Office of the Secretary of Defense,* vol. I: *The Formative Years 1947–1950.* Washington, D.C.: Office of the Secretary of Defense Historical Office, 1984.

Reece, Robert K. "Strategic Air Command 74 Hour Duty Week: An Analysis." Maxwell Air Force Base, Ala.: Air War College, 1966.

Rhodes, Richard. *Dark Sun: The Making of the Hydrogen Bomb.* New York: Simon & Schuster, 1995.

Rosenberg, David Alan. "American Atomic Strategy and the Hydrogen Bomb." *The Journal of American History* 66, no. 1 (1979): 62–87.

————. "Smoking Radiating Ruin at the End of Two Hours: Documents on American Plans for Nuclear War with the Soviet Union, 1954–55." *International Security* 6, no. 3 (1981).

————. "The Origins of Overkill: Nuclear Weapons and American Strategy, 1945–1960." *International Security* 7, no. 4 (Spring 1983): 3–71.

Ross, Edwin C. "Flying the B-47." In *Boeing B-47 Stratojet: True Stories of the Cold War*. Edited by Mark Notola. Atglen, Pa.: Schiffer Military History, 2002.

Ross, Steven T. *American War Plans, 1945–1950: Strategies for Defeating the Soviet Union*. Portland, Ore.: Frank Cass, 1996.

SAC Historical Branch. *The Deployment of Strategic Air Command Units to the Far East*. Offutt Air Force Base, Neb.: Strategic Air Command, 1950.

———. *Development of Evasion and Escape and Air Evacuation Program*. Historical Study no. 14. Offutt Air Force Base, Neb.: Strategic Air Command, 1951.

———. *Strategic Air Command Expansion Program*. Historical Study no. 19. Offutt Air Force Base, Neb.: Strategic Air Command, 1951.

———. *Strategic Air Command History*, vol. 1: *January–June 1951*. Offutt Air Force Base, Neb.: Strategic Air Command, 1951.

———. "Radar Bomb Scoring Activities in Strategic Air Command: Origins and Growth through 1952." Offutt Air Force Base, Neb.: Strategic Air Command, 1952.

Sagan, Scott Douglas. *The Limits of Safety: Organizations, Accidents, and Nuclear Weapons*. Princeton, N.J.: Princeton University Press, 1993.

Schein, Edgar H. *Organizational Culture and Leadership*. 3rd ed. San Francisco: Jossey-Bass, 2004.

Schilling, Warner R. "The Politics of National Defense: Fiscal 1950." In *Strategy, Politics, and Defense Budgets*. Edited by William Fox. New York: Columbia University Press, 1962.

Secrist, Grant E. "Combat Crew Duty with the 308th Strategic Missile Wing: Personal Perspective on the Early Years. Unpublished paper. January 24, 2006.

Sherman, William C. *Air Warfare*. 1926. Reprint, Maxwell Air Force Base, Ala.: Air University Press, 2002.

Simpson, Charlie. "Getting Started in the Titan I." *Association of Air Force Missileers Newsletter* 9, no. 4 (December 2001).

———. "Missileers and the Cuban Missile Crisis." *Association of Air Force Missileers Newsletter* 10, no. 4 (September 2002).

Smith, Starr. *Jimmy Stewart: Bomber Pilot*. St. Paul, Minn.: Zenith Press, 2005.

Society of the Strategic Air Command. *America's Shield: The Story of the Strategic Air Command and Its People.* Paducah, Ky.: Turner Publishing Co., 1997.

Sorrells, A. R. "Alert." *Skyline* 16, no. 2 (1958).

———. "Omaha." *Skyline* 16, no. 2 (1958).

Spaatz, Carl A. "The Air-Power Odds against Us." *Reader's Digest,* June 1951, 11–14.

Suid, Lawrence H. *Guts & Glory: The Making of the American Military Image in Film.* Rev. ed. Lexington: University Press of Kentucky, 2002.

Tate, James P. *The Army and Its Air Corps: Army Policy toward Aviation, 1919–1941.* Maxwell Air Force Base, Ala.: Air University Press, 1998.

Time. "Man in the First Plane." September 4, 1950, 16–19.

Trice, Harrison Miller, and Janice M. Beyer. *The Cultures of Work Organizations.* Englewood Cliffs, N.J.: Prentice Hall, 1993.

The United States Strategic Bombing Surveys: Summary Report. 1945. Reprint, Maxwell Air Force Base, Ala.: Air University Press, 1987.

U.S. Lady. "How Wives Are Organized to Serve in Our Strategic Air Command." Vol. 1, no. 6 (May 1956): 9, 42–43.

Wade, David. "SAC Security: How SAC Tackles Its Security Problems." *Air Force Magazine* 39, no. 4 (April 1956).

Waggoner, Walter H. "First in History." *New York Times.* March 3, 1949.

Watson, George M. *The Office of Secretary of the Air Force, 1947–1965.* Washington, D.C.: U.S. Government Printing Office, 1993.

Weinkle, Robert K. "The Progression of the Standardization/Evaluation Program in Strategic Air Command." Maxwell Air Force Base, Ala.: Air University, 1965.

Werrell, Kenneth P. *Blankets of Fire: U.S. Bombers over Japan During World War II.* Washington, D.C.: Smithsonian Institution Press, 1996.

Widder, Arthur. "ICBM: Prelude to Pushbutton Pilots." *The National Guardsman,* no. 10 (May 1956).

Wolk, Herman S. "The Quest for Independence." In *Winged Shield, Winged Sword,* vol. I. Edited by Bernard C. Nalty. Washington, D.C.: U.S. Government Printing Office, 1997.

Worden, R. Michael. *Rise of the Fighter Generals: The Problem of Air Force Leadership, 1945–1982.* Maxwell Air Force Base, Ala.: Air University Press, 1998.

Index

About the Author

Melvin G. Deaile is an associate professor at the Air Command and Staff College. He is a retired Air Force colonel who flew the B-52 Stratofortress and the B-2 Spirit. He has flown combat operations as part of Operation Desert Storm and Operation Enduring Freedom, including a record-setting 44.3-hour combat mission. He is the recipient of the Distinguished Flying Cross and is a distinguished graduate of the U.S. Air Force Weapon School.

The Naval Institute Press is the book-publishing arm of the U.S. Naval Institute, a private, nonprofit, membership society for sea service professionals and others who share an interest in naval and maritime affairs. Established in 1873 at the U.S. Naval Academy in Annapolis, Maryland, where its offices remain today, the Naval Institute has members worldwide.

Members of the Naval Institute support the education programs of the society and receive the influential monthly magazine *Proceedings* or the colorful bimonthly magazine *Naval History* and discounts on fine nautical prints and on ship and aircraft photos. They also have access to the transcripts of the Institute's Oral History Program and get discounted admission to any of the Institute-sponsored seminars offered around the country.

The Naval Institute's book-publishing program, begun in 1898 with basic guides to naval practices, has broadened its scope to include books of more general interest. Now the Naval Institute Press publishes about seventy titles each year, ranging from how-to books on boating and navigation to battle histories, biographies, ship and aircraft guides, and novels. Institute members receive significant discounts on the Press' more than eight hundred books in print.

Full-time students are eligible for special half-price membership rates. Life memberships are also available.

For a free catalog describing Naval Institute Press books currently available, and for further information about joining the U.S. Naval Institute, please write to:

Member Services
U.S. Naval Institute
291 Wood Road
Annapolis, MD 21402-5034
Telephone: (800) 233-8764
Fax: (410) 571-1703
Web address: www.usni.org